D1550938

Power and Military Effectiveness

Power and Military Effectiveness

The Fallacy of Democratic Triumphalism

MICHAEL C. DESCH

The Johns Hopkins University Press

Baltimore

© 2008 The Johns Hopkins University Press
All rights reserved. Published 2008
Printed in the United States of America on acid-free paper

2   4   6   8   9   7   5   3   1

The Johns Hopkins University Press
2715 North Charles Street
Baltimore, Maryland 21218-4363
www.press.jhu.edu

Library of Congress Cataloging-in-Publication Data

Desch, Michael C. (Michael Charles), 1960–
Power and military effectiveness : the fallacy of democratic triumphalism /
Michael C. Desch.
p. cm.
Includes bibliographical references and index.
ISBN-13: 978-0-8018-8801-4 (hardcover : alk. paper)
ISBN-10: 0-8018-8801-8 (hardcover : alk. paper)
1. Strategy. 2. Democracy. 3. War. 4. Military readiness. 5. Military policy—
United States—21st century. I. Title
U21.2.D349 2008
355.02—dc22
2007031884

A catalog record for this book is available from the British Library.

Special discounts are available for bulk purchases of this book. For more information,
please contact Special Sales at 410-516-6936 or specialsales@press.jhu.edu.

Before the eyes of men, that never, being
Mortal, ought we cast our thoughts too high.
Insolence, once blossoming, bears
Its fruit, a tasseled field of doom, from which
A weeping harvest's reaped, all tears.
Behold the punishments of these! Remember
Greece or Athens! Lest you disdain
Your present fortune, and lust after more,
Squandering great prosperity.
Zeus is the chastener of overboastful
Minds, a grievous corrector.

Aeschylus, *The Persians,* 819–29
(trans. Seth G. Benardete)

Contents

Acknowledgments

This book began as an article in *International Security* and a subsequent exchange with a number of scholars whose work I critiqued, including Ajin Choi, David Lake, Dani Reiter, and Allan Stam. For extremely helpful comments on parts of earlier drafts of this book I thank them, as well as Alexander Downes, Jeffrey Engel, James Galbraith, Eugene Gholz, Douglass Gibler, Hein Goemans, Samuel Huntington, Stuart Kaufman, Edward Mansfield, Daniel Markey, John Mueller, John Odell, Clifford Orwin, Robert Pape, Helena Truszczynska, Steven Voss, and Stephen Walt, and especially John Mearsheimer, Sebastian Rosato, and Amr Youssef. The anonymous reviewers for *International Security* and for the Johns Hopkins University Press provided valuable comments as well.

I also wish to thank participants in seminars at the Program for International Security Policy at the University of Chicago; the Belfer Center for Science and International Affairs at the John F. Kennedy School of Government, Harvard University; the David Kennedy Center for International Studies at Brigham Young University; the Joan B. Kroc Institute for International Peace Studies, the Helen Kellogg Institute for International Studies, and the Department of Political Science at the University of Notre Dame; the George Bush School of Government and Public Service at Texas A&M University; the Christopher H. Browne Center for International Politics at the University of Pennsylvania; and the Lyndon B. Johnson School of Government at the University of Texas. In addition, fellow panelists at the International Studies Association annual convention and the American Political Science Association annual convention provided thoughtful and thought-provoking criticisms and suggestions. The Liberty Fund's excellent symposium, "Liberty, Leadership, and Images of the Battle of Salamis," in June 2004 particularly shaped my thinking about the problem of democratic hubris.

Finally, I gratefully acknowledge the indispensable research support of John Hajner, Glenn Rudolph, Kenneth Vincent, and Sydney Woodington.

Despite these many intellectual debts, I alone am responsible for any remaining errors in the book.

I received generous financial support during the course of writing this book from the Smith Richardson Foundation, the John M. Olin Institute for Strategic Studies at Harvard University, the Patterson School of Diplomacy and International Commerce at the University of Kentucky, and the George Bush School of Government and Public Service at Texas A&M University.

Earlier versions of parts of this book were published previously as "Democracy and Victory: Why Regime Type Hardly Matters," *International Security*, Vol. 27, No. 2 (Fall 2002): 5–47; "The Wartime Impact of Peacetime War Planning," *Joint Forces Quarterly*, Spring 2002, 94–104; and "Democratic Victory Reconsidered," *International Security*, Vol. 28, No. 1 (Summer 2003): 142–94, and are used here by permission of MIT Press and the National Defense University.

I dedicate this book to my father, Charles A. Desch (*requiescat in pace*), my lifelong mentor and role model.

Power and Military Effectiveness

Introduction

One of the most significant developments in world politics in the later half of the twentieth century has been the spread of democracy around the globe. In 1942 fewer than 20 percent of the states of the world were democratic; by 1990 almost half were, according to data assembled by political scientist Samuel Huntington.[1] Indeed, the march of democracy seemed so inexorable that former State Department official Francis Fukuyama famously declared that we had reached "the End of History." By that he meant simply that while democracy may not have been the only form of political order left in the world, it had become the only legitimate one.[2]

Fukuyama's thesis generated much controversy and debate,[3] but his larger point that democracy was increasingly coming to dominate world politics—and would fundamentally change it—was widely accepted by both scholars and policymakers. Scholarly and policy attention moved away from a focus on the spread of democracy to the consequences of these developments. The first manifestation of this shift was the debate over what has become known as the "democratic peace." The notion that democracies are less likely to go to war with each other derives from classical liberal arguments such as that proposed in Immanuel Kant's system for "Perpetual Peace," which guarantees global amity once "the civil constitution of *every* nation [is] republican."[4] In a series of influential articles, political scientist Michael Doyle adopted Kant's argument but focused on liberalism and democracy rather than republicanism, and based on a survey of the wars of the nineteenth and twentieth centuries, he concluded that liberal and democratic regimes were very unlikely to go to war with each other.[5]

Since that seminal piece, much research has attempted to clarify the mechanisms explaining this "democratic peace"—specifically, is it due to the structure of democratic governments or the externalization of democratic norms among states?—but many scholars agree with international relations scholar Jack Levy's claim that it is "the closest thing we have to a law in international politics."[6]

This theory of the democratic peace not only has been influential in the academy but has also come to undergird America foreign policy in recent years.[7] Both the Clinton and Bush administrations embraced it as their rationale for believing that the spread of democracy will bolster U.S. security. Clinton's 1996 "National Security Strategy" stated explicitly that "the more that democracy and political and economic liberalization take hold in the world . . . the safer our nation is likely to be and the more our people are likely to prosper."[8] In his 2004 State of the Union address, President George W. Bush confirmed that "our aim is a democratic peace."[9] His national security advisor, Condoleezza Rice, subsequently explained that "President Bush's foreign policy is a bold new vision that draws inspiration from the ideas that have guided American foreign policy at its best: That democracies must never lack the will or the means to meet and defeat freedom's enemies, that America's power and purpose must be used to defend freedom, and that the spread of democracy leads to lasting peace."[10] The logic of the democratic peace is widely embraced by political leaders from both parties and will no doubt continue to influence American foreign policy for years to come.

Like previous American presidents, Bush not only thought that the spread of democracy would be good for America, but he was optimistic that it could take root nearly anywhere. "Do not bet against freedom," he advised us.[11] And he backed up his claims against long odds. On Iraq, the president argued, "There was a time when many said that the cultures of Japan and Germany were incapable of sustaining democratic values. Well, they were wrong. Some say the same of Iraq today. They were mistaken. The nation of Iraq—with its proud heritage, abundant resources and skilled and educated people—is fully capable of moving toward democracy and living in freedom."[12] In a discussion of Afghanistan in 2003, Vice President Dick Cheney boasted that the nation's capital has "a lot of people in it who are armchair quarterbacks, or who like to comment on the passing scene. But those who have predicted the demise of our efforts since 9/11, as we fought the war on terror, as we've liberated 50 million people in Iraq and Afghanistan, did not know what they were talking about. And I would submit to you today that we'll succeed in Iraq just like we did in Afghanistan. We'll stand up a new government under an Iraqi draft constitution, we'll defeat the insurgency. And in fact, it will be an enormous success story that will have a huge impact, not just in Iraq but throughout the region."[13] In Bush's view, there was no doubt that "the future belongs to freedom."[14]

Reinforcing the democratic peace's normative appeal is a parallel belief that democracy's spread is also in America's interest. President Bush promoted the idea in his second inaugural address: "The survival of liberty in our land increasingly depends on the success of liberty in other lands. The best hope for peace in our land is the expansion of freedom in all the world."[15] Given that premise, it is not surprising that the president has made it "the policy of the United States to seek and support the growth of democratic movements and institutions in every nation and culture, with the ultimate goal of ending tyranny in our world."[16] In an earlier interview, the president emphasized the point: "I believe the United States is *the* beacon for freedom in the world. And I believe we have a responsibility to promote freedom that is as solemn as the responsibility is to protecting the American people, because the two go hand-in-hand."[17] Bush held up his administration's efforts to democratize Iraq as a prime example of how democracy and U.S. security go together: "A free, democratic, peaceful Iraq will not threaten America or our friends with illegal weapons. A free Iraq will not be a training ground for terrorists, or a funnel of money to terrorists, or provide weapons to terrorists who would be willing to use them to strike our country or our allies. A free Iraq will not destabilize the Middle East. A free Iraq can set a hopeful example to the entire region and lead other nations to choose freedom. And as the pursuits of freedom replace hatred and resentment and terror in the Middle East, the American people will be more secure."[18] The spread and consolidation of democracy has now become a bipartisan foreign policy objective for the United States.

Recently, a related thesis about the benefits of the spread of democracy has begun to capture the attention of scholars and policymakers. Not only does the spread of democracy make the world more benign by reducing the likelihood of wars among liberal states, but democracies also seem to enjoy certain advantages in their relations with nondemocratic states, particularly when they are at war with them.[19] This argument, which I call "democratic triumphalism," also begins with an interesting empirical regularity. Since 1815, democratic states have been on the winning side of most wars.[20] One influential historian argues that this has been the case since ancient Athens.[21] And many today probably agree with historian John Lewis Gaddis that the democratic West's victory over the authoritarian East in the Cold War provides even more compelling evidence that democracies can successfully compete in the realm of high politics.[22] Research

now focuses on what makes democracies so successful at war. Some triumphalists think democracy makes states better at selecting winnable wars before they
start; others believe that democracy confers wartime advantages through the
generation of greater wealth, stronger alliances, better strategic decision making, greater public support, or better effort from troops in the field. Irrespective
of their particular theory, proponents of this view argue that there is a causal relationship between democratic political systems and military effectiveness.

As with the "democratic peace," "democratic triumphalism" has not only
been influential in the academy but has also shaped U.S. national security policy.
The rhetoric of democratic triumphalism has permeated Bush administration
pronouncements. Its clearest articulation was President Bush's claim that "there
is no power like the power of freedom, and no soldier as strong as the soldier
who fights for that freedom."[23]

The link between "democratic triumphalism" and Bush administration foreign policy is more than rhetorical. In fact, one triumphalist scholar whose work
I discuss at length in the following chapters, political scientist Aaron Friedberg,
was tapped by Vice President Dick Cheney to serve as his deputy national security advisor.[24] Another scholar, historian Victor Davis Hanson, met with, was
read by, and was cited regularly by the president, the vice president, and many
senior officials in the Department of Defense.[25] It is Hanson's view that "democracy, and its twin of market capitalism, alone can instantaneously create lethal
armies out of civilians, equip then with horrific engines of war, imbue them
with a near messianic zeal within a set time and place to exterminate what they
understand as evil, have them follow to their deaths the most ruthless of men,
and then melt anonymously back into the culture that produced them. It is democracies, which in the right circumstances, can be imbued with the soul of
battle, and thus turn the horror of killing to a higher purpose of saving lives and
freeing the enslaved."[26] What made him so attractive to the Bush administration
was precisely his argument about the military advantages that democracies supposedly enjoy.[27]

That the "democratic peace" and "democratic triumphalism" would be so attractive to American policymakers is not surprising. If true, these two theories
and the policies based upon them hold out the possibility that the fundamentally
conflictual nature of international politics can be alleviated as more states become democratic and that democratic states can successfully use their military
might to further this end because they will be able to defeat their authoritarian
rivals without their military prowess antagonizing their democratic allies.

The democratic peace has been very thoroughly debated, with some scholars questioning whether its purported mechanisms really operate as stipulated and others raising doubts about its statistical underpinnings.[28] Because democratic triumphalism is now widely embraced among scholars and has become so influential in public policy, it is high time to critically evaluate this argument as well. That is the purpose of this book.

I argue that there are serious problems with the logic and evidence supporting the concept of democratic triumphalism. In order to make the case that there is a causal relationship between the level of democracy in a state and its likelihood of prevailing in war, triumphalists need to show not only a statistical association between the two variables (and a logically compelling theory explaining the relationship) but also evidence that in actual cases the proposed causal mechanisms operate as stipulated. I offer reasons to think that the statistical association between democracy and victory is weak. In the triumphalists' models, democracy plays a very small role in explaining why states win or lose wars. Better specifications of these models suggest that democracy plays no role at all. Through an in-depth process tracing of case studies of victorious democracies, I find that the various prewar and wartime causal mechanisms that triumphalists offer to explain why democracies win their wars do not in fact operate. Thus, the association between democracy and victory appears to be spurious: factors such as wealth and power that make states more likely to win their wars also make it more likely that they will be democratic.

Military effectiveness, I argue, is the result of a constellation of variables. The most important of these is a preponderance in the material power assets available to the state. The reason that democracy seems to be a significant factor in explaining why democracies have been on the winning side of most of their wars over the past 200 years is that wealth is a crucial precondition for both military power and democracy. Of course, this is not to say that democracy represents an obstacle to the successful conduct of war, as democratic defeatists have long maintained; rather, it is just not much of an asset, as democratic triumphalists claim.

This investigation matters not only because it touches on the long-standing debate about the effectiveness of democracies in their relations with other states. This book also has important implications for the ongoing discussion of the sources of military effectiveness. A growing body of literature examines the nonmaterial constituents of military effectiveness.[29] Democratic triumphalists focus on only one nonmaterial factor—democracy—and argue that it helps states wisely choose and then effectively prosecute their wars. As the discussion in this book makes clear, nonmaterial factors seem to be important determinants of military effectiveness in only a handful of cases, and when you look closely at those cases, regime type is not the key factor explaining the outcome.

In addition to contributing to the scholarly debates about democracies and the sources of military effectiveness, this book has an explicit policy agenda. As political scientist Kenneth Waltz rightly warns, democratic triumphalism, if it is uncritically accepted by policymakers, could lead to many unnecessary wars.[30] I believe that American policymakers have learned from the democratic peace and democratic triumphalist literatures that democracies such as our own are uniquely virtuous and effective. This has contributed to an atmosphere in Washington, D.C., of democratic hubris, which, in turn, has led the United States into an unnecessary war in Iraq. My policy objective in this book is to caution policymakers that just because democracy is not an obstacle to the successful prosecution of wars, it does not mean that they ought to believe that it offers unique advantages either.

In order to make this case, I begin in chapter 1 by outlining the long-standing debate about the effectiveness of democracies in the realm of foreign policy and show that it is dominated by a pervasive but unwarranted pessimism. I also show how that debate is linked to the narrower question of whether democracy is a liability in war, which has been the conventional wisdom for more than 2000 years. I challenge the view that democracy is a liability—what I call democratic defeatism—on three grounds: first, the logic undergirding democratic pessimism is either not clear or not compelling; second, the causal mechanisms stipulated by democratic pessimists do not work in what should be an easy case for them, the "strange defeat" of France in the early stages of the Second World War; and, third, the fact that democracies have been on the winning side of most of their wars in the past 200 years clearly shows that democracy is not an obstacle to winning wars.

In chapter 2, I take up the democratic triumphalists' claim that the statistical association between democracy and victory over the past 200 hundred years supports a causal relationship between the two. First, I point out some limitations in the data from which this association comes. Second, I critique the logic and evidence that underpins the various triumphalist arguments that democracies have unique advantages in selecting winnable wars before the fact or waging them more effectively once they are in them.

Chapters 3, 4, and 5, are structured case studies of democratic countries that prevailed in wars. I chose these particular "fair-fight" cases because they are instances of democratic states prevailing when the most likely alternative explanation—material power—would have predicted they would have lost. As I show in the cases of democratic Poland's victory over the Soviet Union in the Russo-Polish War, democratic Israel's victory over its Arab adversaries in 1948, 1956, 1967, 1973, and 1982, and democratic Britain's victory over Argentina in 1982, none of the triumphalists' causal mechanism worked as stipulated. Indeed, alternative explanations based upon power, the nature of the conflict, nationalism, weak adversaries, geography, emulation of the most successful military formats and practices, and the level of development explain these outcomes far better.

Finally, in chapter 6 I offer additional evidence to support my alternative theory that power is the best explanation of victory in war. I also explore some of the nonmaterial sources of military effectiveness. I conclude by highlighting the deleterious policy implications of democratic triumphalism and urge American policymakers to avoid the trap of democratic hubris.

CHAPTER I

Democracy and Victory

Why Democracy Is Not a Liability

In this chapter, after summarizing the long-standing debate about democracy and foreign policy, I turn to a subset of that larger issue: the relationship between democracy and military effectiveness. Although the conventional wisdom holds that democracy is a liability in the successful conduct of war, I suggest three reasons for doubting this view: first, the theoretical propositions of democratic defeatism are not well or systematically laid out; second, the causal mechanisms that democratic defeatists think hinder democratic military effectiveness do not operate in one of their canonical cases; and, third, the aggregate outcomes for democracies at war over the past 200 years contradict what the defeatists would expect, as democracies have been on the winning side more often than not.

THE DEBATE ABOUT DEMOCRACY AND FOREIGN POLICY

Does regime type determine if a state can successfully conduct its foreign relations? The ongoing debate suggests just how complicated this question is. Kenneth Waltz, in an early study of democracy and foreign policy, cautioned that "how much of the success of a nation is caused by the structure of its government and how much by other conditions is difficult to determine."[1]

The conventional wisdom, extending back to the ancient Greek philosopher Plato, was that democratic regimes were at a decided disadvantage in this realm.[2] While generally endorsing democracy, many liberal political theorists were nonetheless skeptical of its ability to conduct its external affairs successfully. For example, John Locke observed that foreign policy "must be left in great part to the prudence of those who have this power committed to them, to be managed to the best of their skill for the advantage of the commonwealth."[3] "Foreign policies," Alexis de Tocqueville later commented in an oft-quoted remark, "demand scarcely any of those qualities which are peculiar to democracy; they require on the contrary, the perfect use of almost all those in which it is deficient."[4]

Many American statesmen share this skepticism about the ability of democracies to handle foreign affairs. Former secretary of state Dean Acheson decried "the limitation imposed by democratic political practices [that] makes it difficult to conduct our foreign affairs in the national interest."[5] Subsequent Cold War secretaries of state agreed. Not surprisingly, Henry Kissinger was no fan of democratic foreign policy. But even Warren Christopher, one of Jimmy Carter's secretaries of state, conceded that "we must accept that American foreign policy making will never be as efficient as it is in undemocratic countries."[6] Reservations about the ability of democracy to conduct foreign policy effectively were not limited to practitioners of democratic diplomacy. Scholars such as Gabriel Almond, Robert Dahl, and V. O. Key expressed some doubts about its ability.[7] Whatever democracy's other virtues, in the conduct of foreign policy large numbers of political theorists, statesmen, and scholars concur that it is weak and ineffective.

The reasons for this deficiency can be found in the character of the masses in democratic states. With some understatement, George Kennan observed that "public opinion, or what passes for public opinion, is not invariably a moderating force in the jungle of politics."[8] In an unfavorable contrast with the elite virtues of pragmatism, farsightedness, and rationality, Hans Morgenthau characterized the general public as overly moralistic, shortsighted, and emotional.[9] Walter Lippmann was searing in his indictment: "Where mass opinion dominates the government, there is a marked derangement of the true functions of power. The derangement brings about the enfeeblement, verging on paralysis of the capacity to govern."[10] Significant mass influence upon foreign policy would therefore be deleterious to its effective conduct.

The answer to democracy's weakness was to make foreign policy as undemocratic as possible. "Almost all nations that have exercised a powerful influence upon the destinies of the world," Tocqueville observed, "following out and executing vast designs, from the Romans to the English, have been governed by aristocratic institutions."[11] "Aristocratic institutions" was a euphemism for elite dominance of foreign policy. Lippmann and others justified leaving the conduct of foreign policy to elites because they believed that "strategic and diplomatic decisions call for a kind of knowledge—not to speak of an experience and seasoned judgement—which cannot be had by glancing at newspapers, listening to snatches of radio comment, watching politicians perform on television, hearing occasional lectures and reading a few books."[12]

The problem that proponents of elite control of foreign policy faced was how to get the masses to go along with it. In the aristocratic era, coercion might suffice. In the modern era of mass democracy, something more subtle was required. Hans Morgenthau laid bare the dilemma: "A tragic choice often confronts those responsible for the conduct of foreign affairs. They must either sacrifice what they consider good policy upon the altar of public opinion, or by *devious means* gain popular support for policies whose true nature they conceal from the public."[13] The doyen of American diplomatic history, Thomas A. Bailey, intimated that "Deception of the people may in fact become necessary. . . . The yielding of some of our democratic control of foreign affairs is the price we have to pay for greater physical security."[14] Bailey was seconded in this by Lippmann, who observed that "democratic politicians can rarely afford the luxury of telling the whole truth to the people."[15] The classic solution to the age-old problem of perceived democratic weakness in the realm of foreign policy was for elites, rather than the masses, to control the content of foreign policy by relying on coercion and trickery rather than candor and consent.

This conventional wisdom about democracy's debility in the realm of foreign policy did not go unchallenged. Enlightenment philosophers Immanuel Kant and Jeremy Bentham, for example, were ardent in their belief that democracy was a distinct asset. This view was shared by some American statesmen, such as President Woodrow Wilson and Secretary of Defense Elihu Root.[16] The source of this more optimistic view of democracy's ability was the belief that the masses could make a positive contribution to the formulation of a rational and coherent foreign policy.[17] James Mill, a disciple of Bentham, argued that the more people involved in foreign policy decision making, the better: "Every man possessed of reason is accustomed to weigh evidence and to be guided and determined by its preponderance. When various conclusions are, with their evidence, presented with equal care and equal skill, there is a moral certainty, though some few may be misguided, that the greatest number will judge right, and that the greatest force of evidence, whatever it is, will produce the greatest impression."[18]

Hearkening back to the arguments of the French physiocrat Condorcet, Bruce Russett argues that greater public involvement in foreign policy decision making will produce better foreign policy. According to the Condorcet's famous jury theorem, if there is a 55 percent chance of an individual making the right decision, and 1,000 people decide using majority rule, then there is a 99.9 percent chance that such a democratic procedure will produce the right outcome.[19] It was essential for the masses to be involved in foreign policy decision making because the elites, left to their own devices, were apt to make the wrong decision out of narrow self-interest or downright foolishness because they were unlikely to directly bear the costs of failure.[20] "Rather than driving relations on a perilously volatile course," Miroslav Nincic concluded, "public opinion is more likely to have had a moderating influence on foreign policy."[21] Thus, far from being a liability, democracy turns out to be a distinct asset for foreign policy decision making, and the masses should be involved, through consent and candor, in the entire foreign policy decision-making process.

Finally, a very small number of philosophers and scholars accept neither the conventional nor the revised wisdom about democracy and foreign policy. "The nature of the masses," Niccolò Machiavelli observed, "is no more reprehensible than is the nature of princes, for all do wrong and to the same extent when there is nothing to prevent them doing wrong."[22] Kenneth Waltz concluded that because democracies had both strengths and weaknesses, regime type was probably not the most important variable explaining foreign policy success or failure. In fact, he argued that designing and executing a rational and coherent foreign policy was a challenge for any type of political system.[23] In a later work, Waltz elaborated on this theme, observing that the functional similarities among states were more important than were internal differences such as regime type.[24] In sum, the nature of a state's regime type matters little for its ability to conduct a successful foreign policy, according to this view.

THE PARALLEL DEBATE ABOUT DEMOCRACY
AND MILITARY EFFECTIVENESS

Mirroring this debate about whether democracy is more, less, or no more or less effective in foreign policy is a parallel debate about whether that type of political system is a liability, is an asset, or makes no difference to a state's ability to prepare for and fight wars.

The conventional wisdom, stretching from Thucydides through Tocqueville to the mid- twentieth-century realists like Lippmann, Carr, and Kennan, is that democracy is a decided liability in preparing for and fighting wars. I refer to this pessimistic view as democratic defeatism. The Greek historian Thucydides' account of democratic Athens' failure in its titanic struggle with authoritarian Sparta in *The Peloponnesian War* is the classic indictment of democracy's inability to successfully fight wars.[25] Almost 2,000 years later, Mao Tse-tung rendered a similar verdict.[26] Even such a leading partisan of democracy as John F. Kennedy conceded that "when [democracy] competes with a system of government . . . built primarily for war, it is at a disadvantage."[27] At the height of the Cold War, French political theorist Jean-François Revel predicted democracy's eventual defeat and even penned its obituary: "Democracy probably could have endured had it been the only type of political organization in the world. But it is not basically structured to defend itself against outside enemies seeking its annihilation, especially since the latest and most dangerous of the external enemies, communism—the current and complete model of totalitarianism—parades as democracy perfected when it is in fact the absolute negation of democracy."[28] Particularly during the Cold War, the pessimistic perspective on the fighting power of democracies was dominant.[29] Despite the successful conclusion of the Cold War, a few Cassandras are still concerned that democracies are unprepared to meet the next major military threat from authoritarian states such as China or international terrorist organizations such as al-Qaeda.[30]

Once again, the root of the problem is that the masses have too much input into national security policy in democracies. "By committing even the conduct of state affairs to the whims of the multitude," Thucydides observed that democratic Athens blundered into "a number of mistakes, amongst which was the Sicilian expedition."[31] Writing in the *Federalist Papers,* Alexander Hamilton noted that "the cries of the nation and the importunities of their representatives have . . . dragged monarchs into war, or continued them . . . sometimes contrary to the real interests of the nation."[32]

Two assumptions about the relative virtues of the elites versus the masses and the relationship between state and society underpin this argument: elites are more competent than the masses in terms of national security decision making. Gabriel Almond suggests that this should be the case because national security issues are of a highly technical character, national security decision making requires secrecy, and the margin for error in national security is quite small.[33] Therefore, coercion and trickery, rather than consent and candor, are the most reliable means of mobilizing society.[34] Because democracy relies upon consent and incorporates the masses, democracies should not do well in war.

Democracy's military effectiveness can be affected through at least five causal mechanisms: democracies, because they are internally divided, should have a harder time pursuing coherent and consistent national security policies; democracies tend to be inwardly focused, and so they are less attentive to external security concerns; democracies are less flexible than authoritarian states; democracies, ruled by emotion rather than reason, tend to behave irrationally and inconsistently; and democracies have shorter time horizons due to the pressures of election cycles.[35] That being the case, the solution is for national security policy to remain the exclusive purview of a small elite. This elite may have to employ coercion—or, more frequently, trickery and deception—in order to keep the masses from meddling in national security decision making.

As with the widely held belief that democracies are unable to conduct successful foreign policies, the conventional wisdom about democracy undermining a state's ability to prepare for and fight wars is also challenged by a powerful revisionist current, what I call democratic triumphalism. The first assumption underpinning this revised wisdom is that the masses can make a positive contribution to the formulation and implementation of a state's national security policy. The Greek historian Herodotus maintained that democracy increased military effectiveness: "Take the case of Athens, which under the rule of princes proved no better in war than any of her neighbors but, once rid of those princes, was far the first of all."[36] In a similar vein, Pericles of Athens maintained that:

> There is a difference between us and our opponents in how we prepare for our military responsibilities in the following ways: we open our city for everyone and do not exclude anyone for fear that he might learn or see something that would be useful to an enemy if it were not concealed. Instead we put our trust not in secret weapons, but in our own courage when we are called upon to act. Our educations are different, too. The Spartans from their earliest childhood, seek to acquire courage by painfully harsh training, but we, living our unrestricted life, are no less ready to meet the same dangers they do. . . . If, therefore, we are prepared to meet danger after leading a relaxed life instead of one filled with burdensome training, with our courage merging naturally from our way of life instead of imposed by law, the advantage is ours. [37]

Because the citizens are an asset in the preparation for and waging of war, the second assumption is that consent and candor are superior to coercion and trickery as means of mobilizing the population for war.[38]

This debate about how regime type affects military effectiveness has continued over the course of nearly 2,000 years. I believe that it is fair to say that democratic defeatism has dominated this debate until quite recently, and so in the next two sections I assess the logic and evidence undergirding the view that democracy is a hindrance to the successful conduct of war.

CONCEPTUAL LAWS WITH DEMOCRATIC DEFEATISM

Most of the democratic defeatists' causal mechanisms do not necessarily follow from the fact that a state is democratic. For example, unless a state is a pure dictatorship, it is just as likely as a democracy to be plagued by differences over what should be the state's national security policy.[39] Similarly, authoritarian dictatorships also tend to be inward looking, perhaps even more so than democracies, because those sorts of regimes are illegitimate and constantly in danger of domestic usurpation.[40] Bureaucratic rigidity has also made both democracies and nondemocracies inflexible.[41] Domestic politics may distort democratic national security policy formulation and implementation, but nondemocracies may also adopt irrational policies.[42] Finally, although electoral cycles can certainly shorten the time horizons of democracies, nondemocracies can also be shortsighted.[43]

Not only does the democratic defeatist argument suffer from significant logical flaws, but it also finds little support in the empirical record. I demonstrate this in the next section in two ways. First, I run the core propositions of democratic defeatism through what should be an easy case for it—the strange defeat of democratic France by Nazi Germany in May–June 1940—and show that, despite arguments to the contrary, France's democratic political system had little to do with that defeat. Second, I report the striking findings of a number of recent studies showing that, over the past 200 years, democracies have been on the winning side of most of the wars they fought.

DID FRANCE DIE OF DEMOCRACY IN MAY–JUNE 1940?

The Battle of France is a "most likely" case for the conventional wisdom that democracies are not very effective militarily.[44] Democratic France, with forces roughly equal to those of Nazi Germany and superior technology, lost that campaign in May and June of 1940 very quickly, and French domestic politics seemed to manifest all of the pathologies commonly attributed to democracies. The Germans, who were slightly less powerful (0.8:1 in iron and steel production, 0.9:1 in military manpower, and 0.8:1 in population) than their democratic adversaries, nonetheless defeated the French decisively.[45] Some accounts attributed this defeat to French democratic politics. "It was entirely owing to our ministers and our assemblies," Marc Bloch later wrote, "that we were so ill-prepared."[46] At the time, France was deeply divided between partisans of the left and the right. Extremists from both sides favored foreign political movements in their internal political disputes,[47] and so most Frenchmen were more preoccupied with domestic events than developments abroad.[48] France's failed alliance bid with the Soviet Union also suggests that it suffered from diplomatic rigidity.[49] There was certainly an element of emotionalism in French foreign policy—especially in its preference for an alignment with Poland instead of the Soviet Union.[50] Finally, it is clear that the time horizons of the French leadership were quite short.[51] Nevertheless, closer inspection of this case reveals that the many problems in French domestic politics actually played little role in France's defeat.

The Battle of France was actually fairly close: the key to its outcome was the changing war plans on both sides.[52] France initially had a very sound operational plan, and Germany did not formulate its war-winning plan until very near to the commencement of hostilities. Had France and Germany stayed with their original battle plans, it is highly likely that the Battle of France would have ended in a stalemate or even a defeat for Germany.

Why France Lost

While France did indeed suffer from serious domestic disorder, the reasons France made the fateful strategic decisions it did had little to do with the domestic political crisis of the Third Republic or even its defensive military doctrine.[53] Indeed, historian Robert Young points out how the debate about the French defeat became highly politicized after the war, with many of the political explanations being driven by later domestic political agendas. Both the French left and the right later blamed the other's domestic political behavior for France's defeat with an eye not toward writing accurate history but rather to scoring future political points.[54]

Some have argued that poor morale in the French military hindered its operational performance. But this was not the view of France's adversaries. As the German historian Hans-Adolph Jacobsen observes, "it must be stressed that Allied troops fought magnificently, and worthily upheld the traditions that had so impressed the Germans in the First World War."[55] Elizabeth Kier suggests that French civilian leaders were more concerned with the domestic threat from the French military than with the international threat from Germany, and so they forced the military to take steps that, given France's particular military organizational culture, made it impossible for it to maintain the offensive military doctrine it had in the 1920s and 1930s. She maintains that the one-year term of service imposed upon the French military by their civilian leaders undermined its combat effectiveness.[56] But Len Deighton concluded that "there were many first-rate

French divisions with high morale and first-class equipment. The low standard of the reservists was more indicative of the *extent* of France's mobilization—one man in eight—than of the state of its regular army formations."[57]

The French military leadership certainly made a strategic blunder by overestimating the difficulty the Germans would have in advancing through the Ardennes; however, this mistake was not attributable to anything particular to French domestic politics because non-Frenchmen, including the eminent British military writer Sir Basil Henry Liddell-Hart and much of the German high command before February 1940, made the same misjudgment.[58] Many analysts have pointed to the lack of an appropriate "armored doctrine" as the source of the French defeat. Although the lack of such a doctrine could not have helped the French, it is not clear that its absence made the critical difference either. As Don Alexander remarks, inappropriate doctrine was less a factor than the maldeployment of French forces: "The French defeat was owing not so much to a faulty conception of mechanized war but to a flagrant disregard by the high command of its own instructions. . . . Far from waiting to determine the main axis of the German advance Gamelin dislocated his strategic reserves by committing the French Seventh Army to the Breda Variant."[59] The positioning of French forces was ultimately a function of this strategy. Thus, the key to the French defeat was that the high command adopted a strategy and formulated a war plan based on that strategy, which put the bulk of its forces too far north in Belgium to blunt the German attack through the Ardennes.[60]

Under their 1939 Plan E, the French would have concentrated upon defending their northern border with only a small advance by the Sixteenth Corps into Belgium to take up positions on the Escaut/Scheldt River (map 1.1). One other important fact to keep in mind about Plan E is that it kept the powerful Seventh Army, comprising one mechanized (DLM), two motorized, and four infantry divisions, in reserve near Riems. German military historians have noted that "if the enemy remained in his positions on the Franco-Belgium northeast frontier then the proposed offensive wedge would drive straight into his deployment."[61] Had the French military stuck with Plan E, it is likely that its forces would have stymied any German attack based on the original Plan Yellow.[62]

Conversely, it was the shift to Plan D/Breda Variant on March 20, 1940, that played a key role in the French defeat. Unlike Plan E, Plan D (map 1.2) advanced French forces far enough into Belgium not only to defend the Channel ports but also to protect major population centers, including the capital, Brussels. By standing on the Dyle River, rather than the Escaut/Scheldt, the French expected to shorten their front by forty miles. The Breda Variant to Plan D was even more

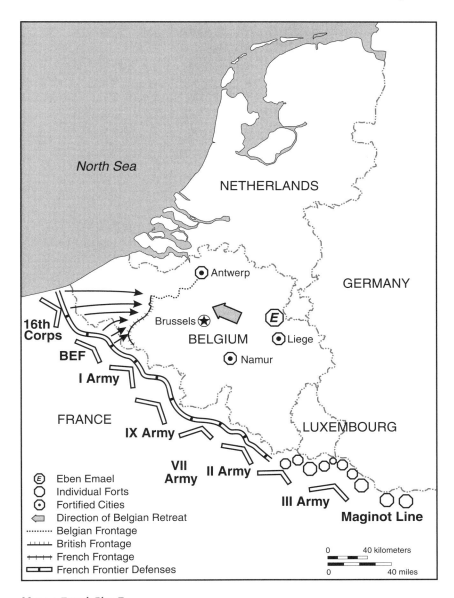

Map 1.1. French Plan E

ambitious: it sent the Seventh Army further north to Breda in the Netherlands in order to establish contact with the Dutch army, which was expected to retreat into a fortified area behind the Peel Marshes (map 1.3). While Plan D shortened Allied lines, Plan D/Breda Variant extended them.[63] More importantly, by mov-

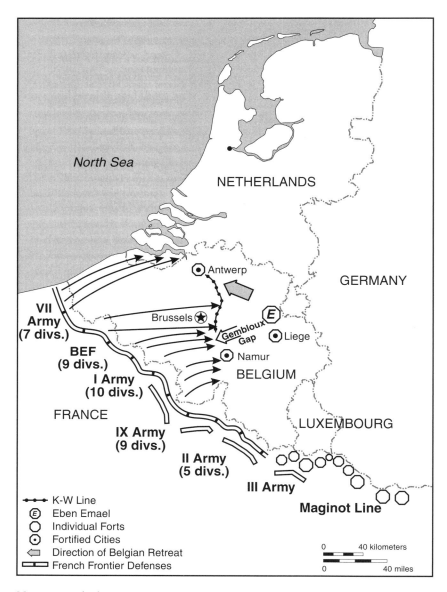

Map 1.2. French Plan D

ing the Seventh Army to southern Holland, both Plan D and Plan D/Breda Variant moved one of the French army's most effective units out of a position from which it could have threatened the southern flank of the Wehrmacht's Army Group A's main axis of attack under the Manstein Plan.[64]

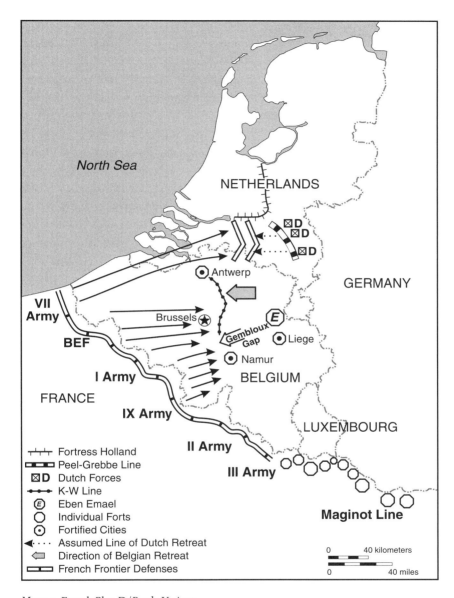

Map 1.3. French Plan D/Breda Variant

Plan D/Breda Variant positioned only reserves and other second-rate forces opposite Ardennes Forest.[65] The reason for this was that the French high command thought it would have eight or nine days' warning of a German attack through Ardennes.[66] Without any first-rate French forces behind the Ninth and

Second Armies, once they were defeated, the battle was over for all of the Allied forces deployed further north. As Deighton reminds us, "A modern army attacked from the rear is as good as defeated. It simply seizes up into a traffic jam of monumental confusion. Thus, the greatest ambition of a strategist is to attack an enemy's rear and then sever the enemy from his supplies. The Manstein plan had achieved both these ambitions."[67]

In short, the key French failing in May 1940 was to embrace precisely the wrong war plan in the face of an imminent German attack. Plan E would surely have foiled Plan Yellow; it might have also impeded the *Sichelschnitt*. Conversely, Plan D/Breda Variant played right into the Germans' hands. The French high command made a crucial strategic misstep in how it deployed its forces against the impending German *Blitzkrieg,* but this mistake had nothing to do with the political crisis of French democracy of the late 1930s.

Why Germany Won

Conversely, the German victory was not attributable to the fact that it was undemocratic. Rather, the key to the German victory also lay in the strategy the German armies adopted. It should be borne in mind that Germany did not initially have a war-winning strategy and plan. The original German plan (Yellow) for attacking France and the Low Countries was only developed in October 1939, after war had been declared and only eight months before active operations began.[68] Plan Yellow has sometimes been characterized, even by German military officers, as a replay of the Schlieffen Plan.[69] This is not quite accurate; the Schlieffen Plan at least aspired to deliver a decisive blow against France by seizing Paris. Plan Yellow was far less ambitious: it sought merely to achieve a tactical victory in Belgium. German forces in the west were organized in two army groups from north to south: Army Group B (facing Belgium) and Army Group A (facing Luxembourg and northeastern France). Army Group B, with thirty infantry and eight armored divisions, was the main attacking force under Plan Yellow. Its mission was to fight through Belgian, French, and British forces and seize the Channel ports. Army Group A, with twenty-two infantry divisions, was expected to launch only limited supporting attacks further south on Belgian and French forces to tie them down on the Meuse and Sambre Rivers (map 1.4). Had the Germans executed this original plan, as they intended, it is likely they would have failed. As Deighton concludes, "had the attack been made according to the earliest PLAN YELLOW, it would almost certainly have come to stalemate in the mud."[70]

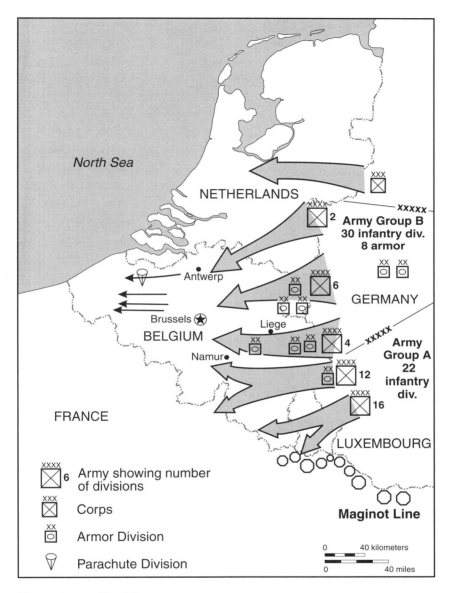

Map 1.4. German Plan Yellow

In contrast, the final plan the Germans developed in February 1940 turned out to be a war winner. The new plan (variously referred to as Plan Yellow [5], the Manstein Plan, or *Sichelschnitt*) had a much more ambitious goal: to cut off and decisively defeat Dutch, Belgian, French, and British forces in the area. It would do this by targeting a weak section of the French front, breaking through it, and cutting off the bulk of the Allied forces in the Netherlands, Belgium, and northern France. Unlike Plan Yellow, *Sichelschnitt* placed the main burden of the attack upon Army Group A with thirty-five infantry and ten armored or motorized divisions. Army Group B was relegated to a supporting role; with its twenty-six infantry and three armored divisions, it was expected only to subdue the Netherlands and to tie down French and Belgium forces in northeastern Belgium and southern Netherlands. Spearheaded by General Heinz Guederian's Nineteenth Panzer Corps, Army Group A was expected to wend its way through the Ardennes Forest, establish a series of beachheads across the Meuse River, drive through the French Ninth and Second Armies, and then race toward the French Channel Coast, thereby cutting off the bulk of the Allied forces in Belgium and northern France[71] (map 1.5). The Germans targeted the French Ninth and Second Armies because they knew that, unlike the French forces manning defensive positions in Belgium, these units consisted largely of reserve and second-rate troops. By attacking at these points, the Germans were able to achieve a 5:1 superiority over the French, and the breakthrough was made quite quickly.[72] The key to victory was that the Manstein Plan exploited the weakest part of the French front and landed a knockout punch on the Allies.

Fate, as much as superior strategic thinking, led the Germans to adopt the Manstein Plan instead of the original Plan Yellow. From the very beginning of the war, Hitler had been dissatisfied with the German army high command's (OKH) Plan Yellow. But he was also initially skeptical of the plan proposed by General Erich von Manstein (then the chief of staff to Army Group A commander General Gerd von Rundstedt) to redirect the main axis of attack through the Ardennes Forest. Three things changed his mind. First, in January 1940 two German air force officers in a light plane lost their way and crashed in Mechlen, Belgium, carrying parts of Plan Yellow, which was thus compromised. Second, German military intelligence ascertained that the new French Plan D/Breda Variant placed the bulk of the Allied forces in Belgium, right in the path of Army Group B's main axis of attack under Plan Yellow. Finally, a series of sand-table exercises in February 1940 demonstrated that *Sichelschnitt* was feasible. As Manstein concluded, "The utter débâcle suffered by the enemy in Northern Belgium was almost certainly due to the fact that, as a result of the changes later made to the operational plan, the tank units of Army Group A were able to cut straight through his lines of communication and push him away from the Somme."[73] The decisive German victory in the Battle of France would not have happened without this change in German plans.

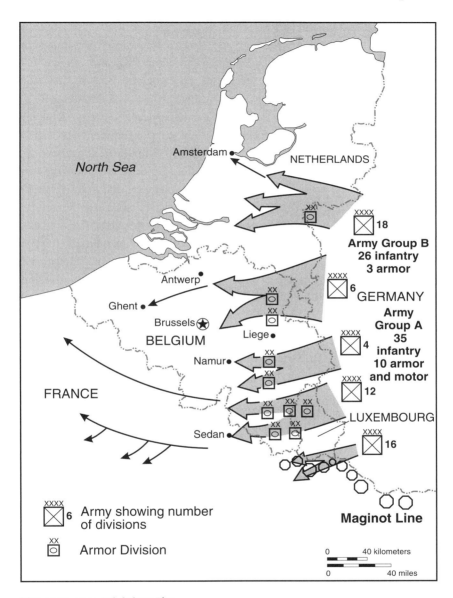

Map 1.5. German *Sichelschnitt* Plan

To be sure, democratic France suffered from a host of domestic problems. However, when you consider why France was defeated so quickly and decisively, it becomes apparent that these many domestic pathologies actually contributed very little, if anything, to that defeat. Rather, at least in this case, the critical changes in the French and German operational plans provide a far more compelling and comprehensive explanation for France's defeat and Germany's stunning victory. In sum, the fact that France was a democracy and Germany an autocracy tells us little about the outcome of the Battle of France.

An obvious objection to this argument is that showing that democratic defeatism does not explain the outcome of one case, even such a prominent one, hardly undermines the whole argument. As I discuss at length in the next chapter, however, over the past two hundred years democratic regimes have been on the winning side of most of their wars. This fact clearly suggests that democratic defeatism is wrong: democracy is certainly not an obstacle to effective preparation for and conduct of wars. The key question now becomes whether this fact also proves that democratic triumphalism is a powerful theory of military effectiveness. One of the central claims of this book is that it does not. All it does is confirm that there is a correlation between democracy and victory—it does not rule out alternative explanations for that correlation or confirm that the causal logics operate as stipulated by democratic triumphalists, both necessary steps in demonstrating a causal relationship.

CHAPTER 2

Democracy and Victory

Why Regime Type Hardly Matters

Democratic triumphalists point out that an examination of all wars since 1815 reveals that the more democratic states have been on the winning side in the overwhelming majority of cases.[1] From this correlation between the level of democracy and the likelihood of victory, they infer that there is a causal link between the two. "There is something about democratic regimes," Dan Reiter and Allan Stam triumphalists suggest, "that makes it easier for them to generate military power and achieve victory in the arena of war."[2] In their book *Democracies at War*, the most recent and comprehensive statement of the democratic triumphalists' case, Reiter and Stam make strong claims about the role of democracy in explaining why democracies have been on the winning side of so many wars. They conclude that "democracy has . . . been the *surest* means to power in the arena of battle" and that "democratic political institutions hold the *key* to prudent and successful foreign policy."[3]

Democratic triumphalists offer different reasons for why this should be the case and sometimes dissent from each other's arguments. Taken as a whole, though, they advance two reasons why democracies tend to win their wars.[4] Some adopt the "selection effects" argument, arguing that democracies are better at picking the wars they get into, starting only those they know they can win. Others embrace the "military effectiveness" argument. The latter maintain that once at war, democracies fight more effectively: they have bigger economies, form stronger alliances, make better decisions, have higher levels of public support, or can count on greater effort from their soldiers.

The aim of this chapter is to assess this sanguine view about democracy and military victory. I argue not only that the triumphalists' historical data are problematic but that their methodological approach does not strongly support their claim that, all other things being equal, democracies are more likely to win their wars. Specifically, there is no reason, nor is there much evidence, to suggest that leaders of democracies are more careful in selecting their wars than their authoritarian counterparts. The same charges can be made against the military effectiveness argument.

My case against the triumphalists should not, however, be read as support for the pessimists' claim that democracies are especially inept at fighting wars and therefore likely to be defeated by rival authoritarian states. Rather, it supports the view that democracies share no particular advantages or disadvantages in selecting and waging wars. In other words, regime type hardly matters for explaining who wins and loses wars.

In the remainder of the chapter, I present the triumphalists' case and then critique the data and approach that undergird the triumphalists' claim that, in war, democracies are more likely to be victorious. Next I analyze the logic and evidence that underpin the triumphalists' case: selection effects and military effectiveness.

THE TRIUMPHALISTS' CASE

The foundation of the triumphalists' claim that democracies are more likely to win wars is based on two studies that employ different sets of cases selected from the same databases. In an early study, David Lake looked at all the wars since 1815 listed in the Correlates of War (COW) dataset and selected those wars involving states with a democracy score of 6 or higher based on the widely used POLITY democracy index.[5] This criterion makes sense because states with such scores exhibit the characteristics we expect of democracies.[6] Using Lake's method, in the most current versions of the COW and POLITY datasets I have determined that there have been thirty-one wars involving democracies, three of which are excluded because they were draws (the Korean War, the 1969 War of Attrition, and the 1982 Lebanon War). Democracies won twenty-three of the remaining twenty-eight wars, or 82 percent (table 2.1).[7]

In a more recent study, Reiter and Stam examine most of the wars since 1815 in the COW dataset to determine how often, controlling for other factors, the more democratic state prevailed over the less democratic state. Reiter and Stam also used the POLITY democracy index to measure the level of democracy in

TABLE 2.1
Outcomes of COW Wars (democracy score = > 6)

Pessimists (5)	Triumphalists (23)	Not Counted (3)
	Mexican-American (1848)	
	Roman Republic (1849)	
	Crimean (1853–56)	
	Anglo-Persian (1856–57)	
	Sino-French (1844–85)	
Greco-Turkish (1897)		
	Spanish-American (1898)	
	Boxer Rebellion (1900)	
	Spanish-Moroccan (1909–10)	
	First Balkan (1912–13)	
	Second Balkan (1913)	
	World War I (1914–18)	
	Hungarian-Allies (1919)	
	Russo-Polish (1919–20)	
Russo-Finnish (1939–40)		
	World War II (1939–45)	
	Palestine (1948)	
		Korean (1950–53)
	Sinai (1956)	
Sino-Indian (1962)		
Second Kashmir (1965)		
Vietnam (1965–75)		
	Six-Day (1967)	
	Football (1969)	
		War of Attrition (1969–70)
	Bangladesh (1971)	
	Yom Kippur (1973)	
	Turko-Cypriot (1974)	
	Falklands (1982)	
		Lebanon (1982)
	Gulf War (1990–91)	

the warring states. Utilizing that criterion and the most current versions of the COW and POLITY III datasets (see the appendix to this chapter), I counted seventy-five wars, twenty-four of which were excluded because data are missing on the level of democracy for all participants, the wars involved states with the same democracy score, the war ended in a draw, or the conflict was still ongoing. The more democratic state won thirty-six of the remaining fifty-one wars, or 71 percent (table 2.2).[8]

In sum, the historical record appears to support the triumphalists' claim that, whether one looks at wars involving states with democracy scores greater than 6 or expands the universe to consider all wars in which more democratic states battled less democratic ones, there is a strong correlation between democracy and victory.

TABLE 2.2
Outcomes of COW Wars (winner democracy > loser democracy)

Pessimists (15)	Triumphalists (36)	Not Counted (24)
	Franco-Spanish (1823)	
		Russo-Turkish (1828–29)
	Mexican-American (1848)	
		Austro-Sardinian (1848–49)
First Schleswig-Holstein (1848–49)		
		Roman Republic (1849)
La Plata (1851–52)		
	Crimean (1853–56)	
	Anglo-Persian (1856–57)	
		Italian Unification (1859)
		Spanish-Moroccan (1859–60)
		Italo-Roman (1860)
	Italian-Sicilian (1860–61)	
	Franco-Mexican (1862–67)	
Ecuador-Columbia (1863)		
Second Schleswig-Holstein (1864)		
	Lopez (1864–70)	
	Spanish-Chilean (1865–66)	
		Seven Weeks' (1866)
		Franco-Prussian (1870–71)
		Russo-Turkish (1877–78)
	Pacific (1879–83)	
	Sino-French (1884–85)	
Central American (1885)		
	Franco-Thai (1893)	
	Sino-Japanese (1894–95)	
Greco-Turkish (1897)		
	Spanish-American (1898)	
	Boxer Rebellion (1900)	
	Russo-Japanese (1904–5)	
Central American (1906)		
		Central American (1907)
	Spanish-Moroccan (1909–10)	
		Italian-Turkey (1911–12)
	First Balkan (1912–13)	
	Second Balkan (1913)	
	World War I (1914–18)	
	Hungarin-Allies (1919)	
	Russo-Polish (1919–20)	
	Lithuanian-Polish (1919–20)	
		Greco-Turkish (1919–22)
		Franco-Turkish (1919–22)
Sino-Soviet War (1929)		
	Manchuria (1931–33)	
Chaco (1932–35)		
Italo-Ethiopian (1935–36)		
	Sino-Japanese (1937–41)	
	Chankufeng (1938)	

Pessimists (15)	Triumphalists (36)	Not Counted (24)
Nomohan (1939)		
Russo-Finnish (1939–40)		
	World War II (1939–45)	
	Franco-Thai (1940–41)	Korean (1950–53)
	Palestine (1948)	
	Sinai (1956)	
		Russo-Hungarian (1956)
Sino-Indian (1962)		
Second Kashmir (1965)		
Vietnam (1965–75)		
	Six-Day (1967)	
	Football (1969)	
		War of Attrition (1969–70)
	Bangladesh (1971)	
	Yom Kippur (1973)	
	Turko-Cypriot (1974)	
		Vietnamese-Cambodian (1975–79)
		Ethiopian-Somali (1977–78)
		Uganda-Tanzanian (1978–79)
		Sino-Vietnamese (1979)
		Iran-Iraq (1980–1988)
	Falklands (1982)	
		Lebanon (1982)
		Sino-Vietnamese (1985–87)
	Gulf War (1990–91)	
		Azeri-Armenian (1992–98)

DO DEMOCRACIES REALLY WIN WARS MORE OFTEN?

To determine whether regime type explains a state's military performance, it is important first to look more closely at both the data and the approach that lead triumphalists to conclude that democracies are more likely to win their wars.

Data

There are at least five problems with the data that the triumphalists bring to bear to support their claim that democracies excel at winning wars.

First, conflicts are misaggregated in a number of cases. Improper disaggregation could—and sometimes does—bias the results in favor of democracy.[9] For example, in Lake's dataset World War II is treated as a single war involving the same belligerents from 1939 to 1945 in which the democracies prevailed. This characterization is inaccurate, however, because the war comprised at least three distinct conflicts involving different actors and different scenarios: the Battle of France (May–June 1940); the European War (June 1941–May 1945); and the Pacific War (December 1941–August 1945). Treating World War II as single war over-states the effectiveness of the democracies and misses the real reasons why they ended up on the winning side.[10]

Second, there are cases of democracies winning wars as members of mixed alliances in which the nondemocracy accounted for the majority of the winning alliance's military strength.[11] A "mixed alliance" is one in which the democratic participant accounts for less than 50 percent of the power potential in two out of three power categories, such as number of troops, iron and steel production, and total population. In the second phase of World War II in Europe, for in-stance, a mixed alliance including Britain, the Soviet Union, and the United States defeated an alliance of fascist states led by Nazi Germany and Italy. Although the democracies—Britain and the United States—were on the win-ning side, this case does not strongly support the triumphalists' claim for two reasons. The Soviet Union—not Britain and the United States, as Reiter and Stam suggest—was principally responsible for defeating Nazi Germany. Most historians agree that the war in Europe was settled mainly on the eastern front.[12] Indeed roughly 85 percent of the Wehrmacht was deployed along that front for most of the war; not surprisingly, about 75 percent of German casualties were suffered there.[13]

Third, many of the cases of wars involve states that cannot really be consid-ered democratic and therefore are not strong tests of the triumphalists' theories. This approach of looking at wars involving states that are relatively more demo-cratic increases the number of relevant cases but also results in the inclusion of many cases of wars between states in which at least one of the belligerents does not score a 6 or higher on the democracy scale—for example, the Pacific War (1879–83), the Sino-Japanese War (1894–95), the Russo-Japanese War (1904–5), the Manchurian War (1931–33), the Sino-Japanese War (1937–41), Changkufeng (1938), or the Football War (1969).

Fourth, in several cases the triumphalists' coding is questionable and, when corrected, weakens their case. Reiter and Stam, for example, code the 1969–70 Israeli-Egyptian War of Attrition and the 1982 Israeli-Syrian War as victories for democratic Israel. Most analysts, including the original compilers of the COW dataset, regard them as draws, however. As Ezer Weizeman concluded, "It is no more than foolishness to claim that we won the War of Attrition. On the con-trary, for all their casualties it was the Egyptians who got the best of it."[14] As I show in chapter 4, the 1982 Lebanon War hardly counts as a clear Israeli victory either. Even a few miscodings can bias the triumphalists' findings about the propensity of democracies to win their wars.

Finally, there are cases in which the belligerents' interests in the outcome of the conflict are so asymmetrical that it is impossible to ascribe the outcome to regime type and not the balance of interests. For example, Israel did well in conventional wars in which its survival was at stake (e.g., 1948 and 1967). In contrast, Israel fought poorly in unconventional wars where its survival was not at stake (e.g., Lebanon in 1982).[15] This is not surprising because, as Martin Gilbert notes, the 1982 Lebanon War "was the first war in Israel's history for which there was no national consensus. Many Israelis regarded it as a war of aggression."[16]

Approach

Many of the cases in the COW dataset are not fair tests of whether regime type affects the likelihood of that state winning wars. A fair test of a theory involves identifying crucial cases that clearly rule out alternative explanations, such as that states with a preponderance of power are more likely to win their wars.[17] In some cases, a democracy was much more powerful than its adversary and used that advantage simply to overwhelm its rivals. A "gross mismatch" is a conflict in which one side has a greater than 2:1 advantage in two out of three power indices. Such gross mismatches should be considered only if the triumphalists' can prove that regime type caused the imbalance of power.[18] The defeat of Nazi Germany by the United States, Great Britain, and the Soviet Union is an example of a gross mismatch. The Allies had a 3.8:1 advantage in iron and steel, a 1.7:1 advantage in military manpower, and a 2.47:1 advantage in population over the Axis. In the Pacific War the United States, with support from Australia, Britain, China, and New Zealand, inflicted a decisive defeat on Japan in 1945. Although the democracies were on the winning side in this conflict, Japan lost because it was far less powerful than its rivals. Although the military manpower balance was roughly even, the Allies had a 13:1 advantage in iron and steel production and a 10:1 advantage in population.

Of the all seventy-five wars since 1815 listed in the most recent version of the COW dataset, fifty-four are clearly unfair tests, with only twenty-one cases classified as fair fights. Of these, the more democratic state won twelve times, while the less democratic state won nine times (table 2.3).[19] There were thirty wars involving states that were clearly democratic; however, twenty-two of these involve misaggregations, mixed alliances, gross mismatches, or asymmetric in-

TABLE 2.3
Fair Tests

War	Misaggregation	Mixed Alliance	Gross Mismatch	Asymmetric Interests	Draw	Fair Test/Favors?
Franco-Spanish			X			No
Russo-Turkish						No[a]
Mexican-American			X			No[b]
Austro-Sardinian			X			No[c]
First Schleswig-Holstein			X			No
Roman Republic			X			No[b]
La Plata			X			No
Crimean		X				No[b]
Anglo-Persian			X			No[b]
Italian Unification						No[c]
Spanish-Moroccan						No[a]
Italo-Roman						No[c]
Italo-Sicilian			X			No
Franco-Mexican						No
Ecuador-Colombian				X		Yes/Pessimists
Second Schleswig-Holstein						Yes/Pessimist
Lopez		X	X			No
Spanish-Chilean				X		No
Seven Weeks'						No[c]
Franco-Prussian						No[c]
Russo-Turkish						No[a]
Pacific						Yes/Triumphalists
Sino-French			X			No[b]
Central American (1885)						Yes/Pessimists
Franco-Thai			X			No
Sino-Japanese						Yes/Triumphalists

War				Assessment
Greco-Turkish			X	No[b]
Spanish-American			X	No[b]
Boxer Rebellion		X		No[b]
Russo-Japanese				Yes/Triumphalists
Central American (1906)				Yes/Pessimists
Central American (1907)				No[c]
Spanish-Moroccan			X	No[b]
Italo-Turkish				No[a]
First Balkan		X		No[b]
Second Balkan		X		No[b]
World War I	X		X	No[b]
Hungarian	X			No[b]
Russo-Polish			X	Yes/Triumphalists[b]
Lithuanian-Polish				No
Greco-Turkish				No[c]
Franco-Turkish				No[c]
Sino-Soviet				Yes/Pessimists
Manchurian				Yes/Triumphalists
Chaco				Yes/Pessimists
Italo-Ethiopian			X	No
Sino-Japanese				Yes/Triumphalists
Changkufeng				Yes/Triumphalists
Nomohan			X	No[b]
Russo-Finnish			X	No
World War II	X		X	No[b]
Franco-Thai			X	No

continued

TABLE 2.3 (continued)

Ware	Misaggregation	Mixed Alliance	Gross Mismatch	Asymmetric Interests	Draw	Fair Test/Favors?
Israeli Independence						Yes/Triumphalists[b]
Korean					X	No[b]
Russo-Hungarian						No[c]
Sinai			X			No[b]
Sino-Indian						Yes/Pessimists[b]
Second Kashmir					?	No[b]
Vietnam				X		No[b]
Six Day						Yes/Triumphalists[b]
Football						Yes/Triumphalists
Attrition					X	No[b]
Bangladesh			X			No[b]
Yom Kippur						Yes/Triumphalists[b]
Turkish-Cypriot			X			No[b]
Vietnamese-Cambodian						No[a]
Ethiopian-Somali						No[a]
Uganda-Tanzanian						No[a]
Sino-Vietnamese						No[a]
Iran-Iraq					X	No
Falklands						Yes/Triumphalists[b]
Lebanon					X	No[b]
Sino-Vietnamese			X			No[a]
Gulf War						No[b]
Azeri-Armenian?					X	No[b]

[a] Equally democratic
[b] Democracy score > 6
[c] Missing democracy scores

terests. Thus, of the remaining eight cases, three support the pessimists and five support the triumphalists.[20] While democracies do better than their rivals in both cases, and better when you consider just wars involving one clearly democratic state (democracies win in 63 percent of the eight cases) than in all wars (democracies win in 57 percent of the twenty-one cases), we cannot have much confidence in the proposition that democracy is the reason that states are more likely to win their wars.

An obvious objection is that excluding cases that are not "fair fights" is methodologically unsound because it deprives us of useful information. There is, however, no methodological problem with focusing on "fair-fight" cases, because doing so has an effect similar to adding control variables in a multivariate equation. The purpose of control variables is to account for variation in the dependent variable that may be wrongly attributed to the independent variable. Adding them thus avoids this "omitted variable bias."[21] In either case, the net result is to discount observations that are not decisive to the theory.[22]

The real question is whether limiting consideration to fair fights provides an equitable test of the various triumphalist theories. Lake maintains that looking at only fair fights is an unfair test of his theory because he believes that one of the wartime advantages of democracies is that they tend to be more successful in generating wealth, which in turn gives them greater military resources with which to wage war. Because wealth is one of the sinews of military power, it is not surprising that wealthier states tend to win their wars. Excluding such cases, in Lake's view, eliminates those cases on which his theory depends.

There are two problems with this argument. First, Lake's theory is impossible to test against the most likely alternative theory: that states win when they have a preponderance of wealth. Second, as Lake acknowledges, it is possible that the relationship between democracy and victory is spurious, inasmuch as wealth may explain both democracy and military success.[23] Lake's subsequent effort to establish the causal chain from democracy to wealth by showing that democracies are more likely to provide public services does not shed much light on the question of whether democracies are likely to produce greater wealth.[24]

Reiter and Stam reject Lake's claim that democracy makes states better able to generate wealth and advance a somewhat different argument.[25] They maintain that democracies start only those wars they can easily win. But, like Lake, they maintain that focusing on "fair fights" is not an adequate test of their theory, because they claim that the main advantage of democracies is finding unfair fights.

After testing Lake's wealth argument, Reiter and Stam conclude that they "can reject two hypotheses: that democracies in general win their wars because they have higher capabilities, and that democratic initiators win wars because they have significantly higher capabilities than do other kinds of initiators." Elsewhere they note that their selection effects argument "does not imply that [democracies] win because they are more powerful, rather that they are better at avoiding wars they would have gone on to lose had they fought them."[26] It is difficult to reconcile these arguments that power imbalances do not explain victory with their claim that democratic initiators tend to win because they are better at selecting "unfair fights" in which they have a decided advantage in military power.[27]

Another possible objection is that the better approach would be to keep the unfair tests in the dataset and control statistically for other factors that may account for why democracies win their wars more often than nondemocracies. The major advantage of this approach is that it offers a large number of cases that make advanced statistical analysis possible. Even if one accepts the validity of all the historical cases and tries to control for competing explanations, there are still reasons to question the triumphalists' claim that democracy is the key to military victory.

First, Lake, as well as Reiter and Stam, employs approaches that utilize data consisting of a number of countries, some of which are involved in multiple wars, to generate each data point. A central assumption of statistical analysis, however, is that each data point is independent (the outcome of one war is not affected by the outcome of previous ones), homogeneous (the wars are roughly comparable), and exchangeable (if a democracy can beat one nondemocracy, it should be able to defeat all similar nondemocracies). Reiter and Stam, for example, have a total sample of 197, but this actually consists of only 66 countries, a small number of which are looked at repeatedly. Among the most democratic states in their dataset (scores of 9 or 10 on the democracy index), only three— Britain, Israel, and the United States— compose approximately 56 percent of the cases. Of the most democratic states that won wars, these three countries account for 75 percent of the results. Given that three states play such a large role in the triumphalists' findings, it makes sense to ask whether there are particular circumstances in each case, or variables not contained in the triumphalists' models, that explain their propensity for winning particular wars. This potential problem of dependencies among observations affects much research using large datasets in international relations.[28] Some triumphalists argue that they can eliminate this problem within a regression framework simply by reporting robust standard errors.[29] The optimal solution to the problem, however, is to collect more and better data that would make it possible to control directly for the unobserved variables that might be unique to each case.[30] This task is by no means easy, however. Unobserved variable bias would not be much of a problem if it were easy to identify and measure those variables. Therefore, another way to solve the problem is through in-depth process tracing to ascertain whether factors unique to those cases explain the outcome.

Second, although there is a correlation between democracy and victory, correlation by itself does not mean causation.[31] To establish causation, the most likely alternative explanations need to be ruled out, and it must be demonstrated that the causal mechanisms of the theory actually operate in the cases. There are, however, alternative explanations that the triumphalists cannot rule out by controlling for them statistically. For example, a large body of scholarship argues that democracy takes root and flourishes as the result of a distinct set of preconditions, including high levels of aggregate wealth, equitable wealth distribution, free markets, high levels of social development, a strong feudal aristocracy, a strong bourgeoisie or middle class, high levels of literacy and education, a liberal political culture (e.g., toleration, compromise, and respect for the law and individual rights), Protestantism, strong intermediary organizations, capable political institutions, low levels of domestic political violence, moderate politics, occupation by a democratic state, geographical security (water, mountains, etc.), strong allies, and weak adversaries.[32]

Some of these preconditions for democracy also confer decided military advantages.[33] For example, wealthy, highly developed, well-educated, highly institutionalized states that are geographically secure and have strong allies and weak adversaries are also more likely to win wars. Rather than democracy explaining this outcome, it is possible that certain preconditions of democracy produce both a democratic political system and an impressive record of military success. If this argument is correct, then the correlation between democracy and military victory is spurious. The common preconditions, not democracy per se, account for both.

In sum, the historical data do not strongly support the triumphalists' claim that democracies are more likely to win wars than nondemocracies. In particular, many of the cases they employ are not fair tests of their claim and therefore cannot be used to support (or refute) it. Nor does the triumphalists' approach effectively rule out alternative factors that may explain why states win wars: the existence of common preconditions for democracy and victory. In the following two sections, I assess the specific causal mechanisms that the triumphalists use to explain why democracies are more likely than other types of regimes to win their wars.

SELECTION EFFECTS

According to the selection effects argument, democracies win more of their wars because democratic leaders start them only if they have a high probability of winning them. There are two versions of the selection effects explanation, both of which employ logics very similar to the effects of "audience costs" on other aspects of the foreign policy behavior of democratic states. The core of the audience costs argument is that democrat leaders are sensitive to the effects of their policies on public opinion, so they have a powerful incentive to cleave to those policies which the public supports.[34]

One approach focuses upon the putatively superior information-gathering and disseminating properties of democratic political systems. The logic of the argument here is that democratic leaders should be better at strategic decision making because they can avail themselves of the open marketplace of ideas, which presumably would give them better information, making it more likely that they would select winnable wars. Another strand of this argument is that democratic publics know more about government decisions and presumably could use that information, either prospectively or retrospectively, to prevent misguided wars.

The other approach depends upon the institutional constraints of democratic political systems. The reason democratic leaders are more selective about their wars, in this view, is that they are regularly subjected to the electoral process and the voters will punish a leader who initiates an unsuccessful war. Because the public will pay the ultimate cost in blood and treasure, democratic leaders will be very careful about starting wars that they cannot win quickly and easily.[35] Authoritarian leaders, on the other hand, are rarely held accountable by their populations and thus can more easily weather a losing war.[36] Here, the assumption is that democratic leaders want to stay in power and democratic publics will punish leaders who start and lose wars but will reward those who start and win them. Given these two assumptions, democratic leaders should be very careful about the wars they start, only doing so when they believe they have a high probability of victory.[37]

Both Lake and Reiter and Stam use statistical methods that aim to show that whether democracies start wars matters tremendously for the outcome. In particular, they point to the positive and significant association between victory and an interaction variable involving democracy and war initiation. From this, they infer that information and institutional constraints must have caused victory

TABLE 2.4
Probit Results (win/lose)

Variables	R&S Model 4
democracy*initiation	0.0675943 *
	(0.0298018)
democracy*target	0.0639582 *
	(0.0275639)
initiation	0.9142049 **
	(0.3422103)
capabilities	3.726842***
	(0.5249923)
allies capabilities	4.721843***
	(0.6837011)
quality ratio	0.0522075
	(0.0329194)
terrain	−10.93261 ***
	(2.937978)
strategy*terrain	3.560021 ***
	(0.9689448)
strategy1	7.235081 *
	(2.886022
strategy2	3.478767
	(1.993146)
strategy3	3.35718 *
	(1.428867)
strategy4	3.069146 *
	(1.252304)
Constant	−5.517191 **
	(1.698374)
Pseudo R2	0.5244
Log Likelihood	−64.886064
N	197

Note: The variables I used were polini, poltarg, init, wl, concap, qualrat, capasst, terrain, strat1, strat2, strat3, strat4, and staterr. These variables are discussed at length in Reiter and Stam, *Democracies at War,* 40–44.

    * ≤ .05 (all tests two-tailed and all standard errors are robust)

     ** ≤ .01

     *** ≤ .001

(table 2.4).[38] Despite this apparent support for the triumphalists' case, there are grounds for skepticism about the extent to which democracy explains the outcome, the logic of the argument, the best way to model the process, and whether the processes in actual cases support the finding.

Victory in war is a complex and overdetermined phenomenon in which many factors play a role. Instead of measuring the size of the relative effect of democracy and other variables that might explain victory, Lake and Reiter and Stam are content merely to show that democracy is statistically significant in their models.[39] But there is more to interpreting the results of models besides the "statistical significance" of the variables. Their "practical significance," which is a function not only of the variables' statistical significance but also of the size of the coefficient and their signs, must also be considered. "Too much focus on statistical significance," one standard text on econometrics reminds us, "can lead to the false conclusion that a variable is 'important' . . . even though its estimated effect is modest."[40] In short, democracy may be statistically significant but still not be the key to victory. In other words, democratic triumphalism is not a very useful theory because its central causal variable does not have "large explanatory power."[41]

As a first cut, table 2.5 presents the results of a calculation of the "marginal effects" for each variable in table 2.4. It shows that democracy has one of the smallest effects of any variable. Marginal effects are derivatives of the probability that the dependent variable will equal 1 (in this case, that the state wins) with respect to each independent variable by itself. The marginal effects measure the sensitivity of that probability of winning to changes in the values of various independent variables. The higher the absolute value of marginal effect of an independent variable (e.g., the larger the value of the dy/dx), the more sensitive the probability of the dependent variable equaling 1 is to changes in each independent variable and thus the greater the effect of that independent variable. In other words, the marginal-effects calculation measures how much one's chance of winning changes because of variations in the various independent variables. The interaction between democracy and initiation has one of the smallest effects (0.0267582), whereas terrain (−4.327838) and power—both the state's (1.475326) and its allies' (1.869212)—and the interaction between strategy and terrain (1.409287) have the largest effects on who wins.[42]

There are two conceivable objections to my approach for assessing the triumphalists' selection effects argument. First, because the democracy variable is included as part of an interaction term with an initiation variable, one might argue that I cannot gauge its relative impact in this fashion. The democracy* initiation interaction variable, however, is just 1 or 0 (whether the state initiated war or not) times its democracy score. There is little reason to think that marginal effects cannot be calculated for it in the same way they would be for the straight democracy variable. Second, because the democracy and power variables have different scales, calculating their relative marginal effects is like comparing apples and oranges. However, if we calculate elasticities (the effects of a percentage increase in the independent variables that makes them more comparable) rather than marginal effects, which should mitigate the problem of different scales, democracy still has a relatively small impact on the likelihood of victory.[43]

TABLE 2.5
Marginal Effects of Variables in Probit

Variables	dy/dx
democracy*initiation	0.0267582
democracy*target	0.0253188
initiation*	0.3469761
capabilities	1.475326
allies' capabilities	1.869212
quality ratio	0.0206671
terrain	−4.327838
strategy*terrain	1.409287
strategy1*	0.6914264
strategy2*	0.5623581
strategy3*	0.851552
strategy4*	0.5051578

Note: (*) dy/dx is for the discrete change of dummy variable from 0 to 1.

The more challenging problem with assessing the marginal effect of a variable in a probit model is that the various independent variables' effects upon the dependent variable are also inextricably linked to their relationships with each other. In an ordinary least squares regression model, one might simply look at the size of the coefficient to determine its effect on the dependent variable, but this approach does not always work for probit models. Because of these potential problems with looking exclusively at the coefficients of the different variables, I also try to ascertain the substantive significance of democracy as opposed to other independent variables in three additional ways.

First, I look at the effect upon the log likelihood of the probit model of adding additional variables. The log likelihood measures the fit of the model with the data. The smaller the log likelihood, the better the fit. In Reiter and Stam's treatment of the selection effect argument, they estimate a model predicting the likelihood of military victory based on just the standard indicators of military power (capabilities, quality, and strategy), which produces a log likelihood of −69.3 (this is their model 3 in their table 2.2). When they add their interaction variables, including democracy and initiation, the resulting model improves slightly to a log likelihood of −64.9 (this is their model 4). However, they also estimate a model that includes only democracy and initiation (model 1) and then one (model 4) that adds these military power variables. The log likelihood goes from −128.3 to −64.9. The standard way to assess whether adding variables improves the fit of the model is to calculate a chi-square statistic for the difference between these two log likelihoods multiplied times two using the number of variables added as the degree of freedom.[44] With this approach, it seems clear that, while adding

TABLE 2.6
Marginal Effects of Democracy*Initiation, Capabilities, and Allies' Capabilities at Minimum, Mean, and Maximum Values

	Democracy*Initiation	Capabilities	Allies' Capabilities
Minimum	.0239869	.7226078	1.429178
Mean	.0267582	1.427326	1.869212
Maximium	.0185021	.0684485	.0164265

democracy*initiation improves the fit of the model slightly, adding military power makes a much bigger difference.

Second, I also calculate the substantive effects of the variables of interest at various levels—such as their minimum, mean, and maximum (holding the rest of the variables in the model at their mean)—to see what their effects are on the likelihood of victory.[45] As table 2.6 shows, the effects of a state's capabilities and those of it allies are much larger than the democracy*initiation interaction variable at their minimum and mean and, for the state's capabilities, at the maximum. Figure 2.1 shows the same relationship graphically. Even at their maximum values, where democracy comes the closest to capabilities (and actually exceeds an ally's capabilities slightly), a state's capabilities still have six times the effect of its regime type.

Finally, I look at how much democracy affects the predicted probabilities of victory by asking the counterfactual question, How many wars would have turned out differently if the democracies had been nondemocracies? To do this, I estimate the war outcome model, which generates estimates of β and γ. Then, for each observation involving a democracy, I calculate two things: the predicted probability of victory based on the model and the predicted probability of victory if the state had not been a democracy. In the latter, I create an artificial observation for each democratic observation that is the same in every way, but the democracy variable is set to its opposite value (e.g., 10 to –10). I then compare the predicted probability of victory for the democracy with the predicted probability of victory in the counterfactual case in which the state was nondemocratic. The key question is, In how many cases was the predicted probability for the democracy greater than 0.5 but the predicted probability in counterfactual cases less than 0.5? Those are the cases in which regime type is predicted to make the difference between being more likely to win and being more likely to lose. If the effect of regime type is substantively small, then there will be few cases in which switching the regime type would have switched the most likely outcome. In fact, what I find is that of fifteen such cases of high democracy, the predicted

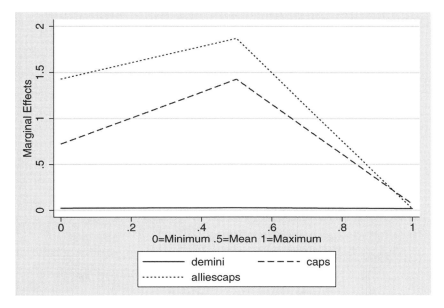

Figure 2.1. Graphic Presentation of Marginal Effects

probabilities change in only two (the 1912–13 First Balkan War and the 1920 Russo-Polish War), one of which is a case in which in-depth process tracing shows that democracy did not operate through any of the triumphalists' hypothesized mechanisms (table 2.7).[46] In sum, if you employ a variety of other means of gauging democracy's substantive effect on the likelihood of victory, it still seems modest at best.

There are also good logical reasons to think that the relationship between democratic leaders and publics is exactly the reverse of that posited by the democratic triumphalists. Rather than the public being the key independent actor constraining the leadership, it is the leadership that really matters in the decision to go to war, with the public being easily led along. This is the case because all leaders, democratic or not, are likely to have greater expertise than the general public, particularly in the abstruse area of national security affairs. It is also perfectly rational for most citizens in a democracy to remain "ignorant" in these realms for the reasons that Anthony Downs and Mancur Olson made clear long ago.[47] Finally, democratic leaders can maintain secrecy about costs, benefits, and probabilities of war because much of the information necessary to judge those things is "private" (i.e., internal to the government) and can be kept from becoming public knowledge.

TABLE 2.7
Hypothetical versus Actual Predicted Probabilities of Victory for High Democracies

Hypothetical	Actual	Country	War	Politics
.994357	.9984682	United Kingdom	Boxer Rebellion (1900)	7
.9748251	.9958367	Czechoslovakia	Hungarian-Allies (1919)	7
.9578193	.9905974	France	Boxer Rebellion (1900)	8
.2770606	**.5127683**	**Poland**	**Russo-Polish (1919–20)**	**8**
.9811564	.9981756	Turkey	Turko-Cypriate (1974)	9
.9865205	.9993396	Israel	Six Day (1967)	9
.7273037	.9036302	Israel	Israeli-Syria (1982)	9
.9329092	.989434	India	Bangladesh (1971)	9
.9407323	.9919492	United States	Mexican-American (1846–48)	10
.9845452	.9985435	United States	Spanish-American (1898)	10
.9993412	.9999142	United States	Boxer Rebellion (1900)	10
.8573618	.9652067	United Kingdom	World War II (1940–45)	10
.1756496	.3955737	Greece	Greco-Turkish (1897)	10
.3900036	**.6749977**	**Greece**	**First Balkan (1912–13)**	**10**
.9999987	1	Israel	Sinai (1956)	10

Note: Boldface indicates those cases where a hypothetical change in the democracy score significantly affects the predicted probability for victory.

In addition, there is little reason to think that caution about starting a war should be unique to democratic leaders. In fact, even some triumphalists concede that leaders in every kind of regime incur significant costs from starting a losing war, and thus they are apt to be careful about blundering into them. As Bruce Bueno de Mesquita and Randolph Siverson note, "the leader—whether president, prime minister, or president-for-life—who adopts policies that reduce the security of the state does so at the risk of affording their political opponents the opportunity of weakening the leader's grasp on power."[48] As this statement makes clear, the general logic of their argument applies equally to democracies and autocracies.

One could even argue that democratic leaders should be less cautious about going to war than their nondemocratic counterparts. After all, the worst fate a democratic leader faces is removal from office and disgrace, whereas authoritarian leaders who lose wars are frequently exiled, imprisoned, or put to death. Given that fact, it seems hard to maintain that an authoritarian leader would be less wary than a democratic leader about losing a war.[49] Although the probability of democratic leaders being ousted may be higher, the costs to autocratic leaders of losing power are so great that the net result should be that both are equally wary of losing a war. Also, if democracies are actually more selective in choosing their wars, and starting only easy ones, they should engage in fewer wars than authoritarian states, because there are not likely to be many sure victories. In fact, it is widely acknowledged by scholars that democracies

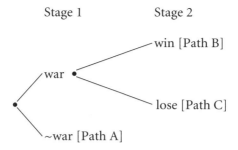

Figure 2.2. The Structure of the Selection
Effects Model

are at least as, if not more, war-prone than other types of regimes.[50] In short, the logic undergirding the triumphalists' selection effects argument is simply not convincing.

It is also questionable whether the triumphalists' approach to modeling the selection effects hypothesis using a single-stage probit model (where the selection effect is measured by the interaction variable between democracy and war initiation) is the best way to test it, given the logic of the argument. As figure 2.2 shows, the structure of the selection effects arguments is two-staged: there is the decision to start the war in phase I (yes/no) and then the outcome in phase II (win/lose). Therefore, the appropriate model for these hypotheses needs to be two-staged as well, incorporating both the decision to start the war and the outcome. Ideally, one would want to employ a two-stage selection model (such as probit with selection) using data that covers both wartime and peacetime cases. Unfortunately, such models are notoriously difficult to implement correctly and are also highly sensitive to otherwise small differences in model specification.[51]

There is, however, an alternative means of testing this hypothesis.[52] The selection effects hypothesis is that states at war should score higher on variables such as aggregate capabilities (cap), military personnel (milper), military expenditures (milex), energy (energy), iron and steel production (irst), and total population (tpop). If democracy is the key to selecting winnable wars, they ought to score higher on these variables than nondemocracies. Stated formally:

$$E(\beta X_i \mid War\&Dem_i = 0) > E(\beta X_i \mid Dem_i = 0) \tag{1}$$

$$E(\beta X_i \mid War\&Dem_i = 1) > E(\beta X_i \mid Dem_i = 1) \tag{2}$$

$$E(\beta X_i \mid War\&Dem_i = 1) > E(\beta X_i \mid War\&Dem_i = 0) \tag{3}$$

To test this hypothesis, I compiled a dataset combining the Militarized Interstate Disputes (MIDs) dataset (which measures conflict behavior of states from 1816 through 2002) with the POLITY IV dataset (which measures democracy for the same period). This dataset contains not only wars over the past 200 years but also significant numbers of peacetime observations ($N = 13,966$). Using that dataset, I estimate a war outcome model on all of the cases leaving out the democracy variable. The results are presented in table 2.8.

Next, I report $\beta^\wedge$, which are the estimated coefficients from this model. This enables me to estimate the effects of the various capabilities variables for every case. From that I can generate an index function for four classes of cases: democracies (7–10 on the POLITY IV democ-autoc index = 1) in peacetime, nondemocracies (–10–6 on the POLITY IV democ-autoc index = 0) in peacetime, democracies at war, and nondemocracies at war (MID-level 5 = 1). We can conclude two things from the results presented in table 2.9. It does seem to be the case that there is some selection going on, inasmuch as the mean for βX_i in wartime and peacetime cases is very different, with the former being two to three times higher than the latter (1 and 2). That is not surprising as states at war have strong incentives to increase their capabilities. However, it also seems evident that whether a country is a democracy or not is not what explains the selection of winnable wars. Indeed, the mean for βX_i for nondemocracies in wartime is ac-

TABLE 2.8
*Probit Results of Effects of Capabilities
on Likelihood of Victory*

Variables	Coefficients
Capabilities	2.143529***
	(.5561899)
Military Personnel	.0002593***
	(.0000197)
Military Expenditures	−1.33e-08*
	(5.77e-09)
Energy	1.28e-07
	(6.17e-07)
Iron and Steel Production	−.0000123
	(8.47e-06)
Total population	−3.16e-07
	(2.33e-07)
Constant	2.227748***
	(.0317206)
Pseudo R2	0.1200
Log likelihood	−1200.3644
N	13,966

* $\leq$ .05 (all tests two-tailed and all standard errors are robust)
** $\leq$ .01
*** $\leq$ .001

TABLE 2.9
Predicted Values for War Outcomes, βX_i, for Model in Table 2.8 across Different Portions of the Sample

Predicted War Outcome	Mean	N	SD	Minimum	Maximum
$E(\beta X_i \mid Dem_i = 0)$	.0192471	8473	.032	2.66e-12	.8328284
$E(\beta X_i \mid Dem_i = 1)$	.0133386	3617	.013	1.55e-11	.221279
$E(\beta X_i \mid War\&Dem_i = 0)$	.0416141	416	.096	.0014479	.8328184
$E(\beta X_i \mid War\&Dem_i = 1)$	.0414154	182	.074	.1.10e-08	.4074664

tually slightly higher than for democracies. In other words, $E(\beta X_i \mid War\&Dem_i = 1) > E(\beta X_i \mid War\&Dem_i = 0)$ (3) does not hold, and so it seems unlikely that democracy is what enables states to select into winnable wars, at least based on these observable factors.

Now it is possible that democracies are selecting into wars based on some statistically unobservable characteristics, such as better information generation and transmission capabilities or the threat of electoral punishment, rather than just finding "unfair fights" in which they outman and outgun their opponents. But to assess those propositions, one would want to focus on what I characterize as "fair fights"—cases in which democracies and nondemocracies are roughly equal on these observable material power indices—to see if process tracing reveals whether these statistically unobservable factors explain the outcome in these cases.

A number of propositions can tell us something about whether triumphalists' proposed causal mechanisms operate as suggested. In the first stage of the model (the decision to go to war or not), if the institutional constraints version of the democratic selection effects argument is right, it should be evident that democratic leaders take into consideration public opinion and the potential audience cost in making their decision to launch a war. If they were irrelevant or unimportant, this suggests that the key mechanism in stage 1 does not operate as hypothesized. On the informational side, we should see democratic decisions to start wars being characterized by full and free debate. If such was not the case, this would count against the argument that democracies are better at selecting winnable wars because their unfettered marketplace of ideas helps them choose more winnable wars.

In the second stage (the outcome of the war), democratic leaders who win their wars should prosper politically by doing so. If they do not, this suggests that a core tenant of the institutional constraints version (i.e., that publics reward or punish democratic leaders based on war outcomes) is not operating. Because the data in the second stage are biased in favor of low-cost wars, findings consistent with the model's predictions (e.g., starting and winning [Path B in figure 2.2]) have evidentiary value, but findings that are inconsistent (i.e., starting and losing [Path C]) may not.[53] For example, some argue, in the analogous tests of the audience costs proposition at work in the process of crisis escalation, that cases of democratic leaders who, having initiated a crisis, subsequently back down but then retain office, do not necessarily falsify the democratic audience costs thesis, because all crises they select into are by definition low cost.[54] Democratic triumphalists could use this same logic to argue that cases of democratic leaders who start losing wars but retain office do not disprove their selection effects theory of democratic victory because they somehow knew they would not pay the price despite losing. But this would make these arguments nearly tautological, as there is potentially no outcome (winning or losing) that falsifies them.

Finally, democratic leaders should not lie or otherwise misrepresent the costs, benefits, or probability of various outcomes. If they can do so in order to start a war (in the first stage) or stay in power after a losing war (in the second stage), this suggests that democratic audience costs actually play little independent role in shaping their decision to go to war. Such behavior is evidence both that leaders knew that war would be unpopular and politically hazardous and that they thought they could get away with it by lying or spinning. If democratic leaders could regularly count on being able to do so, then both the informational and institutional constraints versions of the democratic triumphalists' selection effects argument are faulty.[55]

Although there are daunting methodological and data challenges, it is still possible to test various parts of the triumphalists' selection effects argument. For example, a recent study by Chiozza and Goemans examines whether democratic and autocratic leaders profit by their ability to win wars. Their finding that "democratic leaders do not gain at home from victory abroad"[56] calls into question a central proposition for the second stage of the model (Path B), which predicts that democracies should be more likely to win their wars because democratic leaders know that victory will enhance their hold on power.

But given that much of the evidence for this selection effects argument is statistically unobservable, it is not clear that the statistical analysis approach is the best way to test either version of the democratic selection effects argument. All of the data in the triumphalists' models comes from the second, wartime stage, not the peacetime decision-making process in the first stage. But most of the data supporting or falsifying that theory is in the first stage, whether to start the war in the first place (Path A in figure 2.2). Unfortunately, this initial decision of whether to go to war or not is largely unobserved in the democratic triumphalists' wartime datasets.

Case studies, rather than statistical approaches, may be the optimal way of testing the majority of the selection effects propositions.[57] In the case studies in this book, I propose to explore through detailed process tracing in crucial cases both the informational and institutional constraints versions of the democratic triumphalists' selection effects arguments. Process tracing should make it possible to gauge how much potential audience costs affected first-stage decisions and whether they operated in the second stage in the way the triumphalists posit.[58]

A good test should focus on cases in which democracies initiated and then won the conflict. In fact, the triumphalists have only a handful of cases of democracies starting wars, and the coding of many of them is questionable; in many of the others, the triumphalists' causal mechanisms do not operate. While democracies win 94 percent of the wars they start, according to Reiter and Stam's dataset, there are reasons to question whether this success results from democratic political leaders' being more careful because they fear electoral retribution if they lose.[59] There are only sixteen cases of democracies starting wars since 1815, and half of these involve the same three countries: the United States, the United Kingdom, and Israel. Given that only three states account for such a large proportion of the winners, it is fair to ask how generalizable the triumphalists' findings are (table 2.10).

Moreover, the coding of six of these cases is questionable because democracies actually did not initiate the war. Reiter and Stam and other triumphalists credit France, the United Kingdom, and the United States with initiating the Boxer Rebellion in 1900, ignoring the fact that diplomats and citizens of those countries were already under attack by the Boxers when the Western powers sent their relief expedition to China.[60] The 1919 Czech-Hungarian War is widely considered to have begun with Hungarian communist Bela Kun's attack on Slovakia rather than with democratic Czechoslovakia attacking Hungary, as they maintain.[61] Finally, they count the United Kingdom and the United States as having initiated the 1941 through 1945 phase of the Second World War in Europe despite the fact that Germany began that war in 1939 with the attack on Poland. In sum, there are only ten clear cases of democracies starting wars since 1815.

These ten cases need to be examined closely to see whether the triumphalists' causal mechanisms really explain why these democracies won their wars. Although the triumphalists identify specific causal mechanisms that they believe make democracies smarter about the wars they start, they never test them di-

TABLE 2.10
Assessment of Triumphalists' Selection Effects Cases

Status (%)	Cases
Questionable coding (38%)	France/Boxer Rebellion (1900)
	United Kingdom/Boxer Rebellion
	United States/Boxer Rebellion
	Czech-Hungarian War (1919)
	United Kingdom/World War II (1941–45)
	United States/World War II (1941–45)
Process tracing seems to support selection effects (25%)	Spanish-American War (1898)
	First Balkan War (1912–13)
	Bangladesh War (1971)
	Turkey/Cyprus Invasion (1974)
Process tracing does not support selection effects (38%)	Mexican War (1846–48)
	Greco-Turkish War (1897)
	Russo-Polish War (1919–20)
	Sinai War (1956)
	Six Day War (1967)
	Lebanon War (1982)

Note: Percentages add up to more than 100% due to rounding.

rectly. Rather than systematically testing these propositions in detailed case studies, they are largely content with establishing the correlation between the democracy, initiation, and victory variables and inferring that the selection effect explains it.

A closer examination of the ten remaining cases, however, shows that the triumphalists' causal mechanisms do not explain many instances of democratic victory. To be sure, their propositions appear, at least at first glance, to be at work in four cases: the 1898 Spanish-American War, the First Balkan War of 1912–13, the 1971 Bangladesh War, and Turkey's 1974 invasion of Cyprus. However, in the other six—the Mexican War of 1846–48, the 1897 Greco-Turkish War, the Russo-Polish War of 1919–20, the 1956 Sinai War, the 1967 Six Day War, and Israel's Lebanon War of 1982—democracy does not seem to be the explanation for why these countries did or did not launch successful wars. Instead of democracies winning a very impressive 94 percent of the wars they start, democratic selection effects actually explain only 25 percent of these victories.

The U.S.-Mexican War does not support many of the triumphalists' propositions. President James Polk started the war without substantial public and congressional support because many Americans opposed the annexation of Texas, fearing it would upset the delicate balance between free and slaveholding states.[62] Nor was there much open debate about what came to be called "Mr. Polk's War," which the president initiated by secretly sending U.S. forces into a disputed area of the border, where they were sure to be attacked by the

Mexicans.[63] It is difficult to ascertain from this case whether victory helped the domestic fortunes of the Polk regime because he did not run for reelection after the war. His party—the Whigs—lost the election to Zachary Taylor, whose campaign was clearly aided by his role in the victorious war. But, overall, Polk's motive appears to have been not domestic political gain but rather territorial consolidation of U.S. control of North America.[64]

The 1897 Greco-Turkish War case does not support the triumphalists' argument either. The driving force behind the war in Greece was not the democratically elected government but rather the secret military society Ethnike Hetaria, which succeeded in misrepresenting the costs, risks, and benefits of war with Turkey to the Greek public, thus contravening the informational version of the selection effects argument.[65] Moreover, the institutional constraints hypothesis finds only mixed support: while Prime Minister Deliyannis was forced out after the loss to the Turks, Greek crown prince Constantine—the military commander—was not punished for losing the war that the Greek public obviously did not want to lose. Indeed, he would again command Greek military forces in the First Balkan War and eventually become king of Greece.[66]

The Russo-Polish case also provides little support for the triumphalists' causal mechanisms, as I discuss in the next chapter. Neither Israel's 1956 Sinai campaign nor Israel's 1982 war against Syria in Lebanon provides much support for the triumphalists' selection effects argument. And the decision-making process during the run up to Israel's 1967 Six Day War, as shown in chapter 4, provides little support for the selection effects arguments.

Finally, finding cases of democracies not starting losing wars is as important for proving the triumphalists' selection effects argument as identifying cases they start and win. Of course, because this is largely an exercise in counterfactual history, it is not surprising that Reiter and Stam can identify only two candidates: the 1898 Fashoda crisis and the 1911 Moroccan crisis. In neither instance do they show that the specific mechanisms of democracy led France to avoid war. Indeed, in the latter case they quote French prime minister Joseph Caillaux endorsing Napoleon's advice not to go to war unless the chances of victory are higher than 70 percent. Because Napoleonic France was an autocracy, it is not true that only democracies are selective about their wars.[67] The triumphalists need to do much more work to identify cases of democracies not going to war because they thought they would lose and demonstrate that this assessment was the result of the specific mechanisms of their selection effects argument.

In sum, democracy matters relatively little, if at all, in explaining whether states wisely select and then win their wars.

WARTIME EFFECTIVENESS

The triumphalists offer several causal mechanisms to support their claim that democracies are better at fighting wars than nondemocracies. Democracies are wealthier, make better allies, engage in more effective strategic evaluation, enjoy greater public support, and have soldiers who fight more effectively than their counterparts in authoritarian states. It is impossible to do justice to each of these arguments in the space of one chapter. Nevertheless, a brief assessment of these causal mechanisms suggests that none are logically compelling or have much empirical support.

Rent Seeking

Lake maintains that, as a rule, democracies are wealthier than authoritarian states, and because wealth is the foundation of military power, democracies are more likely to win wars.[68] This claim is based on the belief that democracies are less prone to rent seeking—that is, the governments of democracies are less likely to meddle in their economies, thus fostering free markets that produce greater national wealth.

Triumphalists maintain that democracies are better wealth creators than other types of regimes, but they provide no supporting evidence for this claim.[69] There is, however, a large body of scholarship on the relationship between levels of democracy and levels of economic development, but it does not provide much foundation for their assertion. To be sure, there is some evidence that bolsters the triumphalists' contention that democracy makes economic growth more likely,[70] but there is much more evidence for the converse proposition that wealth is a key factor in creating democracy.[71] Thus, there is no consensus in the development literature on which way the causal arrow runs.[72] Therefore there is little basis for believing the triumphalists' claim that democracies produce greater wealth than nondemocracies.

Another reason to doubt the triumphalists' assertion that democracies are superior wealth creators is that the rent-seeking logic that underpins their claim is flawed. There is no reason to think that rent seeking should be less frequent in democracies. Indeed, there are compelling reasons why rent seeking should be more common in democracies.

Rent seeking is the effort by interest groups in a society to gain excess profits through nonmarket mechanisms.[73] For example, tobacco producers receive special tax breaks and subsidies as a result of political lobbying, which injects economic inefficiencies into the marketplace that slow the rest of the economy. Economists offer compelling arguments about how it is more likely that interest groups will be successful rent seekers in a democracy.[74]

Lake identifies governments, not interest groups, as the main rent seekers. Even if it is true that democratic governments are less likely to engage in rent-seeking behavior, the fact remains that interest groups in democracies are more likely to be free to engage in this kind of behavior. Lake provides no evidence, however, that the lack of government interference in a democracy's economy makes up for the negative effects of rent seeking by interest groups.

Moreover, although wealth is necessary for generating military might, it also is essential that a state can mobilize its wealth for military purposes.[75] This two-step process raises a question that Lake does not address but that might be thought essential to his position: are democracies better able to extract resources from their society than nondemocracies? The best available study on the subject maintains that regime type is largely irrelevant: "Politically capable governments can mobilize vast resources from the society under stress of war, but totalitarian, democratic and authoritarian regimes do not determine the level of performance."[76] In short, democracies are no better than nondemocracies at transforming economic might into military power.

In sum, democracies are wealthier than nondemocracies, and it is indisputable that national wealth is a key building block of military power. But contrary to what Lake and others triumphalists believe, democracy does not seem to be the source of that wealth. It seems equally plausible that states become wealthy first and then become democratic, not the other way around. Moreover, democracies enjoy no special advantage over authoritarian states in mobilizing that wealth for military purposes. Finally, even if Lake is right that state rent seeking is less of a problem in democracies, the literature on rent seeking offers a number of logical reasons why rent seeking by interest groups should be more of a problem in democratic political systems.

Alliances

According Randolph Siverson and Juliann Emmons, democracies tend to form alliances with each other because they share a deep-seated commitment to two norms: cooperation and amity.[77] Some scholars argue that democratic alliances are more durable that other types of alliances.[78] This durability leads Lake and others to conclude that, in war, the resulting democratic alliances are more effective than either mixed alliances or alliances comprising only non-democracies.[79] One underlying assumption that could lead to this conclusion is that democratic leaders must worry about "audience costs" if they renege on their alliance commitments, which should make them highly reliable allies.[80] There are reasons to suggest, however, that this is not the case.

The proposition that democracies are likely to align with each other finds little support in the historical record.[81] In fact, history offers few examples of purely democratic alliances; most have been either mixed or between non-democracies exclusively. Siverson and Emmons's own data indicate that democratic alliances accounted for only 3.24 percent of the total in the 1920–39 period and 10.97 percent in the 1946–65 period.[82] These data can be interpreted to mean that the growth of purely democratic alliances was largely a Cold War phenomenon, where the Soviet threat, not ideological affinity, brought democracies together.[83]

There is also little evidence to think that democratic alliances are militarily more effective than mixed or nondemocratic alliances. Triumphalists disagree among themselves about this.[84] Moreover, in the COW dataset there is only one war (the debatable case of the 1956 Sinai War in which Israel, France, and Britain defeated Egypt) where the victorious alliance was composed entirely of democracies. In an overwhelming majority of the other wars in which democracies won in alliance with other states, these alliances included nondemocracies.[85]

Moreover, the assumption that democracies should ally with each other is unconvincing, because there are equally plausible reasons why democracies should ally with nondemocracies. Michael Simon and Erik Gartzke, for example, argue that because democracies and authoritarian states have different strengths and weaknesses (i.e., democracies have a harder time keeping secrets than authoritarian states), they make good allies.[86] Mancur Olson and Richard Zeckhauser suggest an alternative rationale for why different kinds of regimes attract each other. Collective action among democratic allies is likely to be difficult, they argue, because the bonds of friendship may cause democracies to contribute less than their fair share—that is, they might think that their partner will pick up any slack out of a sense of fraternal obligation. In alliances that include nondemocracies, every member is more likely to pull its own weight, because each recognizes that the others are motivated strictly by self-interest. Therefore, it will not tolerate the kind of free-riding that is likely in an alliance made up solely of democracies.[87] In short, there is no good reason why democracies should prefer to ally with each other, rather than with nondemocracies.

There is also reason to question the audience costs argument, which could provide the theoretical foundation for the claim that democratic alliances are es-pecially durable and therefore more militarily effective. Although Joe Eyerman and Robert Hart conclude that crises between democracies are resolved more easily than those between nondemocracies—and they interpret this finding as support for at least some aspects of the audience costs argument—there is still no evidence that these costs make democracies better allies.[88] The level of pub-lic support for foreign attachments within democracies varies widely; in cases in which the public is not seriously engaged, there are no audience costs for failure to honor an obligation.[89] Indeed, there is considerable evidence that democratic publics are not particularly attentive to international affairs, which means that, more often than not, audience costs play little role in the calculations of demo-cratic leaders.[90] Even in those cases where the public strongly supports a com-mitment to another state, such support can evaporate quickly.[91] Finally, leaders have considerable latitude to shape public attitudes toward alliances, which means that they will sometimes be able to explain away broken promises without incur-ring significant audience costs. In the best available study, Kurt Gaubatz concludes that the evidence supports only the more modest conclusion that democracies are no worse than other types of regimes in making "lasting commitments."[92]

In short, democratic leaders are not necessarily constrained by alliance com-mitments, so there is little reason to believe that democratic alliances should be more effective than other types of alliances at winning wars.

Strategic Evaluation

Some triumphalists believe democracies are better strategic decision makers than nondemocracies because the voters and their representatives, not just a handful of elites, have a say in how to wage war. This has two positive effects: greater public involvement in decision making produces better military policies because those who would pay the costs of going to war make the decisions about how it is conducted; and the greater number of individuals participating in the decision-making process lowers the likelihood of strategic blunders, ac-cording to Bruce Russett.[93] Optimal security policies usually prevail in the marketplace of ideas, which is what Stephen Van Evera, Jack Snyder, and others argue occurs in a democratic political system.[94] On close examination, however, these claims are unpersuasive for three reasons.

The first problem is there are no studies available that assess whether democ-racies or nondemocracies make better decisions about how to wage war. The triumphalists offer no systematic evidence to support this claim but make their case by emphasizing the logic that underpins it. There is, however, evidence that suggests that democracies are no better than authoritarian states at making strategy, as I pointed out in the previous chapter.

Second, there is no question that the public wants to avoid strategic blunders. Nobody wants to die if they can avoid it. The key issue, however, is whether there is a mechanism for translating that motivation into better wartime decision making. In fact, there is not. The root of the problem is that the individual soldiers who fight wars hardly ever have the expertise to improve the decision-making process. Invariably, they have significantly less information and expertise than the civilian and military elites charged with directing the war. In the end, how well those at the top make decisions is all that matters. Moreover, the making of strategy in warfare is the preserve of military leaders. They have both the expertise and the power that civilians lack. Once the political decision has been made to go to war, military decision makers are largely unaccountable.

Finally, a political system that gives voice to large numbers of individuals with diverse preferences may not be able to reconcile those differences and produce coherent policies. For example, Kurt Gaubatz employs Kenneth Arrow's famous "paradox of democracy" to illustrate that democracies can struggle to make national security decisions due to their difficulty in aggregating a diversity of opinions.[95] Unfortunately, the marketplace of ideas is not necessarily an efficient producer of sound strategy.[96]

Public Support

According to Aaron Friedberg, democratic leaders can count on greater public support for their wars than their authoritarian counterparts, because elected policymakers are accountable to the people and so will conduct wars in such a way as to ensure that public support remains high.[97] Although there is no question that democratic leaders are answerable to their constituents, it is doubtful that this link translates into greater public support for the state's wars or that it explains why they win them.

Friedberg argues that it is especially difficult for democracies to rely on coercion and centralized control to wage war while maintaining public support, because they place a high premium on the norm of consent and they usually have a limited and decentralized form of government. To maintain public support for the war effort, Friedberg maintains, democratic leaders must conduct wars relying upon the voluntary consent of the public. Doing so, in fact, is likely to increase the prospects of military success. This approach, according to Friedberg, explains why the democratic United States, rather than the authoritarian Soviet Union, prevailed in the Cold War.

First, there are other reasons for why the United States did not become a large, intrusive, and coercive garrison state during the Cold War that could have risked losing public support in the struggle against authoritarian communism. Structural factors such as geographic isolation and possession of nuclear weapons, rather than norms and institutions, offer an equally plausible explanation for why the United States could wage the Cold War while relying on voluntary consent and with a less intrusive government than the Soviet Union. Therefore, the problem with Friedberg's argument is in part one of case selection. Normative, institutional, and structural factors all anticipate a smaller and less coercive U.S. government relative to the Soviet Union. Because during the Cold War the United States had not only antistatist ideas and weak governmental institutions but also geographical insulation and nuclear weapons, ideas and institutions were not necessarily the driving force behind these strategic choices. In fact, this case could just as plausibly be interpreted as indicating that democracy and success in war were both the result of a favorable geographic location and possession of nuclear weapons.

Second, Friedberg's assertion that the U.S. government during the Cold War was smaller and less intrusive than it might have otherwise been is debatable. If the comparative baseline for measuring the expansion of the U.S. Cold War state is either World War II or what some proponents of big government advocated, it was certainly smaller and less intrusive. It was much larger, significantly more intrusive, and somewhat more coercive, however, than the U.S. state was during the interwar period or at various times in the nineteenth century.[98] Indeed, all successful states become more centralized and coercive in wartime.[99] Authoritarian Nazi Germany, which lost World War II, had remarkably little wartime centralization. On the other hand, the victors (i.e., the authoritarian Soviet Union and the democratic United States and United Kingdom) were highly centralized.[100] This suggests both that more centralized and coercive states are more likely to win wars and that regime type may not be the most important factor in explaining which states are able to mobilize societal resources more effectively in wartime.

Third, the triumphalists' claim about democracy and public support is not logically compelling. In particular, there is reason to believe that leaders and their publics often have different time horizons that affect their thinking about the utility of war. As Donna Nincic and Miroslav Nincic suggest, democratic publics, like consumers, tend to focus on short-term considerations when thinking about the use of force: what is the immediate payoff? In contrast, democratic leaders are inclined to think about war like investors: what will be the long-term payoff?[101] Given these different perspectives on the use of force, it is reasonable to expect democratic leaders and their publics will be out of step in their enthusiasm for particular wars.

Fourth, no comprehensive studies back up the triumphalists' claim that democracies enjoy greater public support in wartime than authoritarian states. There is actually plenty of anecdotal evidence that shows that both types of regimes enjoy varied levels of public support in times of conflict and that neither has an apparent advantage over the other. For example, the American public strongly endorsed U.S. participation in World War II (1941–45), while its support for the Vietnam War (1965–73) evaporated over time, leading the U.S. to withdraw from the conflict. Authoritarian Russia, on the other hand, saw public support for World War I disappear between 1914 and 1917, while the Soviet Union enjoyed broad and deep public support throughout World War II.[102] The historical record thus appears to show that regime type has little effect on the level of public support in wartime.

Troops

Reiter and Stam maintain that because democratic governments have greater legitimacy than authoritarian governments, their soldiers perform better on the battlefield. They attribute this finding to the political culture of democracies, which they argue fosters greater individual initiative and better leadership among their soldiers. Because liberalism privileges the individual, soldiers in democracies display greater initiative, and their leaders are both more enthusiastic and more successful.[103] They reject as an alternative explanation that nationalism, rather than democracy, produces superior leadership and initiative, arguing that nationalism results only in higher morale. Thus, their case rests not on explicating an unbroken chain of logical reasoning but on showing that there is a significant statistical correlation between democracy and various combat skills.

At first glance, Reiter and Stam appear to have assembled impressive statistical support for their claim that soldiers from democratic societies display greater leadership and initiative than those from nondemocracies. On close inspection, however, the dataset of battles that provides the basis for these findings—the Combat History Analysis Study Effort (CHASE)—is unreliable. In 1982 the Historical Evaluation and Research Organization (HERO) was commissioned to assemble it for the U.S. Army's Concepts Analysis Agency (CAA). After receiving the initial version of the dataset in 1984, CAA randomly selected eight battles from it and submitted them for analysis to the U.S. Army Military History Institute, the U.S. Army Center for Military History, the Department of History at the U.S. Military Academy, and the U.S. Army Combat Studies Institute. A total of 159 codings were checked in the eight cases. The results seriously called into question the dataset's reliability: 106 codings (67 percent) were judged to be in error, another 29 (18 percent) were deemed questionable, and only 24 (15 percent) were ascertained to be correct by the reviewers.[104]

Despite two revisions, there is still reason to doubt the reliability of the 1990 version of the CHASE dataset that Reiter and Stam employ. The principal problem is that the codings of certain items in the CHASE dataset remain imprecise. The former CAA project manager, for example, concedes that "even with our best efforts error rates of 5 to 30 percent are to be expected."[105] As a result of continuing conflict between CAA and HERO over the reliability of the CHASE dataset, HERO was relieved of responsibility for updating that dataset in 1987. Nevertheless, HERO continues to work on its own to update the 1987 version of the CHASE dataset, which it calls the Land Warfare Data Base (LWDB).[106] Recently, HERO (which is now called the Dupuy Institute) compared the 1990 version of the CHASE dataset with the current LWDB, focusing on 1,196 data points that were common to both datasets. They found that almost half (500) of the codings for those same data points were different.[107]

There were no differences between the CHASE and LWDB datasets in the "leadership" category, but the consistency between the datasets is not evidence that the data on leadership are reliable. In its various revisions to the CHASE dataset after 1987, HERO focused exclusively on relatively hard variables such as order of battles and casualties, while ignoring softer variables such as initiative and leadership. According to a HERO staff member, these two variables were the "least looked at and poorest proofed section of the data base," because their codings were widely regarded as "all a judgement" anyhow.[108]

Problems with the HERO dataset notwithstanding, Reiter and Stam believe that their findings are still valid on two related grounds: first, unless there is systematic bias in the codings, the very large number of cases should still make it possible to trust the findings. Second, because the principal architect of the original CHASE dataset did not regard democracy as a key explanation for military prowess, we can be confident that the data are not biased in favor of their claims about the battlefield advantages of soldiers of democratic states.[109] Although these particular errors do not produce systematic bias in the CHASE dataset, there is so much potential measurement error in the dataset generally, and particularly in the leadership and initiative variables, that Reiter and Stam are left with inefficient models. If the relatively hard variables have a 5 to 30 percent error rate in their coding, consider how much more imprecise the soft variables are.[110]

There are, however, three more serious data problems. First, three countries—the United States (250), the United Kingdom (67), and Israel (52)—account for 40 percent of the 936 cases in the HERO dataset. In other words, this is hardly a random sample of countries at war. Second, as Risa Brooks pointed out, the HERO "initiative" variable does not even measure what Reiter and Stam define as initiative. HERO codes initiative as which army moved first rather than as a characteristic of individual troops' behavior.[111] Finally, there is possible bias or error in the coding of the independent variable—democracy. Ido Oren, for example, makes a convincing case that the POLITY democracy scores are highly subjective—friends are consistently coded as more democratic than enemies—and thus unreliable.[112] The combination of these data problems for both the dependent and independent variables casts doubt on Reiter and Stam's findings that democratic armies demonstrate greater initiative and leadership skills on the battlefield.

Another unbiased source of data on comparative military competence can be used to test the triumphalists' proposition about the relationship between democracy and military performance.[113] Allen Millett, Williamson Murray, and Kenneth Watman's study of the military organizations in World War I, the interwar period, and World War II provides indicators of their military effectiveness.[114] It offers little evidence, however, that democratic armies fight better than nondemocratic armies.[115] Given the problems with the CHASE database and the evidence of at least one other dataset, there are grounds for doubting the triumphalists' claims that democracies are more likely to win their wars because their soldiers fight better.

This conclusion is hardly surprising, given the consensus among military historians that the three most formidable armies of the twentieth century in terms of initiative and leadership were imperial Germany's army during World War I (authoritarian state),[116] Nazi Germany's army during World War II (authoritarian state),[117] and the Israeli army between 1948 and 1973 (democratic state).[118]

There is reason to think, then, that nationalism, rather than democracy, plays the primary role in enhancing individual initiative and leadership. Many scholars believe that the French Revolution transformed warfare precisely because it democratized French society. This, they maintain, fostered a greater sense of loyalty to the regime, which in turn increased the military effectiveness of the

French army in all three areas.[119] This effectiveness, however, had its roots in prerevolutionary France and survived the collapse of French democracy and the coming to power of Napoleon Bonaparte.[120] Prussia and Spain, two highly nationalistic but not democratic regimes, played important roles in defeating Napoleon by employing many of the same tactics that served revolutionary and then Napoleonic France so well.[121] Nationalism and democracy, though they sometimes reinforce each other, are also distinct.[122] Reiter and Stam concede that nationalism, not democratic ideology, may account for combat prowess. Nationalism could also foster greater initiative by increasing the average soldier's commitment to the state and foster leadership by enhancing the loyalty of the troops. Unfortunately, they have not systematically tested nationalism as an alternative explanation for why militaries in their dataset performed well on the battlefield.[123]

Finally, there is good reason to believe that democratic militaries are effective in spite, not because, of the nature of their political systems. Samuel Huntington famously distinguished between the nonliberal mind-set of the American officer corps and the liberalism that characterized the rest of American civilian society. The paradox of democratic societies, in his view, was that an illiberal and often undemocratic military institution was essential for ensuring the security of even a liberal state from its external adversaries.[124] Given this functional imperative deriving from the anarchic nature of the international system, it is not surprising that there is often a gap between the conservative political and social attitudes of military professionals and those of the rest of civilian society in democracies.[125] Rather than liberalism pervading the militaries, it is most often the case that the armed forces are a distinct and isolated caste, particularly in democratic societies.

CONCLUSION

The triumphalists' arguments about the relationship between democracy and the economy, alliances, decision making, public support, and battlefield performance of soldiers, as explanations for why democracies should do well once at war are unconvincing. In the following chapters, I test the various triumphalist propositions through five in-depth case studies: the 1920 Russo-Polish War, the 1948 Israeli War of Independence, the 1967 Six Day War, the 1973 Yom Kippur War, and the 1982 Falklands War. My rationale for choosing these cases is three-fold. First, these are "fair fights," cases in which democracies won without a decisive power advantage, which should make them ideal for ascertaining how

TABLE 2.11
Probit Results of Democracy and Victory Test without
"Fair Fights" Cases

Variables	R&S Model 4 without Fair Fights
democracy*initiation	.0527094
	(.0366214)
democracy*target	.0359063
	(.0256893)
initiation	1.115024**
	(.3603589)
capabilities	4.354383***
	(.6777097)
allies capabilities	5.290121***
	(.8464172)
quality ratio	.1178567*
	(.0543368)
terrain	−17.71267***
	(3.517158)
strategy*terrain	5.831049***
	(1.152215)
strategy 1	13.20898***
	(3.237059)
strategy 2	6.903492***
	(2.037582)
strategy 3	6.317556***
	(1.698945)
strategy 4	5.831049***
	(1.152215)
Constant	−9.068584***
	(2.035165)
Pseudo R2	0.5545
Log likelihood	−54.020561
N	176

* ≤ .05 (all tests two-tailed and all standard errors robust)
** ≤ .01
*** ≤ .001

much of an independent role democracy played in the outcome. Second, without these five cases (which constitute a mere 21 observations out 197) in the triumphalists' dataset, the democracy*initiation variable is no longer significant, as table 2.11 makes clear. This further emphasizes how dependent the triumphalists' findings are upon a handful of cases. Finally, democratic triumphalists often point to the Israeli cases and Britain's victory in the Falklands War as particularly apt illustrations of the military prowess of democracies.[126] In other words, these are widely recognized by proponents of democratic triumphalism as crucial cases for their theories. If the democratic triumphalists' propositions do not work in these cases, there are grounds for skepticism about their more general arguments.

In the following three chapters, I step back from the correlation between de-

mocracy and victory and focus instead on assessing the triumphalists' prewar selection effects and wartime effectiveness arguments though in-depth process
tracing. Instead of looking at the outcome—Was the more democratic state
more likely to win its wars?—I want to see if the process through which democratic states planned and then conducted their wars accords with what the triumphalists' theories suggest. In other words, did the mechanisms of democracy
make it more likely that they would start winnable wars or conduct them more
effectively once engaged in them? I then consider alternative explanations for
the outcome of each war. If democratic triumphalism is correct, the processes
by which democratic states selected and then fought their victorious wars should
reflect the causal mechanisms of their theories. Also, alternative explanations
distinct from regime type ought not to affect the outcome.

APPENDIX

The COW Universe of Interstate Wars since 1815

Franco-Spanish War (1823): The more democratic country (France, −5) won the war
against a less democratic country (Spain, −7) but did so as a result of a greater than 2:1 advantage in military manpower, almost a 20:1 advantage in iron and steel, and nearly a 3:1
advantage in total population. This case is a gross mismatch and so does not support the triumphalists.

Russo-Turkish War (1828–29): Both countries were equally undemocratic (Russia, −10,
and Turkey, −10) and so this case supports neither theory.

Mexican-American War (1846–48): This case is a gross mismatch because the United
States had a greater than 780:1 advantage in iron and steel production, almost a 3:1 advantage
in military manpower, and a 3:1 advantage in population over Mexico.

Austro-Sardinian War (1848–49): There are two problems with this case: we do not have
reliable democracy scores for a number of the participants; and the winner, Austria-Hungary,
won as a result of a greater than 3:1 advantage in military manpower, a 2:1 advantage in military spending, an 8:1 advantage in iron and steel production, and nearly a 6:1 advantage in
total population.

First Schleswig-Holstein War (1848–49): In this case, the less democratic power (Germany, −8) defeated the more democratic power (Denmark, −4) but did so as the result of a
greater than 3:1 advantage in military manpower, greater than a 7:1 advantage in military
spending, a greater than 250:1 advantage in iron and steel production, and an 8:1 advantage
in total population.

War of the Roman Republic (1849): This case is also a gross mismatch inasmuch as the
victorious coalition (Austria and France) had a greater than 610:1 advantage in iron and steel
production, a 42:1 advantage in military manpower, and a 25:1 advantage in population over
the Roman Republic. It is also missing democracy scores for all participants.

War of La Plata (1851–52): Less democratic Brazil (–7) defeated more democratic Argentina but did so with a greater than 3:1 advantage in military manpower and an 7:1 advantage in total population. This case is a gross mismatch and so supports neither the triumphalists nor the defeatists.

Crimean War (1853–56): The Crimean War is certainly a gross mismatch in one power category (the victors France, the United Kingdom, the Kingdom of Sardinia, and the Ottoman Empire had a 16:1 advantage in iron and steel production over Russia) but not in others (it had only a 1.5:1 advantage in military manpower and 1.3:1 advantage in population). However, the democratic contribution to the coalition was rather modest. While democratic England did contribute 80 percent of the iron and steel production, it contributed only 22 percent of the military manpower and 30 percent of the population to the victorious side. This case involves a mixed alliance and so does not support the triumphalists.

Anglo-Persian War (1856–57): This case is clearly a gross mismatch with England having greater than a 3640:1 advantage in iron and steel production, a 6:1 advantage in military manpower, and a 7:1 advantage in population. Given that, this case does not support the triumphalists.

War of Italian Unification (1859): Because democracy scores are unavailable for two our of three participants (France, the Kingdom of Piedmont-Sardina, and the Austrian Empire), it is unclear whether the more or less democratic side won.

Spanish-Moroccan War (1859–60): Both Spain (–7) and Morocco (–7) were equally undemocratic and so this case tells us little about the effect of democracy on military effectiveness.

Italo-Roman War (1860): Because we lack democracy scores for one side, it is not clear what this case tells us about the effectiveness of democracy.

Italo-Sicilian War (1860–61): More democratic Italy (–5) defeated less democratic Sicily (–10) but did so as the result of a gross mismatch with nearly a 2:1 advantage in military manpower, greater than a 40:1 advantage in iron and steel production, and 7:1 advantage in total population. Hence, this case does not really support the triumphalists.

Franco-Mexican War (1862–67): More democratic Mexico (–3) defeated less democratic France (–6) and did so at a decided power disadvantage: a 1:25 disadvantage in military manpower, a 1:30 disadvantage in military spending, and nearly a 1:5 disadvantage in total population. This case seems to support the triumphalists, but because there was a huge disparity of interests at stake, I do not regard it as a fair test of the theory.

Ecuadorian-Colombian War (1863): Less democratic Colombia (–5) defeated more democratic Ecuador (–1), and because the two sides seemed relatively equal in everything except total population, this case is a fair test that favors the defeatists.

Second Schleswig-Holstein War (1864): Because of incomplete democracy data for Denmark, Prussia, and Austria, it is not clear which position this case supports.

Lopez War (1864–70): The slightly more democratic alliance of Brazil (–7) and Argentina (–3) defeated less democratic Paraguay (–6) but did so in a mixed alliance in which Brazil supplied the bulk of the power resources. That alliance also had a 2:1 advantage in military manpower and a 4:1 advantage in total population, suggesting that it may also have been a gross mismatch as well.

Spanish-Chilean War (1865–66): The more democratic alliance of Peru (–1) and Chile (0) defeated less democratic Spain (–7) and did so at a greater than 1:5 disadvantage in military manpower, 1:10 disadvantage in military spending, a greater than 1:160 disadvantage in iron and steel, and a 1:4 disadvantage in total population. This case therefore supports the triumphalists but is not really a fair test because of the disparity of interests at stake.

Seven Weeks' War (1866): Because so many of the democracy scores are missing for this war between Prussian and Austria, it is not clear what it tells us about the effect of regime type on the outcome of the war.

Franco-Prussian War (1870–71): This case lacks a democracy score for one of the major belligerents and so is not useful for assessing whether regime type matters.

Russo-Turkish War (1877–78): Because both Russia (–10) and Turkey (–10) had the same democracy score, this case also tells us little about the effect of regime type on outcome.

Pacific War (1879–83): More democratic Chile (3) defeated less democratic Bolivia (1) and Peru (–3) and did so in the face of relatively even power balances. This case supports the triumphalists.

Sino-French War (1884–85): This case is miscoded in COW data: France lost rather than won.[127] While the French had a 93:1 advantage in iron and steel production, this was balanced by the Chinese 2:1 advantage in military manpower and 10:1 advantage in population. Because this case was a gross mismatch, it does not support the triumphalists or the defeatists.

Central American War (1885): Less democratic El Salvador (–1) defeated more democratic Guatemala at a 1:3 disadvantage in military manpower and a slight disadvantage in total population. This case clearly supports the defeatists.

Franco-Thai War (1893): More democratic France (7) defeated less democratic Thailand (–10) but did so with a significant advantage in military manpower (122:1), a huge advantage in iron and steel production (2,000:0), and a nearly 8:1 advantage in total population. This case is a gross mismatch and so does not really support the triumphalists.

Sino-Japanese War (1894–95): More democratic Japan (0) defeated less democratic China (–7) while fighting at a significant disadvantage in military manpower (1:10) and population (1:10). This case therefore supports the triumphalists.

Greco-Turkish War (1897): This case is a problem for the triumphalists because democratic Greece lost. I would not count it as a victory for the defeatists, however, because it was also a gross mismatch. Turkey had a greater than 10:1 advantage in iron and steel production, a 12:1 advantage in military manpower, and a 10:1 advantage in population.

Spanish-American War (1898): This case is a gross mismatch (the United States had a 43:1 advantage in iron and steel production, a .65:1 disadvantage in military manpower, but a 4:1 advantage in population).[128]

Boxer Rebellion (1900): This case was something of a mismatch in iron and steel production (the victors France, Russia, the United Kingdom, the United States, Italy, Japan, Germany, and Austria had a greater than 19,096:1 advantage), though the Chinese had slight advantages in military manpower (1.5:1) and population (1.2:1). The real problem with this case is that it is a mixed alliance to which, with the exception of iron and steel production (88 percent), democracies made only a modest contribution in military manpower (29 percent) and population (48 percent).

Russo-Japanese War (1904–5): More democratic Japan (0) defeated less democratic Russia (–10) and did so at a 1:8 disadvantage in military manpower, a 1:3 disadvantage in energy production, a 1:50 disadvantage in iron and steel production, and a 1:30 disadvantage in total population. This case also supports the triumphalists.

Central American War (1906): Less democratic Guatemala (–9) defeated more democratic El Salvador (–6) and Honduras (0) in a relatively even fight. Thus, this case supports the defeatists.

Central American War (1907): Because of missing democracy data for Nicaragua and Honduras, it is not clear what effect regime type had on the outcome of this war.

Spanish-Moroccan War (1909–26): This case is clearly a gross mismatch with Spain having a greater than 308:1 advantage in iron and steel production, a 2.25:1 advantage in military manpower, and a 4:1 advantage in population. Compounding this mismatch, Spain also fought in alliance with France in the later period of this war.[129]

Italo-Turkish War (1911–12): Because both Italy (–2) and Turkey (–2) had the same democracy score, this case also tells us little about the effect of regime type on military performance.

First Balkan War (1912–13): While the victorious coalition of Serbia, Bulgaria, Greece, and Montenegro was at a disadvantage in military manpower (.4:1) and population (.5:1) compared to the Ottoman Empire, the contribution of democracy to that victory was modest: no one had any iron and steel production, but democratic Greece contributed only 23 percent of the military manpower and 27 percent of the population. Because this case was a mixed alliance, it does not really support the triumphalists.

Second Balkan War (1913): This case was both a gross mismatch (no iron and steel production on either side but a 12:1 advantage in military manpower and a 4:1 population advantage for Greece, Serbia, and Rumania over Bulgaria) and a mixed alliance in which democratic Greece contributed only 8 percent of the coalition's military manpower and 14 percent of its population.

World War I (1914–18): There are a number of problems with this case. First, there is the whole question of whether Germany is a democracy.[130] Second, the war ought to be disaggregated into two discrete wars: during the first, from 1914 through 1917, the democratic coalition (France and the United Kingdom) was in serious danger of losing the war.[131] After April 1917, the Entente, with U.S. assistance, won the war. But they did so with a significant power advantage over the Central Powers (3.6:1 in iron and steel, 1.55:1 in military manpower, and 2:1 in population). Because this case is both a misaggregation and a gross mismatch, it is not really a fair test of the theory.

Hungarian War (1919): While democratic Czechoslovakia carried much of the burden of this war, it did so with a huge power advantage over Hungary (a greater than 811:1 advantage in iron and steel, a 9:1 advantage in military manpower, and a 2.89:1 advantage in population). Because this case is a gross mismatch, it does not really support the triumphalists.

Russo-Polish War (1919–20): This case seems to support the triumphalists. While democratic Poland enjoyed something of an advantage in iron and steel production (2.59:1), it was at a disadvantage in military manpower (.6:1) and population (.2:1).

Lithuanian-Polish War (1919–20): More democratic Poland (8) defeated less democratic Lithuania (4) but did so with 13:1 advantage in military manpower, 206:1 advantage in energy production, greater than a 1,500:1 advantage in iron and steel production, and a 13:1 advantage in total population. This case was certainly a gross mismatch and so does not support the triumphalists.

Greco-Turkish War (1919–22): Because we lack a democracy score for Turkey, it is not clear what this case tells us about the effect of regime type on military victory.

Franco-Turkish War (1919–22): In this case we lack a democracy score for Turkey, making it useless for assessing the question of whether democracy makes victory more or less likely.

Sino-Soviet War (1929): Less democratic Russia (–8) defeated more democratic China (–5) in a relatively even matchup, so this case supports the defeatists.

Manchurian War (1931–33): Because more democratic Japan (0) defeated less democratic China (–5), this case supports the triumphalists.

Chaco War (1932–35): In this case less democratic Paraguay (–3) defeated more democratic Bolivia (2). Because Paraguay won despite being at nearly a 1:2 disadvantage in military manpower, 1:7 disadvantage in military spending, 1:6 disadvantage in energy production, and 1:2 disadvantage in population, this case lends much support to the defeatists.

Italo-Ethiopian War (1935–36): Less democratic Italy (–9) defeated more democratic Ethiopia (–5) but did it with a greater than 2:1 advantage in military manpower, a 25:1 advantage in energy production, greater than a 4,000:1 advantage in iron and steel production, and a 3:1 advantage in total population. This case is a gross mismatch.

Sino-Japanese War (1937–41): More democratic Japan (0) defeated less democratic China (–5). Because the two sides were relatively evenly balanced in military manpower, and Japan's advantages in military spending (9:1) and iron and steel production (119:1) were balanced by China's 4:1 advantage in population, I count this case as supporting the triumphalists.

Changkufeng (1938): More democratic Japan (0) defeated less democratic Russia (–9) at a disadvantage in every power category. This case, therefore, supports the triumphalists.

Nomohan (1939): In this case, less democratic Russia (–9) defeated more democratic Japan (0). Because the former had a 4:1 advantage in military spending, a greater than 2:1 advantage in iron and steel production, and over a 2:1 advantage in total population, I would classify this case as a gross mismatch.

Russo-Finnish War (1939–40): This case might have provided the defeatists with support except for the fact that the victorious Soviet Union enjoyed such a massive advantage in iron and steel production (222:1), military manpower (58:1), and population (44:1).

World War II (1939–1945): See discussion in text.

Franco-Thai War (1940–41): More democratic Thailand (–3) defeated less democratic France (–9) and did so with a significant power disadvantage. This case might support the triumphalists except for the disparity of interests in the outcome and also the fact that France had been defeated and occupied by Nazi Germany.

Israeli War for Independence (1948): This case seemingly provides powerful support for the triumphalists because democratic Israel apparently prevailed against adversaries with larger armies (.023:1) and populations (.005:1).

Korean War (1950–53): The Korean War was a draw and so excluded from consideration.

Russo-Hungarian War (1956): We lack a democracy score for Hungary, and so it is not clear what this case tells us.

Sinai War (1956): The Sinai War is a gross mismatch: The democratic coalition of the United Kingdom, France, and Israel had a 5,733:1 advantage in iron and steel production, a 24.5:1 advantage in military manpower, and a 3.7:1 advantage in population.

Sino-Indian War (1962): This case provides some support for the defeatists. China beat democratic India despite the two being relatively even in iron and steel production (1.3:1) and population (1.4:1). China did have a 5.5:1 advantage in military manpower, however.

Second Kashmir War (1965): This case is also wrongly coded in COW/POLITY as a victory for Pakistan.[132] Actually, it was a draw despite Pakistan being at a huge disadvantage in iron and steel production (.0002:1), military manpower (.26:1), and population (.23:1).

Vietnam War (1965–75): The Second Indo-China War should actually be divided into two wars. From 1965 through 1972, the United States and some other democratic states were parties to the conflict. From 1972 through 1975, it was largely a war between two nondemocracies: North and South Vietnam. While many consider this a victory for the defeatists because the democratic coalition had a huge power advantage—1,247:1 in iron and steel production, 14:1 in military manpower, and 17:1 in population—I would not do so because of the asymmetry in interests in the outcome.

Six Day War (1967): This is also a good case for the triumphalists because democratic Israel won despite being at a disadvantage in iron and steel production (.42:1) and population (.07:1) compared to Egypt, Jordan, Syria, and Iraq. However, in military manpower Israel did have a very slight advantage (1.009:1).

Football War (1969): This case also seems to support the triumphalists because more democratic El Salvador, with only a slight advantage in population (1.29:1), no advantage in military manpower (1:1), but a significant advantage in iron and steel production (greater than 3:1) defeated Honduras. However, none of the participants were fully democratic.

War of Attrition (1969–70): This war between Egypt and Israel was a draw and is excluded.

Bangladesh War (1971): This war was a gross mismatch: democratic India defeated Pakistan but did so with a huge advantage in iron and steel production (greater than 6,376:1), military manpower (2.87:1), and population (9:1).

Yom Kippur War (1973): This war seems to support the triumphalists: democratic Israel defeated its Arab adversaries Egypt, Iraq, Jordan, and Syria despite being at a disadvantage in iron and steel production (.41:1), military manpower (.46:1), and population (.005:1).

Turkish-Cypriot War (1974): Democratic Turkey defeated authoritarian Greece, but it was a gross mismatch. Turkey had greater than a 1,458:1 advantage in iron and steel production, a 2.8:1 advantage in military manpower, and a 62:1 advantage in population.

Vietnamese-Cambodian War (1975–79): Because both sides were equally undemocratic (–7,–7), this case is also of little use.

Ethiopian-Somali War (1977–78): All the participants (Cuba, Ethiopia, and Somalia) had the same democracy score (–7), and so this case tells us little about the effect of regime type.

Ugandan-Tanzanian War (1978–79): All the participants (Uganda, Libya, and Tanzania) had the same democracy score (–7), and so this case is not a good test of the effect of variation in regime type.

Sino-Vietnamese War (1979): Both China (–7) and Vietnam (–7) were equally undemocratic, and so this case is also not a good test of the effect of regime type.

Iran-Iraq War (1980–88): This war is a draw and so it is excluded.

Falklands War (1982): Democratic Britain defeated Argentina in this war, and despite being close to a gross mismatch (Britain had a 5:1 advantage in iron and steel production and clearly received significant logistical support from the United States[133] but enjoyed only a 1.85:1 advantage in military manpower and 1.93:1 advantage in population), I still regard it as a victory for the triumphalists.

Lebanon War (1982): This war was a draw and so excluded.

Sino-Vietnamese War (1985–87): As China (–7) and Vietnam (–7) were both equally undemocratic, this case also is of little use in assessing different theories of the effect of regime type on military effectiveness.

Gulf War (1990–91): While the allied coalition, including the United States, Canada, France, Italy, and the United Kingdom was on the winning side of this war, there are two problems with counting it in favor of the triumphalists: First, it was mixed alliance that included some very undemocratic regimes like Bahrain (–10), Egypt (–5), Kuwait (–9), Morocco (–5), Oman (–10), Saudi Arabia (–10), Syria (–9), and the UAE (–10), which were at least as undemocratic as Iraq (–9). Second, it was a gross mismatch.

Azeri-Armenian/Nagorno-Karabakh (1992–98): This conflict was a draw.

CHAPTER 3

Democracy and the Russo-Polish War

At first glance, the Russo-Polish War of 1920 seems like a strong case for the triumphalists' proposition that democracies have a significant advantage over nondemocracies in the wise selection and successful conduct of war. Poland was a democracy, and it launched a successful war. Historian Norman Davies characterized Poland as a parliamentary democracy and the POLITY dataset gives Poland an impressive democracy score of 8, which places it squarely in the "high democracy" category.[1] Given the overwhelming Soviet advantage in military manpower and Poland's newly assembled and untested armed forces, Poland's victory in late summer and fall of 1920 borders on the miraculous.

This stunning victory over the Soviet Union caught almost all foreign observers by surprise. Even Winston Churchill, then secretary of state for war in British prime minister Harold Lloyd George's cabinet, and a staunch supporter of the Polish cause, was taken aback by the magnitude of the Polish reversal of fortune after August 16, 1920. He recalled with amazement the course of the battles in Poland that summer: "there had come a transformation—sudden, mysterious and decisive. Once again armies were advancing, exulting, seemingly irresistible. . . . Once again for no assignable cause they halt . . . and begin to retreat."[2] Given that the Poles were significantly outnumbered and outgunned by the Soviets, it is tempting to attribute this victory to the fact that Poland was a democracy, as the triumphalists do.

In this chapter, I assess through in-depth process tracing whether the outcome of the Russo-Polish War is in fact attributable to Polish democracy. I begin with a brief synopsis of the war. Next, I inquire as to whether the Russo-Polish case supports the triumphalist's selection effects argument that democracies are better at starting wars they can easily win. I look then at each of the triumphalist's wartime effectiveness arguments—rent seeking, alliances, strategic evaluation, public support, and soldiers on the battlefield—to see if any of them explain the outcome. Finally, I explore some alternative explanations, unrelated to regime type, that might explain Poland's remarkable defeat of the Soviet Union.

My conclusion is that neither the triumphalists' prewar selection effects nor their wartime effective arguments persuasively explain the outcome of the Russo-Polish War. While Poland had democratic institutions, its parliamentary system does not seem to have mattered very much for the outcome of the war. Rather, other factors such as the balance of forces, the nature of the conflict, nationalism, a weak adversary, geography, and intelligence provide much more convincing explanations for the war's outcome.

THE RUSSO-POLISH WAR

Poland was part of the Russian Empire, but much of it was occupied by the Central Powers during the First World War. After the February Revolution of 1917, the Provisional Government granted Poland independence but it was not until after the German surrender in November 1918 that it truly gained it. Between November 1918 and December 1919, newly independent Poland engaged in a series of wars to establish its borders with the Ukraine, Czechoslovakia, and Russia. In April 1920 Polish forces invaded the Ukraine and captured Kiev with the intention of setting up an independent and pro-Polish regime. The Poles attacked the Soviet Union because they saw two windows of opportunity: Russia was suffering the ravages of its ongoing Civil War, and the Allies were preoccupied with other issues.[3] Given the former, Russia was vulnerable to attack in the spring of 1920, and the Poles thought they could exploit this vulnerability to establish an independent and pro-Polish government in the Ukraine.[4] Given the latter, the Poles judged that they could execute this plan with little overt opposition from the Allies. In May the Soviet forces launched a major counterattack to recapture the Ukraine and expel the Poles. After retreating most of the summer in the face of a seemingly inexorable Red juggernaut, Poland defeated the Red Army in the Battle of the Vistula literally at the gates of Warsaw during mid-August 1920 and drove it deep into the disputed territories in the Baltic region and Beylorussia.[5] The Soviet Union sued for an armistice in October 1920 and then signed the Treaty of Riga in March 1921, which ratified these Polish conquests.[6]

SELECTION EFFECTS

The essence of the triumphalists' selection effects argument is that democracies tend to prevail in their wars because their leaders are careful about starting only those that they can win. One reason democratic leaders are so cautious about selecting winnable wars is that they are dependent upon the continuing support of the people to stay in office. If democratic leaders begin unsuccessful wars, they are likely to be voted out of office. Hence, they have a powerful electoral incentive to be cautious about the wars they initiate. Another reason that democratic leaders are better at selecting winnable wars is that their open political systems provide them with better information about the costs and risks of war and the probabilities of victory. But for the selection effects argument to hold, it must be the case that Poland made its decisions about going to war democratically, and it has to be clear that Poland started the war.

To be sure, Poland had many of the formal trappings of democracy including a parliament, the Sejm; a civilian government; and regular elections. Despite this veneer of democracy, the reality was that one individual—Marshal Jozef Piłsudski—played an extraordinary role in governing Poland, almost single-handedly conducting its defense and foreign policies.[7] Piłsudski is a legendary figure in modern Polish history. He began his political career as a revolutionary socialist but later became modern Poland's most important military leader, organizing Polish units that fought on various sides during the First World War. The only consistent elements in Piłsudski life were Polish nationalism and the struggle for Poland's independence. Despite Piłsudski's socialist origins, he was not a democrat and, to the extent he had any coherent political leanings, they seemed more inclined toward the restoration of the old Polish aristocracy.[8]

With the establishment of an independent Poland on November 10, 1918, Piłsudski was appointed "supreme commander" by the head of the Polish Provisional Government, Prince Lubomirski.[9] Piłsudski later became "chief of state," a position that was tantamount to a dictator.[10] A new Sejm was elected on February 26, 1919, but immediately ratified Piłsudski's dictatorial powers.[11] During the height of the Russo-Polish War in July 1920, the Sejm established a "State Defense Council" composed of ten civilian leaders of the various political parties, three government ministers, and three members of general staff. It then stopped meeting for the duration of the war. The State Defense Council was given complete authority for running the war.[12] In fact, the Sejm did not become predominant in Polish politics until the Constitution of March 17, 1921, which was adopted well after the war was over.[13] Even this brief period of democracy was short-lived as Piłsudski took power directly again in a coup in May 1926.[14] In short, Poland hardly qualifies as a "high democracy" during the Russo-Polish War, at least in terms of the conduct of it's foreign and defense policies.

The informational version of the triumphalists' selection effects argument assumes that the public and civilian governmental officials have some knowledge of how the war is going. This was clearly not the case in Poland. One Foreign Ministry official asked in 1919: "Where are we going? This question intrigues everybody. . . . To the Dnieper? To the Dvina? And then?"[15] As Richard Watt concludes, "without any appreciable opposition, Piłsudski commanded Poland's army and conducted Poland's foreign affairs. He kept his own counsel and made his own plans, paying no great attention to the desires of the Sejm, the majority of whose members, both on the Left and on the Right, wanted peace with Soviet Russia."[16]

Because Piłsudski was not subject to public opinion in his decisions about when and how to go to war, it is clear that the institutional constraints version of the selection effects argument does not work in the Polish case either. Although most of the Polish public did not support the attack on Ukraine in April 1920, this lack of public support did not stop Piłsudski, whose actions seem inconsistent with the triumphalists' theory that democracies win because they enjoy higher levels of public support than nondemocracies.[17] Finally, Piłsudski reportedly launched the attack on the Ukraine in the spring of 1920 despite serious doubts that it would succeed.[18] He had good reason for concern, given how far it would stretch Polish lines of communication, how tenuous Ukrainian support was for the invasion, and how likely the attack was to rekindle Russian nationalism within the Red Army.[19] Clearly, Piłsudski regarded the possibility of war with the Soviet Union as a risk to the Polish state, which also contradicts the triumphalists' expectations concerning the calculations of leaders contemplating war.

Finally, it is essential to the selection effects argument that the winning side actually initiate the successful war. The Polish case, at first glance, seems to provide evidence for this proposition. Poland arguably initiated four successful military campaigns during this period: in April 1919 the Poles defeated the Soviets and occupied Vilno, in modern day Lithuania.[20] In May 1919 the Poles attacked the Ukrainians and occupied East Galicia.[21] Poland successfully moved into the eastern border regions in December 1919 to establish order with only ineffectual Soviet resistance.[22] Finally, on April 26, 1920, the Poles launched their attack on Soviet-occupied Ukraine, which began their seemingly successful campaign against Russia in 1920.[23]

But a good case can be made that the Russo-Polish War began in 1918 and that the Poles were not solely responsible for starting it. After the war, the Poles themselves, not surprisingly, maintained that the hostilities had began much earlier and blamed the Bolsheviks for starting it: "The war was imposed on Poland when the government of the Soviets, after having taken at the end of 1918 the lands of Lithuania and White Ruthenia, and after having imposed the Soviet regime on them, directed the troops on to the ethnographic territory of Poland against the will of her people. The Polish republic, menaced in its liberty and its recently won independence, was compelled to resist the Soviet invasion."[24] This view was echoed by sympathetic foreign observers such as Churchill.[25]

The Soviets have provided ample rhetorical evidence to support the view that they commenced hostilities against the Poles. In December 1918 Leon Trotsky, Soviet commissar for war, stated that "the straight way to join forces with the Austro-Hungarian Revolution leads over Kiev, as likewise the way to joining forces with the German Revolution leads over Pskov and Vilna."[26] The Soviets launched a number of military operations toward the West, including the invasion of the Ukraine in January 1919.[27] The Poles also "repulsed" Soviet moves toward the Baltic states in March and April 1919.[28] The German General Staff followed these skirmishes closely, noting that the Poles had responded to Soviet moves.[29] However, the most compelling evidence on behalf of the proposition that the Soviet Union initiated hostilities is the admission in its Official History of a plan known as "Target Vistula." The Soviets launched this operation in November 1919 with the objective of occupying territory west to the Bug River, which included territory that was indisputably Polish.[30] Thus, there is at least some evidence for the extreme argument that the Soviets began the war and all Polish operations were essentially defensive in character.[31]

A more reasonable argument can be made that it is not clear which side started the war. Recall that after the First World War much of the territory east of the Bug River and west of Vistula River remained occupied by the imperial German army's *Ober-Ost* (map 3.1). When the Germans finally withdrew westward into East Prussia in compliance with the terms of the Treaty of Versailles, both Poland and the Soviet Union advanced into these territories.[32] As the two sides filled the vacuum left by the withdrawing Germans, Polish and Soviet forces clashed near Bialystok and Brest-Litovsk in December 1918.[33] In February 1919 they skirmished again near Bereza Kartuska.[34] If the Russo-Polish War actually began in late 1918 or early 1919 as the result of both sides advancing into disputed territory, then it is difficult to say for certain who started it. As Adam Zamyoski concludes, "To say when this war started and how is not easy. It was

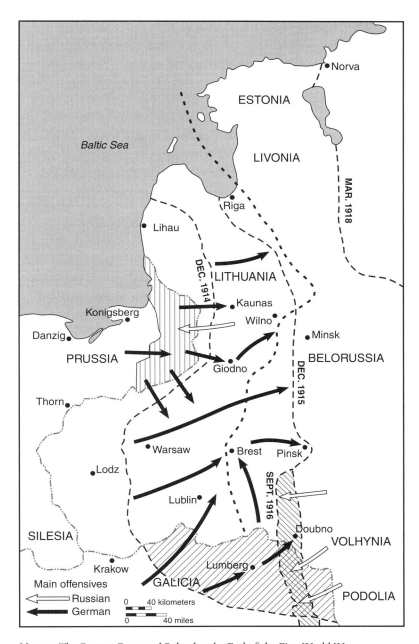

Baltic Sea

Norva

ESTONIA

LIVONIA

MAR. 1918

Riga

Lihau

DEC. 1914

LITHUANIA

Kaunas

Wilno

Minsk

Konigsberg

Danzig

PRUSSIA

Giodno

BELORUSSIA

DEC. 1915

Thorn

Warsaw

Brest

Pinsk

Lodz

SEPT. 1916

Lublin

Doubno

VOLHYNIA

SILESIA

Krakow

Lumberg

GALICIA

PODOLIA

Main offensives

⇐ Russian

⬅ German

0   40 kilometers

0   40 miles

Map 3.1. The Eastern Front and Poland at the End of the First World War

never declared; it never broke out in the normal sense. It merely escalated as both sides were able to field larger armies. For the issues and the causes were already there the day Poland recovered its independence."[35] But it is essential for the triumphalists' selection effects argument that Poland clearly started the war. If the Soviet Union did, or if it is unclear which side did, the Russo-Polish War turns out not to be such strong evidence for their case that democracies are more likely to win because they are better at selecting winnable wars.

WARTIME EFFECTIVENESS

If the Russo-Polish case does not provide much support for the triumphalists' selection effects argument, perhaps it at least offers evidence supporting their arguments that democracies win because they are better at fighting wars once they are in them. A cursory examination of the conflict seems to lend credence to many of the triumphalists' wartime effectiveness arguments. Upon closer examination, though, the Russo-Polish War turns out not support any of them.

Rent Seeking

Some triumphalists maintain that democracies win their wars because they are wealthier, the result of their state bureaucracies being less prone to rent-seeking behavior. If this claim is correct, Poland should have had little state intervention into its economy. An unfettered market economy is more efficient and should have provided Poland with greater military resources than its communist adversary. In fact, Poland did not have much of a market economy, despite its democratic government. According to a contemporary American observer Sidney Brooks: "In Poland excessive governmental control and inefficient bureaucratic administration gummed up the natural mechanisms of trade. Nothing could be done without permit and sometimes it took weeks or months to get official permission for a transaction. By the time permission was obtained the promoter had either lost his ability to act on it or had attained his end by some *sub rosa* arrangement."[36]

A U.S. economic adviser's report noted the predominance of statist economic ideologies in Poland at the time of the Russo-Polish War: "During 1919 and part of 1920 there were certain influences in Poland which tended to exaggerate the importance of the role which the government should play in relation to business and to place too much control of business in the hands of government agencies."[37] Poland had a very high tax rate due to the fact that half the national budget was devoted to military spending, and so it is hard to conclude that Polish democracy prevented excessive state intervention into the Polish economy.[38] Hence, the absence of rent seeking by the Polish state does not seem to explain the outcome of the Russo-Polish War.

Alliances

Other triumphalists suggest that democracies win their wars because their fellow democracies readily join them in alliances, which are durable and hence militarily more effective. Some believe democracies make better allies because they do not engage in conquest or other forms of international rent-seeking behavior. Others maintain that the domestic structure and norms of democracies make them better allies by raising the domestic audience costs for them to renege on their alliance commitments. The Russo-Polish War provides scant evidence to support either of these propositions.

Despite Polish aggression against its various neighbors after independence, the democratic powers of the Entente did endorse the principle of an independent Poland in March 1918, contravening the democratic rent-seeking proposition.[39] In other words, Polish democracy did not prevent it from engaging in imperialistic behavior, and it also did not stop other democracies from aligning themselves with Poland. Indeed, this endorsement initially led Piłsudski and other Polish leaders to anticipate much Allied support for their newly reborn country.[40]

Democracies are supposed to be more transparent than other types of regimes, and this allegedly makes democratic alliances operate more smoothly. In truth, the Poles had a difficult time in divining what policies the Entente was pursuing in Eastern Europe and were never able to coordinate their policies with the alliance.[41] The Polish leaders gradually discovered that, despite some pro-Polish rhetoric, there was little meaningful support for Poland among the democracies.[42] The meager aid that did come from the democracies was motivated not by common democratic fraternity but by crude calculations of national interest. The Entente powers were not averse to manipulating what aid they did give Poland to try to control its behavior. For example, in 1919 the Entente powers cut off aid to Poland in response to its invasion of Galicia.[43] Entente ambivalence about Poland was evident throughout the Russo-Polish War and at the Spa Conference in July 1920 when Poland looked as though it would be overrun by the advancing Red Army.[44] Even after the Poles turned the tide against Soviets in mid-August 1920, Entente enthusiasm for the Polish cause was still decidedly muted.[45] Polish foreign minister Patek succinctly summarized the hard lesson

the Poles had learned: "In one word, we can count only on our forces and, according to that, conduct our policy."[46]

Of all the democratic great powers, the United Kingdom was probably the
least pro-Polish in its foreign policy. With some understatement, one historian
concludes that Britain was "ambivalent at best."[47] To be sure, a few British politicians like Churchill were very supportive of Poland, strongly advocating giving
the Poles aid and even direct military support during the darkest days of the
Russo-Polish War.[48] However, most British leaders, along with much of the public, did not feel a strong affinity for Poland.[49] The British supported an independent Poland in principle, but what they envisioned was that it would be relatively
small and weak.[50] In practice, the British attitudes toward Poland ranged from
indifference to outright hostility.

British prime minister Harold Lloyd George, in particular, had little use for
the Poles concluding that "[n]o one gave more trouble."[51] No only did he regard
the Poles as a nuisance, but he actually believed they were the aggressors in the
Russo-Polish War.[52] "By every rule of war," he argued, "the Russians were entitled to punish the Poles and to exact guarantees against further invasion by
them."[53] This may explain his frantic efforts to get the Poles to come to terms
with the Soviets during the summer of 1920. The Soviets, in turn, recognized
that Lloyd George's anti-Polish sentiments made him willing to force the Poles
to sign even a very bad peace agreement.[54] Even after the dramatic reversal of
Polish fortunes in August 1920, Lloyd George still never warmed to the Polish
cause.[55]

Lloyd George had a number of reasons for his anti-Polish stance. To begin
with, the prime minister was guided by realpolitik and did not regard a strong
Poland as serving Britain's national interest. Lloyd George's scheme for maintaining the post–World War I balance of power envisioned a strong Russia and
Germany to counter French power.[56] Indeed, he explicitly identified Poland and
France as threats to postwar European stability: "There are two nations in Europe who have gone rather mad, the French and the Poles."[57] Another over-
riding concern for Lloyd George was British economic recovery, to which he
also thought Germany and Russia, rather than France and Poland, could contribute far more.[58] Lloyd George seemed little concerned, moreover, with
whether Poland was a fellow democracy or not. The following exchange with
his parliamentary colleague Ernest Bevin is quite revealing on this score:

> *Ernest Bevin:* But, suppose the Polish people themselves agreed upon a constitu-
> tion which did not suit the Allied Powers?

Lloyd George: What have we to do with that? That is their business, not ours.

Ernest Bevin: It is their business?

Lloyd George: Certainly. What have we to say to that? I do not care what the constitution is. If they like to have a Mikado there, that is their business.[59]

The reason for this indifference was that the British government had little confidence that democratic Poland would behave any differently than a nondemocratic Poland.[60] The primary reason the British government could take such a casual view of Poland's fate is that, contradicting the triumphalists' audience costs argument that democratic alliance commitments are stronger because publics are reticent to see them broken, there was little public support for maintaining Britain's commitment to Poland.[61] To be sure, if the Soviet Union had conquered Poland, it would have hurt Lloyd George politically, but still he did very little to support Poland.[62] In fact, domestic politics were very important in shaping British policy, but in a very different way from what the triumphalists' audience costs argument suggests.[63] The powerful British Labour movement actually regarded the Soviet Union as more democratic than newly independent Poland.[64] Pacifism was also widespread among the left, and this dampened public support for aiding Poland.[65] The combination of pro-Soviet and antiwar attitudes on the British left led it to "paralyze any effort the Government might undertake on behalf of the Warsaw regime."[66] Lloyd George concluded that, contrary to the optimist's claim, British democracy made it harder, rather than easier, for Britain to maintain its commitments to Poland during the Russo-Polish War.[67]

While British opinion ranged from ambivalence to outright hostility to Poland during the Russo-Polish War, France was much more sympathetic to the Polish cause, both rhetorically and substantively. However, the evidence does not suggest democracy explains France's more pro-Polish attitude. Rather, the key factor driving Franco-Polish relations was France's national interest. France supported Poland during the Russo-Polish War for straightforward balance-of-power reasons: Poland was to be the keystone in France's post–World War I security architecture in Eastern Europe. The view in Paris was that France faced two potential security threats in Europe: Russia and Germany.[68] As French prime minister Georges Clemenceau observed in December 1918,

The support of Poland was the best way to check Germany. Poland occupies a first-rate strategical position. She has an army of half a million good soldiers inured to hardships and animated by a strong patriotism. Politically she is well disposed to the Allies and sufficiently armed. She only asks the Allies for help. It would be a great mistake if we did not maintain Poland in order to dam up the Russian flood and provide a check to Germany . . . our policy . . . ought to be to fortify Poland in order to keep Russia in check and to contain Germany.[69]

Reinforcing the realpolitik underpinnings of France's aid to Poland was the fact that the French always put very "onerous" conditions on that aid.[70] France made aid conditional on Poland behaving in accordance with French objectives. Unfortunately, the Poles turned out to be very independently minded, and despite their aid, the French frequently found themselves unable to exercise much influence over them. For example, the French were not at all enthusiastic about of Piłsudski's invasion of the Ukraine in the spring of 1920, but the marshal went ahead with that operation despite French reservations.[71] The Franco-Polish alliance was much less an example of democratic fraternity and more of a straightforward, if sometimes rocky, marriage of convenience.

As in Britain, French public opinion was not overwhelmingly in favor of the Franco-Polish alliance. Like the British left, the French workers were often anti-Polish. The Communist paper *L'Humanité* made clear that its sentiments did not favor the Franco-Polish alliance: "Not a man, not a sou, not a shell for reactionary and capitalist Poland. Long live the Russian Revolution. Long live the Workman's International."[72] Thus, the triumphalists' audience costs argument, that democratic publics care deeply about whether their governments keep their alliance commitments with other democracies, does not explain why France supported Poland during the Russo-Polish War.

The United States was an early and fervent supporter of Polish independence, at least rhetorically. In January 1918 President Woodrow Wilson delivered a message to the U.S. Congress in which he laid out his famous Fourteen Points upon which the postwar settlement was to be based. Article 13 specifically endorsed Polish independence.[73] At Versailles, the United States also championed the cause of Polish independence.[74] The United States was seemingly deeply committed to Poland.

In truth, however, the United States government, even President Woodrow Wilson, was, like the leadership of the other democracies, ambivalent about Polish independence.[75] Despite Poland's parliamentary system, American officials nonetheless had serious reservations about its regime. Poland seemed, under Marshal Piłsudski, to be a dangerously militaristic state, especially after its attack upon the Ukrainian separatists in Galicia in 1919. Similarly, American government officials harbored deep concerns about the prevalence of anti-Semitism in Poland.[76] Polish representatives in Washington were never really able to assuage these American concerns.[77] American diplomats in Poland, especially Ambassador Hugh S. Gibson, were quite critical of Poland on these and other issues too.[78] The net result was that the Wilson administration was never enthusiastic about Poland.[79]

This lack of enthusiasm had a number of roots. There were doubts in the U.S. government about whether the United States could do much for Poland in the first place, given the great distance between the two countries and Poland's proximity to its two prime adversaries: Russia and Germany.[80] Moreover, it became clear that Wilson's vision of postwar Eastern Europe was not compatible with the large and powerful Poland that Piłsudski and most other Polish nationalists sought to construct.[81] In fact, much like British prime minister Lloyd George, Wilson's primary concern in the East was Russia rather than Poland.[82] Wilson felt that Russia, due to its size and its tremendous natural resources, was the most important actor in Eastern Europe. Given that Russocentric perspective in Washington, the Wilson administration's pro-Polish rhetoric in Washington was largely lip service.

The ambivalence of the United States about its commitment to Poland is especially problematic for the triumphalists, given the huge pro-Polish "audience" in the United States. At the core of the pro-Poland lobby were the millions of ethnic Poles resident in America. Between 1900 and 1914 alone, 100,000 Poles emigrated to the United States each year.[83] These Polish-Americans remained deeply attached to their motherland and lobbied intensely for stronger U.S. support for Poland, especially during the Russo-Polish War. Despite this huge and influential pro-Polish audience in America, it had remarkably little influence on U.S. policy.[84] The rest of the American public was hardly eager to have the U.S. government make a stronger commitment to Poland.[85] In the end, like Britain and France, the United States framed its policy toward Poland not on the basis of common democratic fraternity but on the dictates of realpolitik, which gave precedence to America's national interest.[86]

The same was true of lesser states. Democratic Czechoslovakia was not surprisingly, given its ongoing border disputes about Teschen, ambivalent about the new Polish republic.[87] Conversely, authoritarian Hungary was a most enthusiastic supporter of Poland, though this enthusiasm derived largely from the fact that Hungary also regarded the Soviet Union as its most dangerous adversary and so saw Poland as a potential ally.[88] What is most striking, given the triumphalists' argument, was how little support there was among the general public in the democracies for Poland.[89]

In point of fact, the best explanation for the Entente powers' relations with

Poland was not common democratic fraternity but rather national interest.[90] Piłsudski himself recognized this, especially regarding the Allies greater concern with Russia: "the Entente, as is no longer a secret, attached more importance to the solution of the Russian problem than to any possible solution of the Polish question."[91] Others also understood that realpolitik was the animating philosophy in Western relations with Poland. "It was not friendship for the Poles," observed German general Hans von Seekt, "that was the reason for the action of the Entente but fear that if we keep fighting we might gradually rebuild our army which, by the way, is our aim."[92] Finally, there is evidence that even among the Entente powers themselves, realpolitik concerns were not absent from their thinking about the Polish issue. Some of the Allies' dithering about what do about Poland was rooted in the fact that the French and British did not quite trust each other and so were always hesitant about supporting the other's initiatives in Poland.[93] In sum, contrary to the triumphalists' claims, the Entente powers did little in Poland that is not explicable in terms of their national interests.

For the triumphalists, one reason democracies win their wars is because their democratic allies increase their military capability either directly through the provision of troops or indirectly through training, supplies, and military advice. It is widely, but erroneously, believed that indirect aid from Britain and France played a key role in Poland's remarkable victory over the Soviet Union in the late summer and fall of 1920. The commander of the Soviet western front, General Mikhail Tukhachevsky, always maintained that Entente assistance was the reason the Poles worked the "miracle of the Vistula" in August 1920.[94] This view was quite prevalent in the West as well.[95] According to the British ambassador to Poland, Lord d'Abernon, "The Allies may fairly claim that considerable portion of the improvement is due to the arrival of the Franco-British Mission, particularly the presence of [French] General [Maxime] Weygand."[96] The American analyst Brooks argued that the most important element of Western aid to Poland was the presence of Weygand in Warsaw: "It will be recalled that at the crucial moment when Polish forces were lowest in morale the French General Weygand was given command of the Polish Army. Receiving instant confidence of the staff and troops he rapidly accomplished order out of confusion."[97]

According to this widely held view, the Allies made four vital contributions to Poland's stunning victory over the Soviet Union. First, Weygand was reputed to have completely reorganized the Polish military, transforming it from a broken rabble into a coherent military force. Second, Weygand and other members of the Inter-Allied Military Mission were supposed to have taken a direct hand in organizing the defenses of Warsaw in the critical weeks of early August 1920.[98]

Third, they allegedly supplied vital provisions and munitions to the Polish armed forces. Finally, they reputedly made it possible for these supplies to get to the Polish army by keeping a lifeline to Warsaw open through the free city of Danzig.[99] If Entente aid and advice were so central to Poland's victory, there would be strong reason to think that the triumphalists were correct that democratic alliances are more effective than other types.

In truth, however, the Entente played little role in Poland's victory over the Soviet Union. First, very little Allied material actually got through to Poland before mid-August 1920.[100] In other words, Poland broke the back of the invading Soviet forces without significant allied resupply. Second, there is no evidence that the Inter-Allied Military Mission, particularly Weygand, played a major role in planning or leading the operations that produced the Polish victory.[101] Weygand himself was quite candid about this: "the victory was completely Polish; the war plan was Polish; the army was Polish."[102] Even Ambassador d'Abernon was forced to concede this as well.[103] The facts speak for themselves: the Inter-Allied Military Mission did not arrive in Warsaw until July 1920, far too late to play an appreciable role in rebuilding the Polish armed forces before the decisive Polish counterattack on August 16, 1920.[104] Moreover, Weygand and the mission originally recommended abandoning Warsaw and fighting the decisive battle further West.[105] And to the extent Entente officers played any role in planning for the defense of Warsaw in early August 1920, it was to push for major Polish operations north, rather than south, of the capitol as Piłsudski ultimately decided.[106] In fact, Allied representatives thought Piłsudski was making a grave error in leaving the north flank of the city so weak and concentrating his forces in the south.[107] Of course, it was precisely Piłsudski's tactical deployment that ultimately unhinged the whole Soviet western front and saved Poland from defeat. In sum, one has to agree with Davies's assessment: "Despite persistent statements to the contrary, the *Entente* did *not* play the role of Poland's protector; the *Entente* did *not* support Poland either politically, morally, or, to any massive extent, materially."[108]

If this is true, why is it so widely believed that Entente saved Poland? The answer lies in the subsequent domestic politics of France and Poland. In France, the right sought to credit Weygand and other members of the French military group for the victory, as many of them were associated with these political parties and the right hoped to accrue domestic political capital from its role in the Polish victory against the Soviet Union. Piłsudski, the architect and operational commander of the victory, also had many political opponents in Poland who sought to minimize his role after the fact. To this end, they fostered the myth that the Allies had played the major role. Together, political opportunists in France and Poland convinced many people at the time and subsequently that without Allied assistance, Poland would have lost the war.[109] The fact remains, however, that Entente support was not a major factor in Poland's victory, and this further undermines the triumphalists' argument that democracies form more effective alliances.

Strategic Evaluation

The triumphalists argue that democracies win wars because they are better than nondemocracies at strategic evaluation. But the truth is that Poland was not very good at it. Part of the problem was domestic politics: the Poles were deeply divided over grand strategy. The National Democrats advocated a policy that regarded Germany as Poland's primary adversary, sought alliance with Russia, and aspired merely to control that territory that was ethnically Polish. Piłsudski and his followers, in contrast, regarded Russia as Poland's primary adversary, were less concerned with a possible German threat, and advocated a "federal" Poland that included large numbers of non-Poles and was to be closely allied with pro-Polish buffer states in the East.[110] These fundamental divisions about grand strategy complicated strategic decision making in Poland.

Moreover, the Poles made a number of questionable strategic decisions during the Russo-Polish War. "In their advance after the Bolshevik attack," Brooks concludes, "the Poles it is true were guilty of excessive zeal, repeating again their mistake of the Middle Ages in seizing more than they could manage."[111] Democratic Poland was not, contrary to triumphalists' expectations, superior to the Soviets in strategic evaluation. Indeed, one could argue that Poland would have gained more not going to war with the Soviet Union. The Soviet leader V. I. Lenin observed that the Treaty of Riga left Poland with 69,650 square kilometers less and 4,477,000 people fewer in March 1921 then it would have received had the Poles accepted Soviet terms offered in January 1920.[112] Modern historians concur with this assessment. According to Thomas Fiddick, "[i]f Poland had agreed to enter into negotiations [in December 1919], its borders would have been wider in the East than those eventually acquired by force of arms, as recognized by the Treaty of Riga in March 1921."[113] Further, this new territory annexed after the Treaty of Riga actually undermined Poland's security by increasing the size of its non-Polish minority populations, a long-standing worry for many Poles. It also exposed Poland to more potential enemies.[114] Finally, this treaty came at the expense of Poland's allies in the Ukraine, whom they had to sell out in order to win Soviet assent to the final agreement.[115]

Public Support

The triumphalists argue that democracies have the advantage of greater public support for their war efforts. That, however, was not always the case in Poland during the Russo-Polish War. Even on the eve of his successful offensive in August 1920, Piłsudski confessed to having grave doubts about how much he could count on the Polish public: "I left [Warsaw on August 12th] with a profound sense of the absurdity of the situation, and even a certain feeling of self-disgust, because the timidity and impotence of my countrymen had forced me to outrage all logic and sound rules of warfare."[116] In short, Poland did not have consistently strong public support for its war effort against the Soviet Union.

Troops

Triumphalists also expect democratic armies to be superior to those of non-democracies because they will have better leadership and their soldiers will exhibit greater initiative. The Polish army consistently demonstrated neither during the course of the Russo-Polish War. For example, the initial Polish successes in the Ukraine in the spring of 1920 were due not to superior leadership by Polish officers and greater initiative by Polish soldiers but rather due to their greater numbers: the invading Poles outnumbered the defending Soviets by nearly three to one.[117] German military intelligence clearly documented this: "Among the young hastily organized troops, which did not yet possess a sufficiently military training, and who were led by superiors without sufficient prestige and experience, military discipline seemed to have been relaxed in places due to the long advance which had been essentially carried out without serious fighting."[118] To be sure, Polish forces did fight well at certain periods of the war, but this tended to be when the Soviets were advancing deep into the Polish heartland.[119] As Davies notes, "In the latter stages, when the war was brought to the gates of Warsaw, the mettle of the Polish soldiers and their devotion to duty was shown to be superior to that of the Red Army."[120] In short, Polish officers did not consistently show greater leadership and Polish soldiers did not regularly demonstrate greater initiative than the Soviets on the battlefield, as the triumphalists would expect.

In sum, none of the triumphalists' wartime effectiveness arguments seem to explain the outcome of the Russo-Polish War either.

If Polish democracy does not explain the outcome of the Russo-Polish War, what does? Soon after the war, Tukhachevsky gave a series of remarkably candid lectures in Moscow in which he tried to account for why the Soviet Union lost the Russo-Polish War.[121] He concluded that five factors played a part in the debacle. First, the Soviet invasion of Poland sparked a powerful nationalist response from almost all classes in Poland. Second, Entente military assistance, especially General Weygand's crucial intervention, helped the Poles win the Battle of the Vistula. Third, the Polish fortifications in front of Warsaw made it possible for the Poles to attack the flank of the advancing western front without endangering Warsaw. Fourth, Poland had ruthlessly suppressed the Polish left, thus depriving Moscow of local allies in the campaign. Finally, the Poles managed to achieve nearly a 2:1 advantage in rifles and sabers against the Soviet forces in front of Warsaw, and this also helped explain Poland's dramatic reversal of fortune.[122] While some of these factors did not play a role in the outcome, and others are decidedly self-serving, it is striking that neither Tukhachevsky nor any subsequent historian has attributed Poland's victory to the fact that it was a democracy.

In my view, there are six plausible explanations for the outcome of the Russo-Polish War that provide much more compelling explanations than the nature of Poland's political system. These include the balance of forces, the nature of the conflict, nationalism, a weak adversary, geography, and intelligence.

Numbers

The conventional wisdom about the Russo-Polish War is that the Poles were decidedly outnumbered by the Soviet Union. A simple "bean count" provides the basis for this conclusion. The Soviet armies numbered about 5 million in 1920, whereas the Poles at their peak could field no more than 1 million. Given this 5:1 ratio, it is not surprising that many regard the Polish victory as a miracle.

In truth, however, the Soviets were incapable of bringing all these forces to bear against Poland on the western and southwestern fronts during the Russo-Polish War. To begin with, the Soviets were never able to field more than one-seventh of their total military manpower as combat troops. The Poles, in contrast, could deploy about one-quarter of their troops in the field as combatants. While that still gave the Soviets a 70 to 20 advantage in divisions, that ratio was not nearly as lopsided as it might seem given that the Soviets were simultaneously engaged in combat against other adversaries besides the Poles during the period between 1919 and 1920.[123] In fact, the only significant Soviet numerical advantage on the western and southwestern fronts was in cavalry: the Soviets had sixty brigades to the Poles' seven.[124]

If the overall military balance somewhat favored the Soviet Union, the balance on particular sectors of the front, which is often what is more important in terms of the outcomes of battles, varied significantly throughout the war.[125] In fact, the course of the war always seemed to mirror the balance of forces. For example, the Poles had a greater than 3:1 advantage over the Soviets in their initially successful attack on Ukraine in the spring of 1920.[126] Tukhachevsky acknowledged that these early Polish successes in the Ukraine were due to the fact that Soviets could not bring most of their forces to bear right away.[127] Eventually, the Soviets managed to gain a 3:1 advantage over the Poles during their counterattack and advance into Poland during the early and midsummer of 1920.[128] However, by mid-August 1920, due to casualties and the need to transfer troops to other fronts, the ratio shifted again in favor of the Poles, and not surprisingly this correlated with a change in their fortunes on the battlefield[129] (see the appendix). Thus, the balance of military forces was a good indicator of the course of the war.

Nature of the Conflict

The nature of the conflict also shaped the course of the war in important ways. Red Army doctrine was heavily influenced by the Civil War experience. This led the Soviets to underestimate both the influence of geography (the further they advanced into Poland, the weaker they became because of their lengthening lines of communication) and the importance of nationalism (the deeper they went into purely Polish territory, the stronger Polish resistance became). The Soviets thought that they were fighting a revolutionary war akin to the Civil War in which long lines of communication were not a problem and national resistance had not been a factor. Conversely, the Poles fought the Russo-Polish War as a conventional war of national defense in which these things mattered.[130] Tukhachevsky and his western front were defeated in Poland in part because they became overextended after advancing so deeply into hostile Polish territory.[131] Conversely, the farther the Poles fell back, the shorter their lines of communication became and the more they could take advantage of interior lines of communication.[132] Because the Russo-Polish War was in reality an interstate war, the Polish approach to fighting it was the more appropriate.

Nationalism

Nationalism was also a decisive factor in the Russo-Polish War. Clearly, both sides fought better when defending their homelands.[133] For example, the tide turned against the Poles in June 1920 when their invasion of the Ukraine rekindled Russian national sentiment.[134] One critical way in which nationalism increased Soviet military capability was that it brought many experienced tsarist military officers over to the Bolshevik side in the war against the invading Poles.[135] Even Piłsudski conceded that the surge in Russian nationalism drove Poland from the Ukraine in the early summer of 1920.[136]

Tukhachevsky, however, did not take to heart this lesson when he transformed the Soviet counterattack to drive the Polish invaders from Mother Russia into a war of revolutionary conquest of Poland. The problem was that Tukhachevsky fought the Russo-Polish war as a class war like the Civil War and mistakenly counted on the support of Polish workers and peasants in what he thought was a revolutionary crusade to free them from the thrall of the Polish landlords.[137] In fact, most of the other Soviet leaders harbored no such illusions. Polish communists such as Karl Radek understood clearly the power of Polish nationalism, especially when roused against Russian invaders.[138] Many of the other Bolsheviks understood this, too. For example, Josef Stalin, then the political commissar for the southwestern front, warned that "class conflicts have not yet reached such a pitch as to undermine the sense of national unity. . . . If the Polish forces were operating in Poland's own territory, it would undoubtedly be difficult to fight against them."[139]

The Soviet commissar for war, Leon Trotsky, also understood that nationalism would stiffen the Poles' willingness to fight.[140] Vladimir Lenin recognized well before the Soviet invasion of Poland the power of Polish national spirit:

> We know that the greatest crime was the partitioning of Poland among German, Austrian, and Russian capital, that this partitioning condemned the Polish people to long years of oppression, when the entire Polish people was brought up on one idea—to free itself from this triple yoke. This is why we understand the hatred that permeates the spirit of the Poles, and we say to them that we shall never cross the boundary upon which our troops now stand—and they stand a great distance from where the Polish people live. We propose peace on this basis, because we know that this will constitute an immense acquisition for Poland.[141]

Surprisingly, despite this knowledge, Lenin did not restrain Tukhachevsky from advancing as far as Warsaw. After the war, Lenin regretted that he had not listened to Radek and Trotsky or even taken to heart his own advice:

> In the Red Army the Poles saw enemies, not brothers and liberators. They felt, thought, and acted not in a social, revolutionary way, but as nationalists, as imperialists. The revolution in Poland on which we counted did not take place. The workers and peasants, deceived by the adherents of Piłsudski and Daszyłski, defended their class enemy, let our brave Red soldiers starve, ambushed them and beat them to death. . . . Even all the excellencies of Budyonny [Budienny] and other revolutionary army leaders could not make up for our deficiencies in military and technical affairs, still less for our political miscalculations—the hope of a revolution in Poland. Radek warned us. I was very angry with him and accused him of defeatism. But he was right in his main contention.[142]

Clearly, the Soviets' failure to take into account Polish nationalism was a costly blunder that surely played a large part in their defeat on the Vistula.

Poland, in general, was an intensely nationalistic country because of its history of partition and recent independence.[143] Marshal Piłsudski, in particular, epitomized Polish national aspirations throughout his career.[144] There is a famous story about Piłsudski meeting some old comrades from his days in the Polish Socialist Party. When they greeted him as "Comrade." Piłsudski dismissed their fraternal greeting coldly: "I rode on the red-painted trolley car of socialism as far as a stop called 'Independence,' but there I got off. You are free to drive on to the terminus if you can, but please address me as 'Sir.'"[145] As Piłsudski's comments make clear, the only ideology he consistently embraced was Polish nationalism.[146] The essence of his appeal as a military leader was this commitment to Polish independence.

Polish nationalism increased the willingness of Polish soldiers to fight hard and effectively.[147] As the Soviets drove deeper into Poland, and the threat to its survival grew, Polish national sentiment soared.[148] According to Watt, "Most Poles simply hated the Russians. It made little difference to them whether Russia was Bolshevik or Tsarist. Practically every Pole believed that any Russian government, no matter what its political orientation, would be the enemy of Polish independence."[149] This anti-Russian sentiment had important military ramifications. General Weygand clearly recognized this: "the national fervour of Poland—where the Government, the Army, and the whole population rose in unison against the invader—imbued the Polish forces with a determination to win far above that of the Russian Army of 1920, with its widely different and conflicting elements."[150] It is a testament to the depth of their nationalist fervor that, of 20,000 Polish prisoners of war, only 123 joined the Soviet army and only 175 Polish civilians joined the Soviet-backed Polish communist government.[151] Nationalism was therefore an important military asset for Poland.

Weak Adversary

Neither the Polish nor the Soviet militaries demonstrated much consistent fighting prowess on the battlefield.[152] But of the two, the Soviet army was the weaker and more inept. The Poles, therefore, had the luxury of fighting a relatively weak and inefficient adversary. This Soviet weakness was a function of two sets of factors. First, the Bolshevik government faced severe internal threats from counterrevolutionaries throughout most of the Russo-Polish War.[153] In fact, Polish military leaders like General Sikorski and others understood that the Red Army was fighting the war with one hand tied behind its back.[154] The major internal threat came from the forces of Baron Piotr Wrangel, which were still operating in the southern Ukraine around the Crimea Peninsula.

This continuing counterrevolutionary threat made Soviet leaders like Lenin much more preoccupied with securing the home front than with marching on Warsaw.[155] They often made clear that defeating the counterrevolutionary threat at home—by 1920 this referred largely to Wrangel—was their main priority. Lenin himself noted in a letter written in July 1920 that "the Crimea must be restored to Russia at all costs . . . even at the expense of other fronts."[156] As Stalin opined at about the same time in *Pravda,* "Only with the liquidation of Wrangel shall we be able to consider our victory over the Polish gentry secure."[157] And Soviet military commander I. I. Latsis noted: "A victory for us on the southern and eastern fronts will deliver into the hands of the Soviet regime the entire territory of the former Russian Empire, and hence a temporary reverse on the Western front will not be reflected in the final result."[158]

Wrangel represented a clear and present danger to the Bolshevik regime as early as June and July 1920, and this threat made the baron a "decisive factor" in the Russo-Polish War.[159] By early August this threat seemed so pressing that General Sergei Kamenev, the commander in chief of the Red Army, sought to transfer two divisions from the Polish theater to the Crimea.[160] Historian John Erickson argues that this movement of forces directly contributed to the Soviet defeat after mid-August 1920. Specifically, Tukhachevsky expected that his western front's southern flank would be covered by the Twelfth Army on the northern end of the southwestern front. The Twelfth Army, however, was too depleted to send units to fight Wrangel.[161] It was precisely in the seam between these two fronts that the Poles struck with devastating effect on August 16. The southwestern front was thinly manned because it was engaged in both the Russo-Polish War and the campaign against Wrangel in Crimea.[162] As legendary Fourth Cavalry Army commander Semyon Budenny remarked, "It is easy to understand the predicament of S. S. Kamenev. The fate of both the Polish and the Wrangel fronts worried *Glavkom* simultaneously, but there were not enough forces to deal with both."[163]

On August 2, 1920, Lenin ordered Stalin to redirect even more resources against Wrangel. When Wrangel began another offensive from Crimea on August 19, 1920, Soviet leaders decided to cut their losses in Poland at any cost and focus their entire military resources on defeating the remaining counterrevolutionary forces.[164] For this reason, Fiddick argues that the Soviets were not really defeated in Poland but rather withdrew for diplomatic and domestic political reasons.[165] Once the Russians and the Poles agreed to a truce in October 1920, the Soviets quickly defeated Wrangel once and for all.

Second, the Red war effort was crippled by factional infighting at many levels. For example, Tukhachevsky and Budenny had very poor personal and professional relations from the very beginning of the war, which inhibited cooperation between the western and southwestern fronts. Relations between Tukhachevsky and Stalin were no more cordial.[166] The top Bolsheviks regarded Tukhachevsky as a double-edged sword: they acknowledged his brilliance as a military commander but doubted his loyalty to the communist regime. Thus, there are reasons to think that Soviet civilian leaders did not have complete control of their military—especially Tukhachevsky—as they should have.[167] This might explain why Lenin acquiesced in Tukhachevsky's continuing advance toward Warsaw despite his concerns about how Polish nationalism would strengthen Piłsudski's forces. The consequence of this was that the Soviets never reconciled their political and military strategies vis-à-vis Poland.

This lack of coordination between the western and southwestern fronts was a major source of Soviet military weakness.[168] The concrete result of this lack of coordination on the Soviet side was the inability to bring Budenny's powerful Fourth Cavalry Army to bear against Polish forces south of Warsaw.[169] Instead of advancing from the south toward Warsaw, forming the anvil for the western front's hammer, the southwestern front—particularly Budenny's Fourth Cavalry Army—instead turned west with the intention of capturing the less important Polish city of Lwow.[170] Had the two Soviet fronts worked in tandem, they might have been able to take Warsaw and defeat Piłsudski. At a minimum, the

Soviets would not have suffered the catastrophic collapse after August 16 because a coordinated southwestern front advance on Warsaw would have prevented Piłsudski's forces south of Warsaw from attacking northward into the
flank of the western front.

Geography

The key to the Polish victory was Piłsudski's decision to hit the weak and divided Soviet forces at precisely their weakest point (see map 3.2). The Soviet
forces were divided into western and southwestern fronts that operated north
and south of Pripet Marshes, respectively.[171] This split was originally mandated
by geography as the Pripet Marshes stood between the two major groups of Soviet forces.[172] As we saw previously, however, growing concerns about the threat
to the southern Soviet Union from Wrangel and intense political rivalries between the leaders of the western and southwestern fronts reinforced and exacer-
bated the split between the two fronts. The lightly defended seam between the
two Soviet fronts was the weak spot that Piłsudski brilliantly exploited on August 16.[173] Attacking northeasterly with five divisions from the city of Wieprz,
which lay south of Warsaw on the Vistula, he punched through the Soviet Mozyr
Group (approximately 12,000 rifles and sabers) and into the flank of Tukhachevsky's Sixteenth Army.[174] This attack shattered the army, effectively rolled up the
western front, and forced the Soviets to withdraw from Poland and sue for peace.

Intelligence

A final factor that may have played a role in the outcome of the war was intelligence. Specifically, the Poles cracked the Soviet's military codes and could deci-
pher many Soviet military communications.[175] This gave them a clear picture of
Soviet war plans. Conversely, while Tukhachevsky acknowledged that the Russians had captured a copy of Piłsudksi's plan of August 16, they regarded it as a
fake and so did not act on it.[176] These intelligence developments also contributed
to the Polish victory and the Soviet defeat. However, it is hard to link them to
the fact that Poland was a democracy or that the Soviet Union was not.

CONCLUSIONS

The Russo-Polish War, which seems to provide the triumphalists with a great
deal of support for both the selection effects and wartime effectiveness argu-

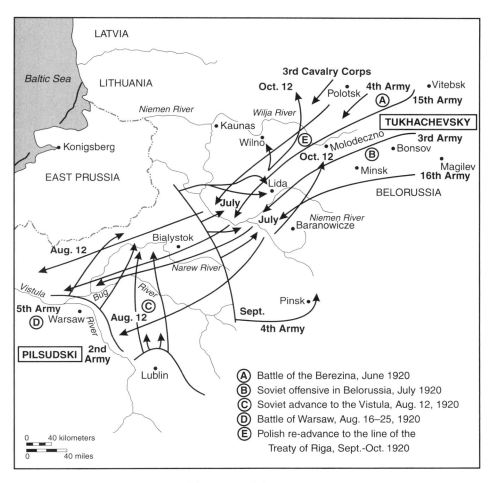

Map 3.2. The Major Campaigns of the Russo-Polish War

ments, upon closer inspection provides little, if any, support for either of these arguments. Contrary to the triumphalists' selection effects argument, the Piłsudski government was not very democratic in terms of how it made the decision to attack the Soviet Union in the spring of 1920. None of the triumphalists' wartime effectiveness arguments work very well either. Poland was an archetypal rent-seeking state, and so was not wealthier than the Soviet Union. Poland could not reliably count on the support of the democratic powers of the Entente. Poland was not much better than the Soviet Union at strategic evaluation. Public support for the Polish war effort was intermittent. Finally, the performance of Polish troops on the battlefield was mixed.

In fact, the most plausible explanations for the outcome of the Russo-Polish War have nothing to do with the nature of the Polish regime. Rather, it was shaped by the balance of forces, the nature of the conflict, nationalism, a weak adversary in the unconsolidated Soviet regime, geography; and a timely intelligence break. In sum, factors other than the nature of the Polish political regime provide a much better explanation for the course and outcome of the Russo-Polish War. What this suggests is that the coincidence between democracy and military success in the Russo-Polish War was precisely that: coincidence.

APPENDIX

Estimates of Polish/Soviet Military Balance, August 16–24, 1920

| | Polish Army [Bayonets (Sabers)] | | | | | |
| | Soviet Source | | | | Polish Source | |
	1	2	3	4	1	2
First Army	28,000	—	22,500	40,000	32,139	36,005
	(2,600)		(38,000)		(1,061)	(1,162)
Second Army	10,000	—	7,500	16,000	7,050	3,513
	(1,000)		(12,500)		(450)	(393)
Third Army	13,000	—	15,000	22,000	30,500	30,6000
	(1,500)		(25,000)		(5,521)	(5,521)
Fourth Army	13,000	—	13,800	22,000	25,700	25,700
	(1,500)		(23,500)		(950)	(950)
Fifth Army	15,000	—	27,000	29,000	22,010	22,010
	(1,700)		(46,000)		(3,826)	(3,826)
Total	66,000	100,200	85,000	107,000	117,399	117,828
	(6,800)	(14,460)	(145,000)		(11,808)	(11,852)

| | Soviet Army [Bayonets (Sabers)] | | | | | |
| | Soviet Source | | | | Polish Source | |
	1	2	3	4	1	2
Mozyr	11,690	6,020	4,000	4,193	11,690	5,020
Group	(?)	(164)	(8,000)	(-)	($\approx$ 1,000)	(7,398)
Third Army	18,710	16,349	10,000	9205	45,539	16,349
	(1,122)	(970)	(20,000)	(914)	(1,911)	(970)
Fourth Army	16,020	23,262	14,000	9,568	16,020	23,262
	(5,083)	(5,122)	(28,000)	(4,861)	(5,083)	(5,122)
Fifteenth Army	26,829	21,294	13,000	12,729	45,539	21,294
	(789)	(580)	(26,000)	(465)	(1,911)	(580)
Sixteenth Army	36,695	26,901	10,500	10,584	31,655	29,901
	(1,041)	(662)	(20,700)	(244)	(1,041)	(662)
Total	104,904	93,826	51,500	46,279	104,904	93,826
	(8,325)	(7,498)	(102,700)	(6,484)	(9,035)	(7,498)

Source: Shewchuk, "The Russo-Polish War of 1920," 350.

CHAPTER 4

Democracy and Israel's Military Effectiveness

Israel seems to be a perfect illustration of how democracy helps states wisely select and effectively prosecute wars. Clearly anticipating later triumphalist arguments, Israeli leaders boasted of the military virtues of their political system. For example, Yigal Allon, the commander of the Palmach, maintained that the fact that Israel was a democracy gave it a number of wartime advantages over the Arabs:

> To be a political and social democracy in the midst of backwards, patriarchal, autocratic or dictatorial regimes was by itself an advantage. . . . The political history of the Middle East has shown that a genuine democracy such as Israel's could command the loyalty of its citizens as the regimes of the Arab countries had never been able to do. It guaranteed (to begin with) their fullest mobilization, both physical and moral, in times of national crisis; it enabled Israel to give arms to each and everyone of her citizens; and it ensured the qualitative superiority of her fighting forces, expressed in their fighting morale, in the qualities of leadership at all levels, and in the efficient use of military equipment. It was conducive to more stable government, and to a greater sense of unity and common purpose. It ensured a conspicuously higher level of government culture and education, of scientific and technological know-how, of basic physical health.[1]

Some contemporary scholars concur with this assessment. "Israel's ability to withstand Arab attempts to destroy it in one of the longest and most lopsided wars ever fought serves as an indelible testimony to the strength of democratic culture" concludes Ruth Wisse.[2]

The standard view is that the Jewish state was a small, embattled democracy that repeatedly won its wars in the face of overwhelming odds.[3] Moreover, its major ally, the United States, supposedly had no real strategic interest in assisting Israel aside from moral obligation and ideological affinity.[4] Finally, of the five wars in the COW/POLITY dataset that seem to indisputably support the triumphalists' view of the wartime superiority of democracy, three (1948, 1967, and 1973) involved Israel. Israel, therefore, constitutes a series of "most likely" cases for the triumphalists' arguments about democracies' ability to win wars and a hard case for theories that downplay the importance of regime type in explaining military effectiveness. If the triumphalists' theories do not actually explain the outcome in these Israeli cases, there are serious grounds for doubt about them.

In this chapter I first provide an overview of Israel's wars and its performance in them. Next, I show that the specific mechanisms optimists argue account for democracy's military advantages—selection effects and wartime effectiveness—in fact do not explain Israel's military performance in the 1948, 1956, 1967, 1969–70, 1973, and 1982 wars. Finally, I conclude by arguing that alternative explanations, such as the balance of military forces, the nature of the conflict, emulation, nationalism, and the level of development, provide more convincing explanations of Israel's military performance since 1948.

ISRAEL'S WARS

Israel's wars constitute a significant fraction of the victorious democracies in the triumphalists' datasets. Israel fought and won its War of Independence in two phases, first against indigenous Palestinians and then against Arabs from neighboring countries between May 1948 and January 1949. Israel joined France and the United Kingdom in the Suez War in October and November 1956, inflicting a significant tactical defeat upon the Egyptians, but was denied a strategic victory when the United States forced it and its allies to withdraw from captured Egyptian territory. In 1967 Israel launched the Six Day War and handily defeated Egypt, Jordan, and Syria in short order. Israel and Egypt fought a series of indecisive skirmishes in the occupied Sinai during 1969 and 1970, which collectively are referred to as the War of Attrition. In October 1973 Egypt and Syria surprised the Israelis in the Yom Kippur War and made significant gains in the occupied Sinai Peninsula and Golan Heights before being thrown back. Finally, in the summer of 1982, Israel invaded Lebanon and inflicted tactical defeats on Syria and PLO forces but was eventually forced to withdraw without achieving its

TABLE 4.1
Initiative and Outcome of Israel's Wars

War	Israel Started?	Israel Won?
1948	No	Yes
1956	Yes	Yes/No
1967	Yes	Yes
1969–70	No	Draw
1973	No	Yes
1982	Yes	Draw

larger strategic goal of evicting Syria and installing a pro-Israel government in Beirut. Table 4.1 summarizes Israel's military record from 1948 through 1982.

Very few democracies have fought in so many wars in such a short period of time and amassed such an impressive record of victories. Not surprisingly, Israel represents the poster child for democratic triumphalists. But do the triumphalists' prewar selection effects or wartime effectiveness hypotheses really explain this track record?

SELECTION EFFECTS

Israel initiated three wars between 1948 and 1982. In 1956 Israel fought as part of an overwhelming coalition against Egypt, winning a decisive tactical victory, which was eventually reversed by the United States. The Israeli invasion of Lebanon in 1982 again met with some tactical success but hardly constituted a clear strategic victory. Only the Six Day War of 1967 appears, at least at the correlational level, to support the triumphalists' theory. But it is important to go beyond this correlation between democracy, war initiation, and victory and determine whether democracy was the key causal factor. Triumphalists attribute the propensity of democratic states to win their wars to the fact that democratic statesmen, desiring to remain in office, or democratic publics, unwilling to pay the price for long and costly wars, should be more cautious and therefore smarter about starting wars, only initiating those they believe they can win.[5] The informational version of this argument suggests that democracies can undertake superior strategic assessment due to their open societies; the institutional version emphasizes the readily available mechanisms through which democratic publics can punish leaders who start unsuccessful wars. In order to test the triumphalists' selection effects argument through process tracing in the Israeli cases, we need first to ascertain how democratic national security decision making really was. Next, we need to see if Israeli leaders took public opinion into account as they considered whether to go to war. Also, debates about going to war should be full and fair and completely transparent to the public. Finally, successful wars should benefit Israeli political leaders, whereas costly unsuccessful wars should impose a political cost upon them.

How Democratic Was Israeli National Security Decision Making?

An essential precondition for the triumphalists' selection effects argument is that the state be democratic and that decisions about war be subject to the democratic process. The conventional wisdom is that Israel has been a robust democracy from the very beginning of statehood in 1948.[6] Indeed, many believe that Israel's democratic roots extend from the prestate Yishuv as far back as biblical times.[7] Reflecting this view, the widely used POLITY dataset, consistently rates Israel as a "high democracy." On its twenty-one point Democracy Composite Index (–10–10), Israel scores 10 in 1948; 10 in 1956; 9 in 1967; 9 in 1969–70; 9 in 1973; and 9 in 1982 (the slight drop in Israel's democracy score was the result of its occupation of the West Bank and Gaza Strip after 1967).

While Israel has been politically open for most of its history, this image of it being a consistently robust liberal democracy needs to be qualified. Dan Horowitz and Moshe Lissak noted that "the democratic element in the ideologies of most movements in the Yishuv was mainly on the operative level, while on the fundamental level most parties carried traces of a predemocratic or even undemocratic position."[8] This was certainly evident in the early years of the Jewish state which saw its nearly complete dominance by Prime Minister David Ben-Gurion and his Mapai party.[9] His Labor Party colleague Golda Meir recounted a revealing exchange that highlighted the extent to which Ben-Gurion was first among equals in the new Israeli government: "Peretz Naphtali looked at [Ben-Gurion] for a moment, smiled his charming smile and answered thoughtfully, 'No, I wouldn't say that [you conduct meetings democratically]. I would say rather that in the most democratic fashion possible, the party always decides to vote the way you want it to.'"[10] Looking back, Israeli historian Tom Segev concluded that while Ben-Gurion and his colleagues were in principle committed to democratic political procedures, in practice they often flouted them when they thought it necessary "'for the good of the state,' 'for security reasons,' or even 'for the good of the party.'"[11] Contrary to the conventional wisdom, Israel was a much weaker democratic polity in the early days of statehood than it would later become.

Moreover, Israel was never really a "liberal" democracy in the European sense.[12] Antiliberal aspects of Israel's political system included the restriction of ownership of much of the land in Israel to Jews; the continuing presence of Mandate-era Emergency Laws, used primarily against the Arabs; the Basic Laws of 1992, making Israel a "Jewish" state; the absence of any bill of rights protecting personal liberties, such as freedom of speech or the press; and the lack of separation of church and state.[13] The continuing threat from the Arab world was one major source of Israel's lack of commitment to liberalism. The rights of Israeli Arabs were widely circumscribed for fear of them becoming a fifth column.[14] This has led many Israeli historians and Arab scholars to deny that Israeli Arabs even live in a democratic political system.[15]

Despite the overtly secular orientation of the Zionist movement, another important obstacle to liberalism in Israel was the fact that from the beginning Orthodox religious Jews exercised significant influence within the avowedly secular government.[16] Rather than being a liberal democracy in the classic European sense of recognizing the inviolability of individual rights, Israel was a "communitarian democracy" committed to advancing the rights of Jews over other groups and guided by a legal tradition and political culture based exclusively upon Judaism.[17]

Finally, Israel is widely regarded as something of a "dysfunctional democracy."[18] The fact that Israel has a multiparty proportional representation system gives small, ideologically extreme parties disproportionate influence. This political structure makes it very hard for Israeli voters to know beforehand what policies a government would pursue because the content of coalition agreements is not always predictable beforehand. All of this is not to deny that Israel is a democracy; rather, it is to suggest that Israel's democracy has matured and consolidated over time but that it also remains illiberal and prone to instability.

There are, however, a few areas in which Israel has hardly been democratic at all: in the formulation of its foreign policy and in the conduct of its wars.[19] Israel's parliament, the Knesset, has historically played little role in foreign policy decision making.[20] In the areas of national defense and war, Israeli democracy has been most compromised.[21] Ben-Gurion set the tone from the very beginning of the state: "I have never brought security issues to my party. . . . I always accepted a majority decision in my party, in the Histadrut, and in the Cabinet as self-understood. . . . But in security matters as I see them, there exists for me only my own conscience."[22] True to this principle and virtually by himself, Ben-Gurion made the decision in 1956 to join France and the United Kingdom in their plot to foil Egyptian leader Gamal Abdel Nasser's plan to nationalize the Suez Canal.[23] Similarly, Ben-Gurion gave the Knesset no say in the decision to build the nuclear reactor at Dimona, the cradle of Israel's nuclear weapons program.[24]

This tradition of exempting national security and war from normal democratic politics continued under Ben-Gurion's successors. When you look, for example, at the actual decision-making processes leading up to the initiation of the 1967 Six Day War, there is little evidence of democratic procedures at work. During the crisis preceding the war, then prime minister Levi Eshkol was forced to take Ben-Gurion's young protégés Moshe Dayan and Shimon Peres into his government. This government reshuffling was hardly the result of normal democratic procedure. Indeed, "it was a real putsch," Eshkol's wife Miriam maintained, "everyone was worried and nobody cared about the democratic process."[25] Defense minister and former general Moshe Dayan had little patience for the democratic process. "I oppose decisions made on majority vote on matters of security," he boasted, and, like Ben-Gurion, Dayan maintained that "in security matters, there is no democracy."[26] Dayan was as good as his word when he was defense minister in Eshkol's cabinet, launching the assault on the Golan Heights without securing the prime minister's approval.

Probably the most egregious example of how war was exempted from normal democratic procedures in Israel was Defense Minister Ariel Sharon's decision to invade Lebanon in June 1982. Sharon used the pretext of an assassination attempt against Israel's ambassador to London, Shlomo Agrov, by the anti-PLO Abu Nidal faction to justify an invasion of Lebanon. Publicly adhering to a "Little Plan" designed only to drive the PLO forty kilometers away from Israel's northern border, Sharon secretly implemented his "Big Plan" in Lebanon to destroy the Palestine Liberation Organization, weaken Syria, and fundamentally remake the Middle East, all without a formal cabinet vote.[27] Along with Sharon, a small cabal comprising Prime Minister Menachem Begin, Foreign Minister Yitzak Shamir, and Chief of Staff Rafael Eitan set into motion the Big Plan with no regard for the rest of the Israeli government or public.[28] As Israeli journalists Ze'ev Schiff and Ehud Ya'ari noted,

> On the surface, Sharon was very careful to adapt his moves to Israel's accepted democratic and political conventions. He invested considerable energy in building the image of a reformed recalcitrant who would not dream of embarking on any consequential action without first submitting a detailed report, receiving prior authority, and explaining himself to the public. The paradox is that exactly the opposite was true: the image of obedience and cooperation was a thin but effective

veneer masking a highly original method of circumventing democratic procedures. Instead of trying to takeover or disperse governmental institutions, as is the
usual course of a coup d'etat, Sharon devised a formula for bypassing the decision-
making process and evading the supervisory prerogatives of the country's parliamentary system. Through chinks in that system, he gained the freedom of maneuver necessary to implement his plan.[29]

Sharon enjoyed nearly complete authority to run the Israeli war effort in Lebanon
until the cabinet finally reasserted its authority on August 12, by which point Israel was bogged down in what would become a costly and fruitless war.[30]

Thus, the conventional wisdom about Israeli democracy needs to be qualified
in three respects: first, contrary to the POLITY dataset, Israel began as a weak
democracy that only became more robust over time; second, Israel has never
been a liberal democracy, as evidenced both by its treatment of the Arab minority and by its lack of separation of church and state; finally, and most importantly, Israel was scarcely democratic in terms of national security decision making. All three of these points pose serious challenges to the triumphalists' claims
that it was liberal democracy that made Israel so militarily effective.

Did Israeli Leaders Take Public Opinion into Consideration?

If the institutional constraints version of the selection effects argument is
correct in stage 1, democratic leaders should be very sensitive to public opinion
as they make their decisions about going to war. According to Michael Brecher's
exhaustive study of Israeli foreign policy decision making, however, domestic
political considerations played only a "marginal" role in 75 percent of its major
foreign policy decisions.[31] For example, in the early days of the state, it was evident that Ben-Gurion paid scant attention to his domestic popularity.[32] Nor does
Israel's successful 1956 Sinai campaign support this part of the selection effects
argument. Neither the Israeli public nor the cabinet strongly supported the war,
as evidenced by the fact that Ben-Gurion went to great lengths to keep prepara-
tions for the operation secret from them.[33] There is not much evidence that domestic political concerns were of much importance to Ben-Gurion, who seemed
to make strategic decisions overwhelmingly in terms of what he thought best
for Israel's survival and prosperity.

We now know that Prime Minister Eshkol did not push for the 1967 Six Day
War in order to bolster his public standing. Eshkol was reportedly "worried,
worried, worried" throughout the debate over whether to strike first.[34] The gen-

eral mood among Israelis was not one of optimism about victory, but rather fear that the Arabs were gearing up to annihilate the Jewish state. As Interior Minister Moshe Shapira observed apropos of public sentiment, "we must remember that the general mood in those days was that we could not reasonably expect the emphatic victory which ensued.'"[35] The only optimists in Israel were the army chief of staff, General Yitzak Rabin, and the director of military intelligence, General Aharon Yariv. While Rabin, Yariv, and their colleagues in the Israeli Defense Forces (IDF) were "spoiling for a fight," Eshkol was hesitant about launching a war against Egypt and Syria. Rather than persuading the prime minister that going to war would result in an easy victory that would enhance his political prospects, Rabin and Yariv instead painted the situation in the bleakest terms and argued that Israel needed to preempt an imminent Arab attack upon the Jewish state that they undoubtedly knew was not in the offing.[36]

Israel's 1982 war against Syria in Lebanon also undercuts the triumphalists' institutional constraints version of the selection effects argument. Prime Minister Menachem Begin and Defense Minister Ariel Sharon began the war despite overwhelming opposition from the cabinet and the public, which opposed transforming a retaliatory raid against Palestine Liberation Organization forces in south Lebanon into a war with Syria.[37] As the chief of military intelligence, Major General Yehoshua Saguy, observed, "One of the worst things a country can do is go to war when it is divided. I fear there's lack of consensus within the army itself, and that's no way to march off to war."[38] Whatever one might think of the wisdom of the Lebanon War, there is little evidence that their domestic political fates affected either Begin's or Sharon's calculations about the advisability of the war with Syria. For Begin, intervention in Lebanon was largely about saving the Christian community from a Holocaust at the hands of the Muslims.[39] Sharon, in contrast, just wanted to use the war to advance his plan to fundamentally reshape the Middle East in order to increase Israel's security. In either case, the institutional constraints version of the selection effects argument did not seem to operate.

Was There Full and Free Public Debate about Starting Wars?

Contradicting the triumphalists' argument that democracies win their wars because they generate better information at the first-stage decision about starting a war or not, in both the 1956 Suez War and the 1982 Lebanon War, Israeli leaders like David Ben-Gurion and Ariel Sharon were able to use secrecy and outright deception to mislead the Israel public about the costs, benefits, risks, and even outcome of these wars. As Schiff and Ya'ari note about the Lebanon War, "Ariel Sharon did not reveal his grand design for a war in Lebanon all at once. On the contrary, he began his term as defense minister by making numerous public statements to the effect that 'war is not good for Israel' and piously vowing that Israel would not initiate hostilities. Within the privacy of the defense establishment, however, he sang a very different tune."[40] Thus, the informational version of the selection effects argument did not influence Israeli leaders' decisions about starting those wars.

Did Israeli Leaders Prosper When They Won and Were They Punished When They Lost?

One important causal mechanism in the second stage of the triumphalists' institutional constraints version of the selection effects argument is that democratic leaders are more cautious because they are more easily "punished" than authoritarian leaders when they start costly losing wars. The Israeli cases pose problems for this proposition. To begin with, Israeli leaders were not regularly punished for losing wars. The arguably mixed results of the Suez War (Israel reduced the *fedeyeen* threat from Egypt but was forced to unilaterally withdraw from the Sinai and became increasingly isolated globally) did not adversely affect Ben-Gurion's political career.[41] True, both Defense Minister Moshe Dayan and Prime Minister Golda Meir resigned in disgrace due to their many missteps during the Yom Kippur War. Despite these resignations, the Labor Party remained in power for four more years. Nor did Dayan remain in the political wilderness very long, as he returned as foreign minister in Menachem Begin's government in 1977. Even Israel's most dramatic military failure in Lebanon did not impose serious political costs on Begin and Sharon. To be sure, Begin did resign in 1983, but he did so largely for personal reasons.[42] Sharon lost his defense portfolio (primarily because of the massacres at Sabra and Shatila), but he remained in the cabinet and eventually became Israel's prime minister. Foreign Minister Shamir also later became prime minister. Israeli statesmen rarely suffered as severe punishments as their Arab adversaries when they lost their wars. The worst fate that befell an unsuccessful Israeli leader was an (often temporary) loss of office.

Conversely, Arab leaders who lost wars lost their positions permanently and often paid a far higher price. For example, Husni Za'im in Syria was deposed and executed after 1948; King Abdullah of Jordan was assassinated in 1951; King Faruq of Egypt was ousted in 1952; and King Faisel and Prime Minister Nuri al-Sa'id of Iraq were assassinated in 1958 for trying to make peace with Israel.

After the 1967 debacle, hundreds of Egyptian military leaders were "punished" by being demoted and even put on trial. Abdel Haim Amer, the vice president and vice commander in chief was immediately relieved from all his posts and either committed suicide or, as some suspect, was murdered by Nasser's agents for his part in the defeat. Shams Badran, the minister of war, and Salah Nasr, the chief of intelligence, were tried, convicted, and sentenced to hard labor for their roles in Egypt's loss. King Hussein of Jordan also feared public retribution in 1967 after he lost the West Bank and Jerusalem. Ironically, undemocratic Arab leaders faced more regular and severe punishments than did their Israeli adversaries when they lost wars. By the triumphalists' selection effects logic, Arab leaders had at least as much, if not more, incentive to be cautious about starting their wars.

In sum, the Israeli cases provide support for neither the institutional nor the informational versions of the selection effects argument. Israel did not regularly start winning wars. Moreover, Israeli leaders were rarely seriously punished for poor wartime performance. There is also scant evidence that Israeli leaders spent much time worrying about how their military performance would affect their domestic political standing anyway. Finally, Israeli leaders were regularly able to avoid punishment for failure not because the public thought that the stakes were low but rather because they could manipulate information in such a way as to distort the public's calculation of the costs, risks, and outcomes of less-than-successful wars.

WARTIME EFFECTIVENESS
Rent Seeking

The triumphalists' argue that democracies suffer less rent-seeking behavior by their governments and therefore tend to be wealthier. One important benefit of this is that it gives democracies greater wealth with which they can buy more military resources. Hence, they are more apt to win their wars.

But lack of rent seeking could not explain Israel's military successes because Israel was a classic example of a state with one of the major manifestations of rent seeking: massive government intervention in the economy. This is not surprising inasmuch as the economic ideology of Israel has always been socialist and collectivist. As one historian of Israel points out, "[Israel] had originally been created by East Europeans who brought with them not the ideas of Western liberal, bourgeois democracy but the collective socialism of the old Russian intelligentsia."[43] Hence, Ben-Gurion's view that "the state of Israel is not a capitalist state."[44] Elsewhere he admitted that "I cannot yet call Israel a Socialist country, for we also encourage private capital, but in agriculture, industry and transport we can claim Socialist achievements, and even the beginnings of a truly communist society in the labor settlements known as *kibbutzim,* to which—so far as I know—there is no parallel anywhere else in the world."[45]

Democracy has done little to constrain the rise of state intervention and thereby provide Israel with more economic resources than its Arab adversaries. Indeed, Israel is one of the most centralized of democratic states.[46] It has one of the highest tax rates in the world at 65 percent.[47] Also, the Israeli government spends more per capita than any other country in the world.[48] Not surprisingly, the Heritage Foundation ranks Israel very high (4 on a scale of 5) in terms of the level of government intervention into the economy.[49]

Ironically, Israel became less statist after 1967, just as its economic (and military) performance began to decline. Indeed, Israel achieved spectacular growth rates approaching 10 percent per year under a relatively centralized economic system; as its economy liberalized, however, these growth rates shrank to 1 percent per year by the mid-1960s.[50] In sum, because Israeli democracy has not served as a check on government intervention into the economy, that reason cannot explain why Israel has won so many of its wars.

Alliances

Triumphalists suggest that another reason that democracies are more likely to win their wars is that they are better able to attract and keep alliance partners. Some believe that the lack of rent seeking curtails imperialistic behavior, which makes democracies less threatening to other states and hence more attractive as alliance partners. Others maintain that because democracies incur substantial domestic audience costs if they break a commitment to another democracy, they are less likely than a nondemocratic ally to do so. Neither of these arguments works in the Israeli cases.

It is hard to argue that Israeli democracy made the Jewish state averse to the conquest of additional territory, as some proponents of the rent-seeking argument suggest. In 1948 the Jewish state colluded with Jordan and seized territory well beyond the original United Nations mandate. In 1956 Israel joined with France and the United Kingdom to seize large chunks of the Sinai Peninsula from Egypt and withdrew only after the United States put pressure on it. In 1967

Israel again occupied the Sinai Peninsula and also conquered the West Bank and Golan Heights. In 1973 Israel fought to maintain control of the Sinai and Golan and even crossed the Suez and occupied more Egyptian territory. Finally, in 1982 Israel invaded and occupied southern Lebanon with the objective of discrediting the PLO among Palestinians in the Occupied Territories, expelling Syria, installing a pro-Israel government in Lebanon, and precipitating a major regional transformation in the Middle East. As former Mapam party leader Simha Flapan lamented, "the concept of a democratic Jewish society might conceivably provide an alternative were it free from the impulse toward territorial expansionism"[51] Clearly, Israel did not attract other democratic allies because it was unthreatening to its neighbors.

The Israeli cases also do not lend much support to the argument that democracies will form stronger and more durable alliances because domestic audience costs make it hard for them to break their commitments. Historically, Israel has made three types of appeals for support from other democratic countries: moral obligation, strategic interest, and common democracy.[52] Despite much rhetoric to the contrary, it is clear that Israeli leaders did not regard common democracy or moral obligation as a strong bond between states. Golda Meir was particularly skeptical of the reliability of other democracies as allies: "The world is harsh, selfish, and materialistic. Even the most enlightened of governments, democracies that are led by decent leaders who represent fine, decent people, are not much inclined today to concern themselves with problems of justice in international relations."[53] This pessimism was shared by the former head of the Haganah, Yisrael Galili: "We belong to the generation that has witnessed the abandonment of the cause of democratic Spain, and is witnessing today the events in Greece and Indonesia. And it was only yesterday six million were abandoned to their fate and massacred?"[54]

Indeed, the most consistent element in Israeli alliance strategy has been to align with states that best serve its interests. As Shlaim explains, Israeli leaders had a quite pragmatic attitude about which states they aligned with dating from the days of the Yishuv, the prestate Jewish community: "Ben Gurion's appreciation of the strength of the Arab opposition led him to seek the support of an external power in order to compensate for the weakness of the Zionist movement. *His orientation was practical rather than ideological.* In the course of his career he advocated an Ottoman, a British, and an American orientation. Changes in orientation were dictated by the rise and fall in the influence of these great powers."[55] Despite frequent appeals to other democratic countries couched in terms of obligation or common democracy, Israeli leaders understood that the only solid basis for alliance was mutual interest. Israel's status as a democracy did little, save perhaps at the rhetorical level, to cement its bonds with other democratic states.

Nothing could make this clearer than the fact that in the early days of the Jewish state the Israelis had a difficult time finding allies in the democratic world. Democracies such as France, Germany, the United Kingdom, and the United States were not inclined to lend much support to the Jewish state during the War of Independence. Nor was the all-democratic alliance that Israel joined to fight the Suez War particularly a model of harmony and cooperation.[56] Moreover, it is a myth that the democratic world came to Israel's aid in 1967 and saved the day. In fact, most of the democratic world tried to remain neutral during the Six Day War.[57] Indeed, Israeli leaders felt that Israel had to win quickly before the democratic states intervened to impose a stalemate and save the Arabs from an even worse defeat.[58] Nor did the democratic world, with the exception of the United States, rally to Israel's aid in its moment of greatest peril in 1973. As Meir recounts, "One day, weeks after the [Yom Kippur] war, I phoned Willy Brandt, who is much respected in the Socialist International, and said ' . . . I need to know what possible meaning socialism can have when not a single socialist country in all of Europe was prepared to come to the aid of the only democratic nation in the Middle East. Is it possible that democracy and fraternity do not apply in our case?' "[59]

The democratic world failed to support Israel in 1973 despite substantial pro-Israel "audiences" in many countries because of their dependence on Arab oil. Europe and Japan imported 85 to 90 percent of their oil from the region and not surprisingly they tilted toward the Arabs; in contrast, the United States imported only 7 percent of its oil from the Arab world, so it could afford to be more supportive of Israel.[60] Subsequently, many democratic nations abstained rather than voting against the 1978 UN General Assembly resolution equating Zionism with racism. Israel could not even sustain good relations with democratic Austria under the premiership of Bruno Kriesky, a fellow Jew.[61] Finally, there was widespread condemnation in the democratic world of Israel's invasion of Lebanon.

Despite common democracy, Israel could not, and indeed did not, count on consistent support from the democratic world. While Israel did at times have close alliances with democratic states such as the United States, France, the United Kingdom, and Germany, these alliances were by no means permanent, and they were based on common interests rather than democratic fraternity.

Moreover, Israel also made common cause with nondemocratic states such as the Soviet Union, Czechoslovakia, South Africa, and Jordan. Let us examine these cases more closely.

United States

The United States has been Israel's most important ally. The key question is why this has been the case. Nadav Safran, for example, suggests that the fact that Israel was a democracy was central to the United States' willingness to align with the Jewish state.[62] However, the United States was quite ambivalent about Israeli independence in 1948, opposed the democratic coalition Israel fought with in 1956, and hamstrung the Israelis in 1967. Not until after 1967 did the U.S.-Israeli alignment become the quasi alliance it is today. Not surprisingly, even once the U.S.-Israeli alliance was consolidated, the Israelis were never very confident in it.[63]

The U.S.-Israeli alliance was clearly based not on common democratic norms but rather on U.S. strategic interest in having allies in the Middle East as a balance against the Soviet Union and later Iran and Iraq.[64] Realizing that this realpolitik motivation on the part of the United States might some day lead it to abandon Israel, the Israelis and their supporters have sought to cloak the alliance in the mantle of common democratic fraternity.

Moreover, the Israelis candidly acknowledge that, despite common democracy, there remain many sources of friction in the relationship. Indeed, Israeli leaders regularly complained that "the American 'connection' has usually acted as the main direct constraint on Israeli decision makers."[65] True, the Israel lobby, a loose connection of individuals and organizations committed to fostering and sustaining a close relationship between the United States and Israel, has been one of the most vocal and influential interest groups in American political history.[66] But despite this important pro-Israel "audience," the Israeli-American relationship has hardly been a model of consistent and strong alignment.[67] The ups and downs of the United States' relationship with Israel are best explained by changes in U.S. interests rather than common democracy.

The U.S. government was divided over the establishment of the state of Israel. President Harry S. Truman was initially supportive of the Jewish state, in part for domestic political reasons and in part because he felt that the world owed the Jews their own state in partial recompense for the international community's inaction during the Holocaust. However, Secretary of State George Marshall and many bureaucrats in the State and War Departments believed that for strategic reasons the United States should be more "evenhanded" in its view of the future of Palestine.[68] Truman's pro-Israel policy initially prevailed, and the United States was one of the first countries to support partition and the establishment of an independent Jewish state.

By March 1948, however, the Truman administration did an about-face and, instead of advocating Israeli independence, endorsed a United Nations trusteeship over the whole of Palestine. The primary reason for this reversal was the United States' desire not to alienate the Arabs as the Cold War intensified.[69] This same concern led the United States to try to thwart Israel's crucial arms deal with Czechoslovakia during the War of Independence.[70]

After Israel's victory in the War of Independence, the U.S. government took the position that Israel was in violation of the UN partition resolution by occupying Arab territory and forced Israel to withdraw from Gaza in 1949. Truman also became increasingly anxious about the Palestinian refugee problem caused by Israel's victory in the War of Independence and began pushing for a resolution of the Arab-Israeli conflict in order to construct an Islamic alliance against the Soviet Union.

By 1950 the United States began to view Israel and the Middle East almost exclusively in the context of the Cold War rivalry with the Soviet Union. On the one hand, the United States "leaned" on Israel to side with the United Nations in the Korean War. On the other, it also issued the Tripartite Declaration of May 1950, which excluded Israel from U.S. regional defense planning. Further, the United States placed an arms embargo on the region, which hurt Israel disproportionately.[71] As Ben-Gurion noted in his diary, "America did not raise a finger to save us, and moreover, imposed an arms embargo, and had we been destroyed they would not have resurrected us."[72] In 1953 the U.S. government imposed sanctions on Israel to stop it from diverting the Jordan River. The United States would not supply Israel with arms before the Suez War because it opposed Israel's retaliatory policy against Arab states harboring anti-Israel *fedeyeen*. Also, the Eisenhower administration refused to recognize Jerusalem as Israel's capital, forcing the American ambassador to boycott Israel's Foreign Ministry until 1956. Finally, during this period Ben-Gurion was never officially invited to United States because of the ambivalence of both the Truman and Eisenhower administrations.[73]

The tenuous nature of U.S. support for the Jewish state was not lost on Israeli leaders. Yisrael Galili warned his colleagues that: "It is irrelevant and even despicable to indulge in clever speculations about 'whether,' 'can it be,' or 'would they dare?' to set loose the Arab states against us? Or whether America 'would' or 'would not let them.' We must constantly remind ourselves that we have to defend ourselves. We have to cleave to the tangible. And what is the tangible? It is Jewish land, Jewish economy, Jewish arms, Jewish fighting men in the Land of Israel."[74] Israeli leaders were under no illusions about the strength of the U.S. commitment to the state of Israel in the early years.

This uncertainty about the U.S. commitment continued into the mid-1950s.[75] Concerned about a possible rapprochement between the United States and Egypt, Israeli intelligence agents initiated terrorist attacks against U.S. facilities, which they hoped the Americans would blame on Nasser. Safran argues that continuing doubts also led Israel to undertake the ill-fated Suez operation.[76] Israeli concerns about the firmness of the U.S. commitment were justified because the United States opposed Israel and its democratic allies France and the United Kingdom during Sinai campaign and was responsible for their ultimate failure. Reflecting Eisenhower's frustrations with the Jewish state's reckless policies, Secretary of State John Foster Dulles began to privately refer to Israel as "the millstone around our necks."[77]

Eventually, this brinksmanship achieved some of Israel's goals. The United States clearly became more solicitous of Israel's security concerns after Suez, fearing that if America did not back the Jewish state, it might undertake other precipitous actions. But continuing uncertainty led Israel to take an even more dramatic step in the mid-1950s to ensure continuing U.S. support. Israel's decision to begin a secret nuclear weapons program had as it central objective to guarantee that any war that threatened the survival of the state of Israel would also threaten the survival of the United States. Employing a biblical metaphor, Seymour Hersh characterized Israel's strategy as the "Samson Option" after the legendary Jewish hero who brought down the Philistines' temple, killing himself along with 3,000 of his enemies. Following a similar logic, the Israelis designed their nuclear program as a means to bolster the U.S. commitment to Israel's survival. Their strategy was to aim their nuclear weapons not just at the capitals of their Arab adversaries but also at targets inside the United States' Cold War rival, the Soviet Union.[78] The reasoning behind this was that, because the Soviet Union would retaliate for any Israeli strike by attacking the United States itself, U.S. leaders could never allow the Jewish state to face so serious a threat that might lead it to undertake such a desperate act in the first place. Francis Perrin, a French nuclear scientist intimately involved in collaboration with Israel's nuclear program, recalled that "We thought the Israeli bomb was aimed against the Americans. . . . Not to launch it against America but to say , *If you don't want to help us in a critical situation we will require you to help us. Otherwise we will use our nuclear bombs.*"[79] One Israeli associated with the nuclear program confirmed that this was Israeli thinking: "We got the message. We can still remember the smell of Auschwitz and Treblinka. Next time we'll take all of you with us."[80]

The United States understood the threat implicit in Israel's nuclear program and sought to derail it. Initially, the United States offered Israel participation in its peaceful nuclear program, Atoms for Peace. This effort failed, as Israel refused to participate and continued to develop nuclear weapons. Next, the United States tried to use the emerging global nonproliferation regime to coerce Israel to open to international inspection its secret nuclear facilities at Dimona in the Negev Desert, but U.S. opposition to its nuclear weapons program merely led Israel to pursue it secretly.

Blackmail, both conventional and nuclear, was one part of Israel's strategy for ensuring closer relations with the United States. Another, more positive element in this strategy was Israel's efforts to make the case that it could serve as a strategic asset for the United States in its rivalry with the Soviet Union. This strategy made sense inasmuch as by 1955 the United States increasingly had come to view Nasser's Egypt as a full member of the Soviet camp. As the conviction spread within the U.S. government that the Egyptian leader was a communist dupe, the consensus grew in those same precincts that the United States should rethink its previously distant relationship with Israel.

The real watershed in U.S.-Israeli relations came during the presidency of John F. Kennedy. The main impetus for improving U.S.-Israel relations was the growing realization that the two states had a common interest in containing Arab radicalism and excluding Soviet influence from the region. The clearest manifestation of this increasingly close alignment was the decision by the United States to sell to Israel one of its most advanced military systems: the HAWK antiaircraft missile.

Lurking behind this veneer of common strategic interests remained continuing U.S. concerns about slowing the Israeli nuclear weapons program. Failing with Atoms for Peace and inspections, the U.S. government sought to use conventional arms transfers to try to forestall the Israeli nuclear program. In a May 1965 memorandum, National Security Council staffer Robert Komer explicitly asked whether selling Israel twenty-four Skyhawk jets would keep it from going further down the path to an operational nuclear arsenal: *"Can we use the planes to keep Israel from going nuclear? Desperation is what could most likely drive Israel to this choice. Should it come to feel that the conventional balance was running against it. So judicious US arms supply aimed at maintaining a deterrent balance, is as good an inhibitor as we've got."*[81] In sum, the increasingly close relations between the United States and Israel were the result of two factors: shared strategic interests in the Cold War Middle East and Israel's implicit threat of nuclear blackmail.

Despite some common strategic goals and Israel's nuclear blackmail, the U.S.-Israeli relationship hardly constituted a tight alliance. In the run-up to the Six Day War in June 1967, the United States sought to minimize its military commitment to Israel in the hopes of preventing the war, which U.S. leaders feared would undermine its position in the region. Anticipating Israel's preemptive strike on the Egyptian air force, President Lyndon Johnson warned Israeli foreign minister, Abba Eban, that *"Israel will not be alone unless it decides to go it alone."*[82] Defense Minister Dayan interpreted this to mean that "the United States was not prepared to complicate her relations with Egypt in order to guarantee freedom of shipping for us."[83] He and other Israeli leaders questioned the depth of the U.S. commitment to Israel's security. There was ample reason for them to doubt U.S. support for their war effort. The United States restricted arms shipments to Israel, tried to prevent the Jewish state from starting the war, and then sought to limit Israel's gains once the war began by urging it not to take Jerusalem. The United States also tried to restrain Israel from attacking Syria at the end of the war.

The most dramatic evidence of the tension just below the surface in U.S.-Israeli relations was Israel's attack on the USS *Liberty,* an American electronic intelligence collection ship. Despite Israeli protestations to the contrary, many in the U.S. government and military believe that the attack on the American spy ship by Israeli aircraft and ships was no accident.[84] The presence of this U.S. signals intelligence platform off the Sinai Peninsula, as the IDF was completing operations against the Egyptians, was evidence that the United States was spying on Israel. James Bamford, a well-connected expert on the U.S. National Security Agency, suggested that the motive for the attack was Israeli concern that the *Liberty* had collected electronic evidence of IDF massacres of Egyptian prisoners of war in the area of al-Arish.[85] Whether the attack was deliberate or not, it certainly demonstrated that the U.S.-Israeli alignment during the Six Day War was not free of strain.

The United States did not really embrace Israel until after the Six Day War was won. Certainly, there was a nonstrategic component to the increasingly close ties between America and the Jewish state. As historian Peter Novick has documented, the Holocaust became much more salient among the American public—especially Jews—around the time of the Six Day War.[86] Many Gentiles also regarded Israel's apparently miraculous victory as providential. President

Johnson, who had visited the Nazi concentration camp at Dachau just after World War II and was deeply affected by the experience, was like many other Americans inclined to be sympathetic toward the beleaguered Jewish state.[87] Certainly, a growing sense that the security of Israel was a debt the world owed the Jews for the Holocaust played some role in closer U.S.-Israeli ties.

Much more than moral obligation, however, led to the increasingly close U.S.-Israeli relations. Israel's stunning and decisive victory over the Arabs made clear that the Jewish state had become the strongest military power in the region. Many American officials therefore felt that closer relations would advance U.S. interests in the region. But undergirding this common strategic interest was also the continuing Israeli threat to use nuclear weapons in the event they faced a serious threat to the survival of the state of Israel. If anything, Israel's threat of nuclear "blackmail" became much more important under the administration of Prime Minister Levi Eshkol.[88] The result was the arms agreement of February 1968 that transformed the United States into Israel's largest arms supplier.

In many respects, the period after the Six Day War was the apex of U.S.-Israeli relations. Even during this time, however, the relationship was not without friction. The 1969-70 War of Attrition is a case in point: some Israeli scholars believe that U.S. pressure forced Israel to end deep penetration raids against Egypt and agree to a cease-fire on less than optimal terms. Despite Israel's ongoing conflict with Egypt, in January 1970 the United States put on hold the sale of forty-five Phantom and eighty Skyhawk jets to Israel, at a time of increasing Soviet military aid to Egypt. Another instance of the gap between the two democracies was President Richard Nixon's endorsement of a more "evenhanded" approach to the Arab-Israeli conflict. Nixon and his secretary of state, William Rogers, shocked the Israelis by advocating a unilateral Israeli withdrawal from the territories Israel had occupied in 1967.

Like Johnson after the Six Day War, Nixon and his national security advisor, Henry Kissinger, regarded Israel as one of the key Cold War proxies in the Middle East. They believed that Israel could help the United States check growing Soviet influence in the region. Israel's support of the embattled King Hussein of Jordan during the "Black September" crisis of 1970 also demonstrated its potential as a "strategic asset" in the region to counter regional threats to U.S. interests. Arab leaders in Egypt and Saudi Arabia certainly recognized the increasing harmony of interests between Israel and the United States due to the Cold War. As with Johnson, Nixon's support for Israel was based primarily on his calculation that it would further U.S. strategic interests.

But even this relatively close U.S.-Israeli alignment did not deter the Egyptians from intensifying their conflict with Israel. President Anwar Sadat believed that despite their support for Israel, Nixon and Kissinger were not averse to the Egyptians turning up the heat on Israel along the canal in 1972 to get them to negotiate a withdrawal from the occupied Sinai. The United States also sought to limit its military support for Israel in order to maintain a regional balance of power. In October 1973, as in May 1967, Israeli leaders like Moshe Dayan claimed that U.S. pressure caused Israel to delay full mobilization and eschew preemptive strikes in order to assure the United States that Israel had not provoked the war. Both Kissinger and American ambassador Kenneth Keating told the Israelis that there would be no U.S. aid if they started the war.[89] Once the Yom Kippur War began, Israel did not rely solely on democratic fraternity and moral obligation but also used the threat of nuclear blackmail to force the United States to undertake a massive resupply effort to make up the early losses of equipment and ammunition.[90]

Despite the military support the United States rushed to Israel during and after the war, there were clearly limits to its support for Israel. For example, Kissinger prevented the Israelis from dealing the Egyptians a knockout blow by destroying the beleaguered Third Army trapped on the east side of the Suez Canal.[91] Moshe Dayan later recounted that this caused great tension between the two democracies: "A crisis followed after we cut off and surrounded the Egyptian Third Army. At first it seemed that the two superpowers alone were involved. But it was soon evident that the United States and the Soviet Union had resolved matters between themselves, and the crisis turned into one between the U.S. and Israel."[92] Dayan was sure that the United States would sell out Israel in the cease-fire negotiations in order to lift the Arab oil embargo. "During one of my talks with Dr. Kissinger," Dayan remembered, "though I happened to remark that the United States was the only country that was ready to stand by us, my silent reflection was that the United States would really rather support the Arabs."[93] There were indeed grounds for Israeli leaders to question whether U.S. support would be unconditional. President Gerald Ford subsequently threatened to reassess U.S. relations with Israel due to what he regarded as Israeli intransigence in its peace negotiations with Egypt. Under President Carter, the United States was much closer to the Egyptian than Israeli position at the Camp David peace talks in 1979.

During the Reagan administration, the United States and Israel signed an "Agreement for Strategic Cooperation" in 1981 that came close to establishing a formal alliance between the two democracies. But even with the formal codification of the U.S.-Israel strategic partnership, Israeli leaders were under no illusions that common democracy, by itself, represented much of the basis for an enduring alliance. Despite the strategic partnership agreement, U.S.-Israeli relations were never completely harmonious. In 1981 U.S.-Israeli ties were strained by Israel's bombing of the Iraqi nuclear facility at Osirik and its attack on the PLO's headquarter in Beirut. Prime Minister Menachem Begin was completely pragmatic in his view of the alliance with the United States. Begin understood that he needed to persuade President Reagan that Israel could be a strategic asset in the Cold War.

The most vexing issue in U.S.-Israeli relations during the Reagan administration was the invasion of Lebanon. Triumphalists might point to the fact that Secretary of State Alexander Haig probably gave the Israeli defense minister, Ariel Sharon, the "green light" for a limited operation in Lebanon, as evidence of the close alignment between the two democracies. However, Haig authorized only the Little Plan to drive the PLO forty kilometers north of Israel's borders, which Sharon briefed to Begin's cabinet.[94] Sharon and Begin recognized that there were limits to U.S. support and that neither Haig nor Reagan would support their more ambitious Big Plan to use their victory in Lebanon to fundamentally remake the Middle East. Begin and Sharon intended to launch the Big Plan without notifying the Reagan administration and hoped to win its acquiescence by presenting it with a fait accompli.[95]

Once it became clear that Sharon had mislead them about the purpose and scope of the incursion into Lebanon, Haig and Reagan sought to rein in Israel. The U.S.-imposed cease-fire of June 11, 1982, saved the Syrian army in Lebanon from complete destruction at the hands of the IDF.[96] There were many other instances during the Lebanon War where Israel and the United States worked at cross-purposes, thus belying the notion that America and the Jewish state where working hand in glove.

Probably nothing could better illustrate the discord just below the surface in U.S.-Israeli relations at the time than the Pollard Affair. Jonathan Pollard, an American Jew, was working for the Office of U.S. Naval Intelligence when he was recruited to spy for Israel's Ministry of Defense. Sharon himself initiated this operation because he was dissatisfied with the extent of intelligence sharing with the United States, which had been curtailed after the Lebanon War.[97] Pollard turned over highly classified intelligence and military operational data, some of which the Israelis later sold to Moscow.[98] It is hard to reconcile the Pollard Affair with the widely held image of two democratic states working together seamlessly. Indeed, to this day, the Pollard case complicates U.S.-Israeli relations.[99]

Overall, strategic interests, rather than common democracy, better explain the ebb and flow of U.S.-Israeli relations. During the period between 1948 and 1982, with the few caveats mentioned here, common democracy has been a constant feature of the relationship. However, U.S.-Israeli relations have varied quite dramatically from the cool, arm's-length attitude of the Eisenhower administration to the relatively warm and close relations of the late 1960s and early 1970s. Even though he argues that common democracy explained the close U.S.-Israeli relationship, Safran's account actually provides ample evidence that variation in strategic interests correlates quite closely with the state of U.S.-Israeli relations. They were strained during the period from 1948 through 1957, which Safran attributes to the U.S. desire to have Arab allies for the Cold War, uninterrupted access to oil, and access to air bases in the Middle East from which to launch nuclear strikes against the Soviet Union. Conversely, U.S.-Israeli relations improved between 1957 and 1967. Safran suggests that this improvement came about because the United States had become less dependent upon Middle Eastern nuclear bases; had realized that the Arabs were unlikely to be U.S. allies in the Cold War; and U.S. dependence on Middle Eastern oil was deemed less critical. U.S.-Israeli relations were particularly close between 1967 and 1973. This was because the United States had concluded from the outcome of the Six Day War that Israel was the most potent military force in the region and alignment with the Jewish state could best further U.S. interests. In contrast, the period after 1973 saw a loosening of the relationship between the two democracies. This was due in part to the fact that the Yom Kippur War demonstrated the limits of Israel's military power in the region. Also, the Arab members of the Organization of Petroleum Exporting Countries (OPEC) wielded the oil weapon with devastating effect against the economies of the developed world. The war also drew the Soviet Union more deeply into the region and increased its influence there. Finally, Europe decisively broke ranks with the United States in the Middle East, particularly over the issue of support for Israel. In sum, interests, rather than ideology, are the best explanation for American alignment decisions with Israel.

France

France is another democracy with which Israel has had quite variable relations. Like much of the democratic world, the French were initially reluctant to recognize Israeli independence for fear of antagonizing the Arabs. As its North African colonies became more restive in the mid-1950s, however, France began to realize that the Fourth Republic and the Jewish state shared some common strategic interests. This belief was carefully cultivated by Moshe Dayan in his efforts to get the French Ministry of Defense to sell Israel much needed arms:

"We face a common enemy, the Arabs. You are on the home front, while we are in the firing lines. Don't you think that when the front lines are ablaze the arms should be transferred from the home front to the forward positions."[100] This line of reasoning was persuasive, and France became one of the first democratic countries to sell arms to Israel. France was Israel's "great power patron" from the mid-1950s through the mid-1960s.

To be sure, there was a lot of rhetoric about common democracy as the basis for the Franco-Israeli alignment. "At this dangerous time," Ben-Gurion appealed to French prime minister Guy Mollet in 1956, "the small and young republic of Israel appeals to the older and great French Republic with the certainty of mutual understanding."[101] But France and Israel did not become close for reasons of common democratic fraternity but rather because of their shared belief that Nasser's Egypt was the common cause of all their troubles in the Middle East.[102] The French, in particular, blamed Nasser for supporting the rebels who were making their life miserable in Algeria. Also, France's own nascent nuclear program was critically dependent upon the computer skills of Israeli scientists.[103] Throughout this whole period, however, the Israelis never lost sight of the fact that their alignment with France was based on temporary common interests rather than permanent ideological fraternity.[104]

Nothing could make this clearer than the fact that Israel's once quite close alliance did not survive the Six Day War. Indeed, France refused to support Israel in the run-up to that war and even ended its long-standing policy of selling weapons to Israel on the eve of hostilities. French president Charles DeGaulle concluded that France's strategic interests dictated that it must remain neutral in that conflict, and he resisted supporting Israel despite substantial domestic audience costs "merely because public opinion felt some superficial sympathy for Israel as a small country with an unhappy history."[105] Common democracy did not prevent France from later developing quite close relations with one of Israel's deadliest enemies: Saddam Hussein's Iraq. In fact, the French were deeply implicated in the development of Saddam's nascent nuclear program that the Israelis sought to preempt in 1981.[106] Clearly, democratic fraternity tells us far less than strategic interests about the course of Franco-Israeli relations over time.

United Kingdom

Relations between the democratic United Kingdom and Israel have waxed and waned despite their common democracy. Britain's involvement with the Zionist movement predated the establishment of the state of Israel. During the First World War, the British government expressed support in principle for the establishment of a Jewish homeland in Palestine with the issuance of the Balfour Declaration on November 2, 1917. However, this endorsement of Jewish national aspirations had nothing to do with the political complexion of the Yishuv, the prestate Jewish community in Palestine. Rather, it arose from some very straightforward strategic calculations. In endorsing Jewish statehood, the British hoped to keep Russia in the war through appealing to Russian Jews; get the United States more committed to the Entente by pleasing American Jews; take the moral high ground in Europe by endorsing the principle of national self-determination for a small but important European minority; and preempt a likely German declaration of support for an independent Jewish state. Overall, Britain's objective was to improve its position in the Middle East rather than foster a democracy in the region.[107]

If strategic interest could in some contexts lead Britain to support the Yishuv, in other situations it had precisely the opposite effect. For example, Britain's ardor for Zionism was dampened by the Arab Revolt and the Second World War. The need to keep the Middle East quiescent in preparation for a major war against the Axis led Britain in 1939 to issue a White Paper restricting Jewish immigration to Palestine, hindering the establishment of the Jewish state. Even after the end of the Second World War, the newly elected Labour government in the United Kingdom continued to enforce the White Paper's restrictions on Jewish immigration into Palestine because it believed that good relations with the Arabs remained vital to England's Cold War position in the region.

Relations between Britain and the Yishuv became so strained by the United Kingdom's opposition to an independent Palestinian state that the two democracies were virtually at war with each other. As Israeli journalist Moshe Brilliant recalled:

> As a result [of the White Paper], His Britannic Majesty's bayonets barred the gates of the Jewish National Home to European Jews fleeing Nazi gas chambers and furnaces. Some shiploads which reached the Middle East were turned back to Europe to perish.
>
> This disastrous experience made an indelible impression upon the Jews of Palestine. They became less sensitive to what the world thought of them, and less scrupulous about Marquess of Queensbury rules in their struggle for Palestine.[108]

The bloody and costly war with the Yishuv lead Britain ultimately to withdraw from Palestine and relinquish its mandate. It refused, though, to support Israel's declaration of independence. The United Kingdom also expelled Israel from the pound sterling bloc. British and Israeli air forces even engaged in combat over the Sinai in the latter stages of the War of Independence. Until the mid-1950s, relations between the two democracies were anything but cordial.

Triumphalists might point to the fact that Britain joined its sister democracies France and Israel in the victorious Suez War coalition as evidence that common democracy leads to more effective alliances. Upon closer inspection, however, the Suez War provides little support for the proposition that democracies win their wars because they make stronger alliance partners. To begin with, despite common democracy, the United Kingdom was initially reluctant to side with Israel in the Suez War due to residual hard feelings from the independence struggle. Also, Britain did not want to antagonize the Arabs by openly siding with the Jewish state against Egypt. Finally, the United Kingdom remained wary of Israel due to the latter's policy of retaliations against Jordan, Britain's most important ally in the region.[109]

Of course, Britain did eventually side with Israel in the Suez War, but it did so not out of democratic fraternity but rather because of their common interest in toppling Nasser. Despite common democracy, Ben-Gurion remained skeptical of the reliability of "perfidious Albion" as an ally during the Suez War. "Personally, I have great admiration for the British people, for its democratic regime," he recalled, " but I doubt the strength and honesty of [Prime Minister Anthony] Eden."[110] Ben-Gurion's distrust was well warranted inasmuch as Britain tried to maintain the fiction after Suez that Britain and France were merely intervening to separate Israel and Egypt rather than operating in collusion with the Jewish state.

Finally, as with France, once Britain concluded that alignment with Israel was no longer in its strategic interest, democratic audience costs did nothing to prevent a rupture. Like France, Britain refused to support Israel in the Six Day War. Nor did Britain side with the embattled democracy during its greatest hour of need: the Yom Kippur War. In sum, changing interests, rather than common democracy, best accounts for Britain's varying relationship with Israel throughout the twentieth century.

Germany

Another democracy with which Israel had an up-and-down relationship was the Federal Republic of Germany. A closer examination of this alignment also makes clear that interest, rather than democratic fraternity, provides the best account of its vagaries. The primary impetus for the Israel's rapprochement with the perpetrators of the Holocaust was not that Conrad Adenauer's Federal Republic of Germany was democratic. Despite Germany's transition to democracy, most Israelis were hardly ready to forgive and forget. Indeed, polls showed that 80 percent of Israelis opposed negotiations with even a democratic Germany.[111] Ben-Gurion understood that negotiating reparations and establishing relations with the Federal Republic would cause a huge crisis in Israel—as it in fact did—but he was willing to ignore majority opinion and base his policy toward Germany on realpolitik considerations of Israel's national interest: Israel's economy was in terrible shape after 1948 and needed substantial financial aid. German reparations would produce a huge cash infusion for the Israeli economy.

Ben-Gurion also reckoned that establishing relations with Germany could help to integrate Israel into the U.S. Cold War alliance system. Ben-Gurion rationalized his efforts to establish relations with Hitler's former countrymen as the best means of ensuring Israel's security:

> When I say that the Germany of today, the Germany of Adenauer and the Social Democrats, is not the Germany of Hitler, I am referring not only to the new regime . . . but also to the geopolitical transformation that has taken place in Western Europe and the world. . . . Germany as a force hostile to Israel . . . also endangers the friendship of the other countries of Western Europe and might even have an undesirable influence on the United States and the other countries of America. She is a rising force . . . and her attitude to us will have no small influence on the attitude of other countries that are allied with her.
>
> In my profound conviction, the injunction bequeathed to us by the martyrs of the Holocaust is the rebuilding, the strengthening, the progress and the security of Israel. For that purpose we need friends . . . especially friends who are able and willing to equip the Israel Defence Forces in order to ensure our survival. . . . But if we regard Germany, or any other country—as Satan, we shall not receive arms.[112]

According to Israeli historian Tom Segev, Adenauer made a similar calculation, agreeing to pay substantial reparations to Israel for the Holocaust in return for Germany's rehabilitation as a full member of the Western alliance. The result was that the Federal Republic gave Israel $812 million which covered 29 percent of its balance-of-payments deficit.[113] This aid played a key role in the economic and military development of the state of Israel in the 1950s and early 1960s. As with France and England, this close relationship did not continue through the Six Day and Yom Kippur Wars. The fact that common democracy did not make other states consistently reliable allies calls into question the triumphalists' claim that the reason democracies tend to win their wars is that they enjoy better alliances.

Another problem with this triumphalist claim is that, in many instances, the most important allies of the Jewish state were not democracies at all. Because of their pragmatic views, the Israelis were willing to align themselves with a variety of nondemocratic, and sometimes quite unsavory, regimes if they thought it would increase the security of the state. This precedent was established from the early days of statehood. As we saw previously, the democratic world did not rush to Israel's side after independence. Israel did, however, find significant support in the eastern bloc from the Soviet Union, Czechoslovakia, and Yugoslavia. Subsequently, it would gain important allies in other undemocratic regions of the world.

Soviet Union

The Soviet Union was one of the first states to recognize Israel's independence. The Soviet representative to the United Nations, Andrei Gromyko, strongly endorsed statehood for Israel in a speech on November 29, 1947: "The Jewish people had been closely linked with Palestine for a considerable period in history. As a result of the war, the Jews as a people have suffered more than any other people. The total number of the Jewish population who perished at the hands of the Nazi executioners is estimated at approximately six million. The Jewish people were therefore striving to create a State of their own, and it would be unjust to deny them that right."[114] Despite the high-sounding rhetoric about history and the international community's debt for its inaction during the Holocaust, the Soviets recognized the new Jewish state primarily to undermine the United Kingdom's position in the Middle East and keep it from establishing a military base in the Negev.

Soviet aid to Israel was more than just rhetorical. The communist bloc provided arms to Israel before the United States did.[115] Without Soviet acquiescence, Israel would not have received large numbers of weapons and munitions from satellite states and likely would have lost the War of Independence.[116] Also, the Soviet Union permitted eastern bloc Jews with military experience to emigrate to Israel, which significantly bolstered the IDF's fighting power in the War of Independence. These individuals made much better soldiers than did inexperienced Arabs.[117] Despite a lack of common democracy, the Soviet Union provided Israel with decisive aid early in its existence.

Czechoslovakia

The main conduit for eastern bloc military aid to Israel during the War of Independence was Czechoslovakia. True, the Czech arms deal was negotiated when Czechoslovakia was still a democracy, but this vital military aid continued under communist rule.[118] It was essential to Israel's victory in the War of Independence, constituting more than 60 percent of Israel's weapons acquisitions on the Continent.[119] Golda Meir concluded that "[h]ad it not been for the arms and ammunition that we were able to buy in Czechoslovakia and transport through Yugoslavia and other Balkan countries in those days at the start of the war, I do not know whether we actually could have held out until the tide changed, as it did by June of 1948."[120] Yitzak Rabin concurred: "Without the arms from Czechoslovakia . . . it is very doubtful whether we would have been able to conduct the war."[121] Ben-Gurion was even more categorical about the impact of the Czech arms: "They saved the State. There is no doubt of this. Without these weapons, it's doubtful whether we could have won. The arms deal with the Czechs was the greatest assistance we received."[122] These Czech arms came when no democratic country would sell Israel weapons and most certainly were provided with Soviet acquiescence.

South Africa

Israel has also made common cause with nondemocratic states such as the apartheid regime in South Africa. In fact, Israel and the apartheid regime were so closely aligned that they may even have secretly cooperated in developing each other's nuclear programs, despite South Africa's abhorrent domestic political system.[123]

Jordan

Israel's most important and consistent nondemocratic partner has been the Hashemite Kingdom of Jordan. Cooperation between the Yishuv and King Abdullah began even before the establishment of the state of Israel. Indeed, this "collusion across the Jordan" was an important precipitant of the international phase of Israel's War of Independence. Both Israel and Jordan sought to forestall the emergence of an independent Palestinian state and connived with each other to accomplish that end in 1948. The Israelis allowed King Abdullah to occupy the West Bank; in return, the Hashemite monarch looked the other way when Israel seized other Arab areas in Palestine.[124] Though Jordan and Israel did engage in combat during the War of Independence, King Abdullah had no intention of destroying Israel.[125] "Abdullah and the Zionists spoke the same language, the language of realism," concludes historian Avi Shlaim, though "from different scripts."[126] This Israeli-Jordanian "special relationship" made possible Israel's decisive victory in 1948.

The Israeli-Jordanian "informal alliance" survived King Abdullah's assassination and the ascension to the throne of his grandson Hussein. Israeli leaders understood that both Israel and Jordan suffered from cross-border "raiding" by

Palestinian forces in the 1950s and therefore had a common interest in suppress-ing it.[127] Subsequently, Jordan did not really want to get involved in the Six Day War but Israel's harsh retaliatory policy pushed King Hussein into Nasser's arms.[128] Israel and Jordan fought for Jerusalem and the West Bank for a few days in June 1967 with Israel driving the king's forces back across the Jordan River. That conflict, however, did not stop Israel from coming to Jordan's aid in its hour of need during Black September, the Palestinian uprising in 1970. Israel mobilized its forces to prevent Syrian intervention in support of the Palestini-ans.[129] Jordan reciprocated a few years later when King Hussein gave Golda Meir advanced warning in September 1973 of the planned Egyptian-Syrian Yom Kip-pur attack.[130] Jordan also sat out most of the Yom Kippur War except for sending some token forces to defend Syria. Overall, the Jewish state and the Hashemite Kingdom cooperated much more than they fought over the years.

At various times, Israel also had cordial relations with other nondemocratic or sometimes-democratic states, including the shah's Iran, Turkey, and the Lebanese Christian Phalange in 1982. In all of these cases, the main concern was not the nature of the potential ally's domestic regime but whether alignment with that group furthered Israel's interests.

Israel has been willing to ally with both democracies and nondemocracies as its interests dictated, but Israeli leaders regarded Jews in the Diaspora as their only truly reliable supporters. As Yigal Allon put it, "Israel has had, has and will have, but one faithful ally: the Jewish people in its diaspora."[131] This is why Ben-Gurion and other Israeli leaders have looked to Jews within the United States and other countries as reliable lobbies on Israel's behalf.[132] Common religion and ethnicity, the twin pillars of nationalism, rather than common democracy, have been the only sound basis for alliance in the view of most Israeli leaders.

Common democracy has not guaranteed that Israel and the United States, France, Britain, or Germany have maintained close alliances. Moreover, Israel has often found nondemocracies such as the Soviet Union, Czechoslovakia, South Africa, and Jordan to be reliable strategic partners. In all of these cases, the most important factor explaining Israeli alignments has been strategic inter-ests rather than the domestic character of the regimes involved.

Strategic Evaluation

Triumphalists believe that democracies benefit from better strategic evalua-tion in wartime, and this ability explains their propensity to win their wars.

There are two possible reasons why democracy might help states make better strategic decisions. Some believe that since democracies involve more people in the decision-making process, this increases the likelihood that the right decision will be made. Others argue that democracy fosters a marketplace of ideas out of which emerge the best policies. Either way, democracies are more likely to win their wars because they make better wartime decisions. There is, as will quickly become apparent, significant overlap with the logic of the triumphalists' selection effects arguments. The mechanisms are very similar; the major difference is that they affect the actual conduct of the war, rather than just influencing the decision to begin one.

It is not clear, however, that Israeli democracy fostered better strategic evaluation and decision making. Neither of the causal mechanisms that triumphalists argue produce better decision making adequately explains Israel's military victories. Although Israel is a robust democracy, in the areas of national security very few Israelis have much meaningful input into the decision-making process. Members of the Israeli Parliament play little role in national security decision making because the Knesset has no independent sources of information with which to make strategic assessments.[133] Also, the public in Israel tends to be very trusting of the government and the military and rarely desires to second-guess national security decisions.[134] The net effect is that wartime decisions are made by a very small number of people in Israel.

Moreover, there is really not much of a marketplace of ideas in Israel on national security issues. One reason for this is the very draconian system of censorship that severely constricts the amount of information that the otherwise quite free and lively Israeli press can publish about national security matters. This was a legacy of the British Mandate's security regulations, which Israel's democratic leaders have found no reason to amend. Moshe Dayan, for example, once even conceded that "UN reports are often more accurate than ours."[135] It is not clear, though, that lack of information was the only problem. The legacy of the Holocaust has also made Israelis unwilling to evaluate their country and its policies critically.[136] Finally, Israel has few truly independent civilian defense analysts who provide alternative information and analyses on national security policy.[137] With no information, little desire to question official policy, and few independent experts, it is impossible to have an effective marketplace of ideas vetting national security policy in Israel.

Historically, Israeli national security decision making has not worked the way the triumphalists believe that it should in an open political system. For example, many Israelis believed that Ben-Gurion's Suez gambit was not carefully thought out. The Israeli cabinet was informed only the night before military operations began. The Labor Party's coalition partners were notified just hours before the attack began.[138] The quality of the debate about Operation Kadesh could hardly have been very good because only ten Israeli civilians aside from Ben-Gurion knew about the war before October 25, 1956. In essence, Ben-Gurion alone made all the decisions about the war. As his protégé Shimon Peres recounted:

> I saw Ben-Gurion when he faced momentous decisions, but I shall never forget that evening and night which followed it—between October 24 and 25, 1956. . . . In a certain place, a certain man had to make the decision, despite the fact that some of the essential data, for and against, were unknowable. . . . We sat—Moshe Dayan, the late Nehemia Argov and this writer—with Ben Gurion: not one of us envied him the long night that lay before him. The next morning we saw him . . . the decision made.[139]

This decision-making process was hardly democratic, and it was characteristic of how Ben-Gurion operated in the security realm more generally.

Israel's nuclear program was a prime example of a major strategic initiative that involved only a small number of decision makers and about which the public knew virtually nothing. The program was begun in great secrecy in the 1950s. Ben-Gurion allowed no public debate about it. What little discussion there was within the government was kept to a very small number of officials. Whatever the merits of Israel's decision to pursue a nuclear weapons program, it is clear that Israeli democracy had little influence upon it.[140]

Arguably, the Six Day War was Israel's greatest military victory. In less than a week, Israel defeated the combined forces of Egypt, Jordan, and Syria and conquered the Sinai Peninsula, the West Bank, and the Golan Heights. But even this striking victory was hardly the result of flawless strategic evaluation. No one would claim that Israel's strategy was better as a result of the thorough vetting it got in the marketplace of ideas because the Israeli public knew less about the course of the war than the public in any other state in the region.[141] But the real strategic misstep in the war was Israel's inability to decide what to do with the Occupied Territories. As far back as the Yishuv, Israeli leaders including Ben-Gurion had foreseen that the occupation of territory with a majority Arab population would threaten the Jewish and democratic nature of the state of Israel.[142] Despite early recognition of this dilemma, the Israelis were incapable of formulating a clear strategy for the disposition of the Occupied Territories because the opposition to giving them up by a fraction of the electorate paralyzed the Israeli government. Ironically, it was precisely the electoral dynamics of Israeli democracy that made it difficult for any leader to unilaterally pull out of the territories.[143]

Israeli strategic evaluation during the War of Attrition was not very good either. Israeli leaders made a mistake in thinking that the thin series of fortifications on the Suez Canal known as the Bar-Lev line would constitute sufficient protection of its forward deployed forces.[144] After the end of the War of Attrition, Golda Meir stifled discussion within her cabinet about Egyptian president Anwar Sadat's 1971 peace overture. As a result, Israel missed this possible opportunity to prevent yet another Arab-Israeli war.[145]

The 1973 Yom Kippur War was nearly a strategic debacle of catastrophic proportions for Israel. On the Sinai front, the Egyptians achieved complete strategic surprise and successfully executed a very difficult military operation by crossing the canal. Israeli military intelligence was caught completely by surprise.[146] On the Golan front, the Syrians achieved a decisive breakthrough and little stood between them and Israel proper. Israeli strategic evaluation prior to the war left much to be desired. Hubris and ethnocentrism led Israeli political and military leaders to underestimate both the motives and the capabilities of their Arab adversaries.[147]

There was plenty of evidence available to the Israelis that an attack was imminent but their overconfidence led them to discount it. To give the Egyptians their due, they executed a brilliant plan of strategic deception by mobilizing and demobilizing their forces twenty-two times before launching their actual attack from five separate locations. But the Israelis committed a variety of blunders too. For instance, the Israelis foolishly embraced the notion that tanks by themselves were sufficient for waging ground combat. Also, the Israelis completely misunderstood the Egyptians' attrition strategy, which aimed not to reconquer the whole of the Sinai but rather just to gain a firm foothold on the Israeli side of the Suez Canal and then to bleed the IDF until Israel agreed to negotiate a withdrawal from the rest of the occupied Sinai. Relatedly, the Israelis misjudged the effectiveness of the Egyptian surface-to-air missile (SAM) system. It was also an error to allow the Egyptians to take the initiative in hostilities. Finally, the Israelis underestimated the impact that the Arab oil embargo would have on its main ally, the United States.[148] Despite Israeli democracy, there was no marketplace of ideas in defense policy, because many Israeli cabinet members "voted for [Defense Minister Moshe] Dayan's proposals regularly because they accepted him as *the* authority in security matters."[149] Israel ultimately prevailed in the Yom Kippur War; but it did so in spite, not because, of its strategic evaluation.[150]

Israel's June 1982 invasion of Lebanon was a strategic blunder of major proportions, but Israeli democracy did little to prevent it.[151] Israel's open political system did not foster thoughtful debate. Begin refused to listen to the Israeli intelligence community when it provided the prime minister with evidence that the attack on the Israeli ambassador in London was not instigated by Arafat's PLO. No one in the cabinet bothered to check on PLO involvement. Moreover, both the Israeli civilian intelligence service Mossad and military intelligence had grave reservations about Sharon's Lebanon operation. But Begin and Sharon completely ignored the intelligence experts' assessments in planning the operation in Lebanon.[152] In addition, Sharon kept the scope of the Israeli operation from the cabinet and thwarted efforts by Israel's press to inform the public about what was going on.[153] Begin's cabinet thought it was supporting a limited operation to drive back Arafat's forces forty kilometers from the border rather than authorizing an all-out war against Syria and the PLO. There was remarkably little internal debate, inasmuch as Sharon promoted his Little Plan while in reality intending to execute his Big Plan. Sharon similarly misled the Israeli public about what he was doing in Lebanon. Begin and Sharon also used the Reagan administration's support for the Little Plan to silence domestic critics of the Big Plan. Despite an elected legislature and a free press, Sharon was able to launch his Big Plan without subjecting it to debate in Israel's otherwise vibrant marketplace of ideas.

Moreover, all the major decisions about the war were made by a small group of individuals: Sharon, Begin, Foreign Minister Yitzak Shamir, and the chief of staff, General Rafael Eitan. Begin and Sharon treated the cabinet as a "rubber stamp" rather than as an advisory or consultive body in the discussions of the Lebanon operation.[154] Israeli democracy did not ensure that large numbers of individuals participated in the decision-making process.

As a result, Israeli democracy did not guarantee sound strategic evaluation. Censorship and security restrictions severely constricted the public debate about national security affairs. Moreover, these same security regulations and a deeply entrenched willingness to defer to the government and the military on national security matters also ensured that only a very small number of individuals would be involved in the decision-making process.

Ironically, this relatively undemocratic system of national security decision making sometimes worked to Israel's advantage. Former Israeli prime minister Moshe Sharett reluctantly conceded that Ben-Gurion was correct that Israel's security policy could not be run democratically: "I have learned that the state of Israel cannot be ruled in our generation without deceit and adventurism. These are historical facts that cannot be altered. . . . In the end, history will justify both the stratagems of deceit and acts of adventurism. All I know is that I, Moshe Sharett, am not capable of them, and I am therefore unsuited to lead the country."[155] Former Israeli president Chaim Herzog reflected similarly on the situation during the 1973 Yom Kippur War:

> Mrs. Meir's method of government brought about a system whereby there were not checks and balances and no alternative evaluations. Her doctrinaire, inflexible approach to problems and the government was to contribute to the failings of the government before the war. She was very much the overbearing mother who ruled the roost with an iron hand. She had very little idea of orderly administration and preferred to work closely with her cronies, creating an *ad hoc* system of government based on what was known as her "kitchen." But once war had broken out these very traits proved to be an asset.[156]

Thus, contradicting the triumphalists' marketplace-of-ideas argument, this undemocratic system often worked well in wartime. The fact that Israel is a democracy has not necessarily ensured better Israeli security policies, but the lack of public input has not uniformly been a problem either.

Public Support

There can be little doubt that, until quite recently, the state of Israel could count on the overwhelming support of its citizens and soldiers when it went to war. But rather than democracy per se, the fact that the state was often fighting for its very existence between 1948 and 1973 surely provides a better explanation for that support.[157] Moshe Dayan explained that Israeli society came together in wartime despite seemingly overwhelming odds because "the state of Israel had come into existence in the shadow of imminent destruction, and the memories of escape from fearful dangers have attended the people of Israel from the very dawn of their independence. These memories abide with us still, and go far to explain the depth of our preoccupation with security."[158] Golda Meir concurred that "we couldn't afford the luxury of pessimism either, so we made an altogether different kind of calculation based on the fact that the 650,000 of us were more highly motivated to stay alive than anyone outside Israel could be expected to understand and that the only option available to us, if we didn't want to be pushed into the sea, was to win the war."[159]

The death of 6 million Jews in the Holocaust was obviously an important source of the sense of urgency among Israelis about the need to ensure that Israel did not lose its wars.[160] As the Adolf Eichmann trial in Jerusalem in April

1961 demonstrated, Israeli leaders understood that the Holocaust could be used to construct a new Israeli national identity that superseded deep ethnic, religious, and political differences that would otherwise have divided the Jewish state.[161] The Arab threat provided a powerful impetus for unity among an otherwise very fractious Israeli society.[162]

The sense that the Jewish community was fighting for its existence was already clear before the Holocaust in the Yishuv period. From the very inception of the Jewish state, the sense that national survival was at stake played a key role in forging wartime unity. "All knew in this opening round of our War of Independence," Moshe Dayan recalled, "that there could be no retreat and no surrender."[163] Yisrael Galili concurred: "And if some stubbornly persist in asking, Is it within our power to stand up against an all-Arab assault?—our answer is: This is a foolish question! Is it within our power *not* to stand-up against them? Have we any alternative? Have we any prospect of survival, other than by facing up to them with our full strength?"[164] Similarly, there was little public dissent during the Suez War, though this may have been due as much to lack of public knowledge as to the overwhelming sense of common threat from Nasser's regime.

Ironically, given how quickly the Six Day War was won, Israelis felt most imperiled in the run-up to this war. The sense of threat was felt acutely throughout the country. It provided Israelis with a powerful incentive to support their government's war effort. As Herut Party Knesset member Arye Ben-Eliezer remembered, "We were not so few in number as there is a tendency to believe. By our side fought the six million, who whispered in our ear the eleventh commandment: Do not get murdered—the commandment that was omitted at Mount Sinai and was given back to us in the recent battles in Sinai."[165]

"When I think back on these days [in 1967]," Golda Meir recalled, "what stands out in my mind is the miraculous sense of unity and purpose that transformed us within only a week or two from a small, rather claustrophobic community, coping—not always well—with all sorts of economic, political, and social discontents into 2,500,000 Jews, each and everyone of whom felt personally responsible for the survival of the state of Israel and each and everyone of whom knew that the enemy we faced was committed to our annihilation."[166] Then chief of staff Yitzak Rabin attributed Israel's remarkable victory in the Six Day War to the sense of national unity fostered by a sense of imminent peril: "I said at the time: 'we have no alternative but to answer the challenge forced upon us, because the problem is not freedom of navigation, the challenge is the existence of the state of Israel, and this is a war for that very existence. . . . ' This feeling that the war was to secure our very existence was shared by all the people in Israel. . . . Above all else, our victory was due to this sense."[167] The Six Day War was one of Israel's most popular wars, not because the public thought it would be easy, but rather because of the widespread sense that Israel's survival was at stake.

In contrast, the 1969-70 War of Attrition generated significant dissent among Israelis because the threat did not seem so pressing and the Sinai Peninsula was not considered part of the Jewish homeland.[168] Indeed, Israeli democracy may have actually undermined public support for the war through the widespread public complaining about the war's growing cost in blood and treasure.

There was, however, no such hesitancy in Israel during the Yom Kippur War. Golda Meir recalled the mind-set at the time: "We know that giving up means death, means destruction of our sovereignty and physical destruction of our entire people. Against that we will fight with everything that we have within us."[169] But, again, it was the sense of threat, rather than democracy, that brought the public squarely behind government's war effort.

Lebanon, though, was a far different story. Initially, there was considerable public support for the invasion of Lebanon, but it was based on the belief that the war would be limited to a forty-kilometer operation to push PLO forces from Israel's northern border. There was little public support for the more ambitious goals envisioned in Sharon's Big Plan.[170] Of course, this lack of public enthusiasm did not prevent Sharon from implementing the Big Plan. Israeli democracy did little to bolster support for the wider war. As with the War of Attrition, some analysts suggest that Israel's democratic political system contributed to the failure in Lebanon by allowing open dissent to sap public support for the war. As Geoffrey Wheatcroft observes, "Lebanon was the first of Israel's wars openly to divide rather than unite the country."[171]

Troops

Triumphalists believe that the culture of liberal individualism inherent in democratic armies makes their soldiers superior: in their view, officers lead better, and soldiers fight with greater initiative. There is no doubt that the IDF produced officers with superior leadership skills to those of the Arab armies. But Yigal Allon attributed this not to Israel's democracy but rather to necessity: "Israel, in her unique situation, may under no circumstances lose in war, neither in great battles nor in minor actions. Thus Israel's command personnel—whose task it is to prevent defeat and achieve victory—are entrusted with a responsibility the gravity of which has no parallel in any administrative authority in the country's civilian life."[172] Likewise, most analysts attributed the combat prowess of Israeli soldiers not to their culture of liberal individualism but rather to the fact they faced no other choice but to fight well or face national extinction.[173] As one Israeli air force pilot recalled, "We have no alternative but to be the best. Losing supremacy in the air is the equivalent of having the nation walk into the sea. I don't think it's likely to happen."[174] Finally, the triumphalists' explanation does not work very well in the Israeli case because the IDF's ethos was more "aristocratic" than democratic. This elitist ethos, in turn, contributed to the IDF's military effectiveness, in the view of many analysts.[175]

There is little doubt, for instance, that the IDF enjoyed better leadership and superior initiative in the 1948 War of Independence. But this was due more to the sense of greater urgency on the part of the Jews, fighting only two years after the end of the Holocaust, than to the democratic nature of the state. Yigal Allon noted that the Arab threat appeared ominous at the time:

> As a whole, the Israeli forces were still inferior to those of the enemy in numbers, equipment and geostrategic conditions but superior in organization, discipline, fighting spirit, unity, and a sense of *no alternative.* "Either you win the war, or you will be driven into the Mediterranean—you individually along with the whole nation": this was the meaning of no alternative, a phrase widely used at this time by troops and civilians alike to express the nation's consciousness that it was fighting for its survival.[176]

This sense of no alternative contributed markedly to the willingness of Israeli soldiers to fight effectively in Israel's War of Independence.

The Holocaust image was also regularly invoked in Israel's other wars, including the Six Day War.[177] As Brigadier General Israel Tal, a division commander on the Sinai front, noted, "Other people, other armies can afford to lose a second and third battle. They have strategic depth for retreat, recuperation, reorganization and can initiate a new counter-offensive—we cannot. *We cannot afford to fail in the first battle.*"[178] His colleague Colonel Shmuel Gonen echoed this sentiment: "if we do not win, we will have nowhere to come back to."[179] This sense of "no alternative" fostered superior initiative among the soldiers of the IDF during the Six Day War, as Yitzak Rabin explained:

> Our airmen, who struck the enemies' planes so accurately that no one in the world understands how it was done and people seek technological explanations and secret weapons; our armored troops who beat the enemy even when their equipment was inferior to his; our soldiers in other branches. . . . Who overcame our

enemies everywhere, despite the latter's superior numbers and fortifications—all these revealed not only coolness and courage in battle but . . . an understanding that only their personal stand against the greatest dangers would achieve victory for their country and for their families, and that if victory was not theirs the alternative was annihilation.[180]

There is a widespread recognition, which was amply confirmed by the Israeli experience in the Six Day War, that men do not fight primarily for ideologies like democracy.[181] Rather, because of the greater danger facing the Israelis in 1967, they had much greater motivation to fight than their Arab adversaries, who had little reason to fear that defeat would mean national extinction.

Conversely, the 1982 War in Lebanon demonstrates that when the need is not seen as pressing, soldiers in democratic armies can manifest serious deficiencies in both leadership and initiative. There was no consensus among Israelis that the PLO threat from Lebanon represented more than a nuisance. Given this assessment, military discontent with the prolonged war grew quickly as the operation appeared to have bogged down and losses mounted. Leadership was adversely affected by Israeli military dissatisfaction with the Lebanon operation. For example, an IDF brigade commander resigned his commission rather than lead his troop into what promised to be bloody urban combat in Beirut.[182] Senior IDF officers also admitted that their troops in Lebanon demonstrated little of the initiative that they had shown in previous wars.[183] Yair Yoram, an IDF paratroop commander, testified to this fact after the war:

Q: There was a claim that [IDF] commanders hesitated to take the initiative once they suffered some casualties.
A: In this war there was some problem in the realm you are talking about, since no pressure was felt. You did not face enemy pressure.
Q: But there were operational orders to complete missions by the hour . . .
A: I am trying to explain the phenomena, not to justify it. There was a feeling that it was preferable to go slow but be safe [rather] than to [advance] rapidly but at a risk.[184]

The Lebanon operation sapped the morale of even the IDF's most elite troops. The key factor here was not Israel's democratic political system but rather the fact that the Lebanon incursion was not seen as necessary to ensure national survival.

As the result of the Lebanon War, the quality of Israel's military leadership declined markedly.[185] This was largely attributable to the fact that many of Israel's best and brightest no longer regarded service in the IDF as necessary to de-

TABLE 4.2
Israel's Military Performance

War	Combat Performance
1948	Good
1956	Good
1967	Good
1969/70	Mixed
1973	Mixed
1982	Mixed

Source: Data compiled from van Creveld,
The Sword and the Olive.

fend the survival of the state of Israel. Rather, as the continuing occupation of Lebanon took its toll, and large chunks of the IDF were tied down in increasingly distasteful occupation duties in the West Bank and Gaza suppressing the Intifada, a general sense of malaise took hold within both Israeli society and its armed forces.[186] Israel was certainly not less democratic in this period than it had been in 1948 or 1967; indeed, overall the Jewish state was more democratic. The explanation for variations in leadership and initiative in the IDF lay elsewhere, primarily in the nature of the conflict. The IDF fought well in wars for national survival; it fought poorly in wars that did not involve such high stakes.

The triumphalists' claim that democracy confers military advantages is inconsistent with Israel's actual military performance. Although Israel has become more democratic overtime,[187] its military performance has actually declined during this same period in the view of one of Israel's leading military historians (table 4.2). In fact, as measured by Israeli troops killed per Arab division engaged, the effectiveness of the IDF has steadily declined from 76:1 in 1956 through 98:1 in 1967 to 200:1 in 1973.[188] In short, Israel's level of democracy increased throughout the period from 1948 through the present but its military performance declined markedly. This is exactly the opposite of what the triumphalists would expect. This presents a real puzzle for the triumphalists' argument that a higher level of democracy increases the likelihood of victory.

There is little doubt that Israel won its 1948 War for Independence. But given the weak and unconsolidated nature of Israeli democracy at the time, it is hard to credit the outcome to the nature of its domestic regime.

Similarly, Israel and its democratic allies France and Britain won a decisive tactical victory over Egypt in the 1956 Suez War. Some analysts question, however, whether it ought to be considered a political victory because Nasser remained in power, the United States forced Israel to withdraw from the Sinai and the Gaza Strip, the defeat set back Egyptian rearmament by only a year, the Jewish state did not succeed in refashioning a new order in the Middle East, the United Nations force in the Sinai provided a shield behind which the Egyptians could rearm without fear of Israeli attack, and the free transit of Gulf of Aqaba still depended largely on Israel's strength alone. Despite these reservations, Suez probably still merits being considered an Israeli victory, but it is not clear that this was the result of Israel's domestic political system.

Israel indisputably scored a decisive victory in the 1967 Six Day War. Opinion varies, though, about Israel's performance in the 1969-70 War of Attrition with Egypt along the Suez Canal. A few analysts count it as a win for the Jewish state.[189] Many others claim that Israel lost because Egypt managed to advance its surface-to-air missile systems to the very edge of the canal and Israel could do nothing to prevent that critical development, which would have an important impact in the early stages of the Yom Kippur War.[190] Given that outcome and Egypt's creditable military performance, it is probably most accurate to consider the final outcome as mixed for Israel.[191]

While Israel is generally credited with victory in the October 1973 Yom Kippur War, there are grounds for regarding the outcome as also mixed. The Israeli public certainly recognized that the war had been close.[192] On the one hand, Israel scored a decisive victory over Syria on the Golan front. On the other hand, the campaign on the Sinai front was less decisive: while Israel pulled out a stunning tactical victory in the end, Egypt eventually achieved its strategic objective of securing Israeli withdrawal from the Sinai. Politically, the war was a disaster for Israel: the Arab members of the Organization of Petroleum Exporting Countries (OPEC) successfully brandished their oil weapon, and the Western alliance split over aid to Israel.[193]

There is less debate about the outcome of Israel's 1982 invasion of Lebanon. While Israel succeeded in driving the PLO forces away from its northern border and later forced them to withdraw from Beirut, nearly two-thirds of the PLO fighters escaped to fight another day, and the status of the PLO among Palestinians in the Occupied Territories actually increased as a result of Chairman Yassir Arafat's defiance of the IDF. Despite Israel's tactical victory over Syria, the general impression among Israelis was that overall that campaign was a failure, too.[194] Syria was never ejected from Lebanon; indeed, by the mid-1980s it was once again the dominant power there. Israel's tactical victory over Syria came at a great cost as it revealed very sensitive Israeli military technology.[195] Israel's Lebanon War was clearly a political failure in that it achieved none of Israel's objectives; indeed, it created a new and more formidable adversary for Israel among Lebanon's Shia Muslims.[196] As Israeli historian Avi Shlaim concludes, "there was no disguising the fact that the once legendary IDF had been compelled to leave Lebanon with its tail between its legs and that the real victor was Hizbullah, the tiny Islamic guerrilla force."[197]

The evidence suggests that Israel's performance in war has steadily deteriorated despite the increasingly democratic nature of Israel's political system, which directly contradicts the triumphalists' expectations that a higher level of democracy should increase the likelihood of victory.

ALTERNATIVE EXPLANATIONS

The triumphalists' argument that Israel's remarkable military performance over the years was the result of its democratic political system also ignores a number of alternative explanations for Israel's military effectiveness.

Numbers

The conventional view was that Israel won its wars despite being consistently outnumbered by the Arabs in men and matériel.[198] As Yigal Allon put it, Israel faced Arab military forces of "overwhelming military superiority."[199] If one looks just at the overall balance in total manpower on each side, Israel appears to be outnumbered any where from 6:1 to 1.4:1 in its wars between 1948 and 1982 (table 4.3). Even today, Israel seems hopelessly outmatched by the Arabs in population (33:1), active duty military forces (12:1), combat aircraft (5:1), and tanks (3:1).

But this widely held image of Israel as a small, outnumbered state facing much larger Arab armies is now regarded as a myth by most contemporary Israeli historians. Indeed, in many of its wars, Israel enjoyed numerical superiority over its Arab adversaries in many key indicators of military power[200] (table 4.4). Also, Israel rarely faced all of the Arab states fighting together simultaneously, so aggregate comparisons of forces do not accurately reflect the real odds that Israel faced. This carefully crafted image of an Israeli David confronting an Arab Goliath was useful for mobilizing domestic support and international sympathy but bears little resemblance to the reality between 1948 and 1993.

Israel's War of Independence is a good illustration of Voltaire's famous dictum that God favors the big battalions. Israel enjoyed two key advantages over the Arab forces in this war. First, the Arab coalition was not a monolith uniformly committed to the eradication of the Jewish state. Rather, it was a fractious and mutually suspicious rabble whose members spent almost as much time furtively glancing back over their shoulders at their putative allies as they

TABLE 4.3
Overall Balance in Manpower in Israel's Wars

War	Egypt	Jordan	Syria	Palestine	Iraq	Israel	France/ United Kingdom	Ratio
1948	300,000	60,000	300,000	50,000	—	140,000	—	5:1
1956	300,000	—	—	—	—	175,000	3,000	1.7:1
1967	400,000	60,000	300,000	—	250,000	200,000	—	5:1
1973	400,000	60,000	350,000	—	400,000	200,000	—	6:1
1982	—	—	222,500	15,000	—	174,000	—	1.4:1

Source: www.onwar.com

TABLE 4.4
Balance in Manpower of Engaged Forces in Israel's Wars

War	Egypt	Jordan	Syria	Palestine	Iraq	Israel	France/ United Kingdom	Ratio
1948 (civil)	—	—	—	7,700	—	21,000	—	1:2.7
1948 (international)	10,000	8,000	6,000	7,700	5,000	96,000	—	1:2.6
1956	30,000	—	—	—	—	45,000	22,000	1:2.2
1967 (6/5–7)	100,000	45,000	—	—	—	110,000	—	1.3:1
1967 (6/9–10)	—	—	60,000	—	—	63,000?	—	1:1.05
1973	310,000	5,000	60,000	—	20,000	310,000	—	1.3:1
1982	—	—	30,000	15,000	—	76,000	—	1:1.7

Sources: Dupuy, *Elusive Victory;* Pollack, *Arabs at War;* and van Creveld, *The Sword and the Olive.*

did glaring ahead at their Jewish adversaries.[201] This lack of unity clearly undermined the effectiveness of the Arab military coalition. Yisrael Galili offered what he thought was "a realistic estimate of the force that the Arab countries can marshal for their 'holy war' in Palestine. Mention was made of the weakness of the Arab armies, their low military standard, and of the lack of ideological motivation among their rank and file. Inter-Arab rivalries and mutual antagonisms were also stressed."[202] Second, Israel actually enjoyed nearly a 3:1 advantage in military manpower over the Arabs by the end of the war. Such a numerical advantage in troops has historically been a reliable predictor of victory, and that was certainly true in 1948.[203]

Nor was it the case that an outnumbered Israel won over a much larger Egyptian force during the Suez War of 1956. Rather, Israel and its allies enjoyed better than a 2:1 advantage over the Egyptian forces in the Sinai.[204] This was largely thanks to the Anglo-French operation against Egyptian forces deployed along the Suez Canal, which reduced Egyptian forces facing the Israelis by half. Because France, Israel, and the United Kingdom overwhelmingly outnumbered the Egyptians, the outcome of the war was inevitable given the preponderance of forces arrayed against Egypt.

Israel was not decisively overmatched in the Six Day War either. The sources summarized in table 4.4 suggest that the balance was roughly even in mobilized forces. But according to CIA estimates done in May 1967, the Israelis may have had between a 2:1 and 3:1 advantage over the Egyptians in mobilized manpower on the Sinai front.[205] The overall balance did not look so grim either: Israel had as many front-line troops as the entire Arab coalition.[206] However, the most important advantage Israel had in 1967 was that Arab unity was largely illusory and the Jewish state never really had to face a united coalition of adversaries. Eric Hammel concludes that a the time of the Six Day War, "Arab unity was a myth . . . and the Arab joint command was a sham."[207] Given this lack of unity, Israel was able to engage and defeat the Egyptians in the Sinai early in the war without facing attacks from either Jordan or Syria. Israel was then able to turn its attention to Jordan without fear of attack from Syria or Egypt. Finally, once Egypt and Jordan were knocked out of the war, Israel was able to turn its full attention to wresting the Golan Heights from Syria. In the Six Day War Israel had the luxury of facing divided Arab adversaries that it could engage and defeat piecemeal. Thus, the overall balance was not a good indicator of the actual numbers of opponents the Jewish state faced.

To be sure, in the 1973 Yom Kippur War, Israel did fight and win against numerically greater forces. However, the actual ratio of forces engaged was not 6:1 but rather 1.3:1. Moreover, there are a number of other plausible explanations for Israel's victory aside from the nature of the regimes on each side.

Finally, Israel's initial military victories in Lebanon against the Syrians and the PLO are also largely attributable to a preponderance of Israeli power. A force of 76,000 Israeli soldiers engaged and defeated roughly 15,000 regular PLO fighters and 30,000 Syrian soldiers, giving Israel almost a 2:1 advantage in Lebanon.[208] In the Bekkah Valley, Israel achieved a 3:1 advantage over the Syrians (six and a half divisions to two divisions). In addition, Israel had qualitative advantages over Syria as well. Moreover, as a result of the peace treaty with Egypt and long-standing amicable relations with King Hussein's Jordan, Israel did not have to worry about Arab forces on other fronts and could devote bulk of its forces to the Lebanon War. This was typical of the situation Israel faced in most of its wars.

Geography

Aside from numbers, Israel also had other military advantages including interior lines of communication. This advantage is not at all attributable to the fact that Israel was a democracy, but it certainly helps explain Israel's remarkable track record in its wars with the Arabs.

Nature of the Conflict

Israeli military performance varied closely with the nature of the conflict in which it was involved. As table 4.2 shows, Israel did well in conventional wars for its survival, especially 1948 and 1967. In contrast, Israel fought poorly in unconventional wars where its survival was not at stake such as Lebanon in 1982. This is not surprising because, as Israeli military historian Martin van Creveld notes, the 1982 Lebanon War "was the first war in Israel's history for which there was not national consensus. Many Israelis regarded it as a war of aggression."[209]

Emulation/Socialization

The Israelis were quite assiduous in studying the world's most successful military powers. A willingness to imitate the world's best militaries, no matter what their political complexion, was certainly an important element in Israeli military prowess. The prestate Haganah was trained by a British military officer named Orde Wingate. His training gave the Yishuv decided advantages over its Arab adversaries. World War II service with the British also gave the nascent Israeli army valuable combat experience the Arabs never had. Thus, even before the establishment of the state of Israel, the Jews had many of the essential elements of a "typical" modern military force.[210]

After the establishment of the state of Israel in 1948, the IDF continued to emulate the most successful military formats of other countries. For example, the IDF copied the military organizations of other advanced, industrial powers, such as Britain and Switzerland.[211] Israel's "short-war" doctrine was dictated by Israel's geographic position, its demographic constraints, and its fragile economy. Recognizing that these factors were very similar to those shaping Prussian and German military strategy, Israeli strategists carefully studied those cases as well.[212] In fact, Israel was scarcely constrained by the political ideology of the countries it emulated. One particularly sensitive issue in Israel is the extent to which Israeli military doctrine and tactics drew from the experience of Nazi Germany. For instance, the IDF employed the Wehrmacht's "mission-oriented" command philosophy of *Auftragstaktik*.[213] The IAF was in many respects modeled on the Nazi Luftwaffe.[214] And Israeli mobilization policy drew heavily upon the German territorial *wehrkreis* model.[215] Finally, much of what Israel learned about the doctrines and practices of armored warfare came from Nazi Germany.[216] A great deal of Israel's military success is attributable to the fact that the IDF patterned itself on the successful militaries of the developed world irrespective of whether they were democratic or not.

Conversely, with only one partial exception, the armies of the Arab world did not emulate the successful armies in other parts of the world. That exception, which actually proves the rule, was Jordan's British-trained and British-led Arab Legion. Formed in the image of the British army, the Arab Legion was the most effective Arab military organization in the Arab world. However, after the Jordanians severed their close ties with Britain and expelled the British military officers, the fighting effectiveness of the Jordanian army declined to the low standard of the rest of the Arab world.[217]

Arab militaries were weak and ineffectual in part as the result of the policies of various colonial powers, which consciously sought to keep them from posing a threat to their rule.[218] Rather than replicating their own military formats in their Arab colonies, the imperial powers created local militaries that were weak and posed no threat to their rule. This legacy, of course, persisted after independence and contributed greatly to Arab military ineffectiveness. Most Arab militaries shared four common weaknesses: poor tactical leadership, poor information management, poor weapons handling, and poor maintenance.[219] Not surprisingly, these problems seriously undermined Arab military effectiveness in the various wars with Israel. "Let us recognize the truth," Ben-Gurion noted, "we won not because we performed wonders, but because the Arab army is rotten."[220]

Throughout the period between 1948 and 1993, the Arab armies facing Israel tended to be more focused on internal security than on fighting external wars.[221] The many internal missions Arab forces had to perform, such as protecting the government from domestic rivals and repressing restive minority groups, seriously undermined their effectiveness in fighting conventional military forces like the IDF. None of the Arab states could devote their full military resources to fighting Israel due to internal threats in their own countries. Thus, the fact that the Arabs faced unconventional threats and had to organize their forces to deal with them put Israel's adversaries at a marked disadvantage.

Nationalism

Ideology did play some role in Israeli military success against the Arabs; however, that ideology was not liberal democracy but nationalism.[222] Zionism was a classic example of a nineteenth-century European nationalist movement. And like many other European nationalist movements, nationalism and liberalism were often in tension in Israel.[223]

Greater national consciousness was an important military asset for the embryonic Jewish state. The Yishuv had many potential divisions (Sephardim vs. Ashkenazim, secular vs. religious, left vs. right). The common Arab threat solidified the sense of Israeli national identity, which in turn increased the willingness of Israeli society and soldiers to support the war effort and fight effectively.[224]

Despite much pan-Arab rhetoric, there was little evidence that the Arab-Israeli wars ever generated much nationalist sentiment in the Arab world beyond Palestine. According to Israeli historian Benny Morris, this put the Arabs at a distinct military disadvantage vis-à-vis the Yishuv: "For the average Arab villager, political independence and nation-hood were vague abstractions; his loyalties were to his family, clan, and village and, occasionally to his region. Moreover, decades of feuding had left Palestinian society deeply divided."[225] It is not surprising that Israel generally was more militarily effective than its Arab adversaries.

This imbalance in nationalist sentiment played a significant role in explaining the outcome of the 1948 War of Israeli Independence. The Arab coalition attacking Israel could rarely act cohesively. This disunity had two sources. First, the Palestinians themselves were divided internally by the feud between the Husseini and the Nashashibi clans.[226] This Arab disunity during the War of Independence greatly aided the Jews. Israeli leaders were well aware that the lack of Palestinian national consciousness reduced the threat they faced. As Ben-Gurion observed, "It is now clear, without the slightest doubt, that were we to face the Palestinians alone, everything would be all right. They, the decisive majority of them, do not want to fight us, and all of them together are unable to stand up to us, even at the present state of our organization and equipment."[227] Most Arabs just did not regard the liberation of Palestine as an issue worth dying for, so there was little enthusiasm for attacking Israel in 1948.

Second, the Arab coalition was divided because the rest of the Arab world was rightly suspicious that King Abdullah and the leaders of the nascent Jewish state had cut a deal to divide Palestine, and their intervention during the international phase of the War of Independence was driven in part by the desire to thwart this deal.[228] These other states each had separate and sometimes incompatible reasons for participating in the war. For example, the Egyptians saw attacking Palestine as means of forestalling further British inroads into Jordanian-controlled Palestine. "The political divisiveness and internal rivalries among the Arab leaders," recalled Flapan, "kept them from mounting a unified drive toward war and made their weak military position inevitable."[229]

The lack of an overarching sense of Arab nationalism clearly undermined Arab military effectiveness in other wars as well. For example, no other Arab state came to Egypt's rescue during the Suez War. During the Six Day War, Syria supported terrorism against Israel as much to counter Nasser's claim to lead the Arab world as to hurt the Jewish state.[230] Few Arab states joined Syria and Egypt's attack on Israel in October 1973. No other Arab states came to Syria and the PLO's rescue during the Israeli invasion of Lebanon in 1982.

Conversely, on a few occasions nationalism also worked to the Arabs' benefit. For example, in the War of Attrition and the early stages of the Yom Kippur War, the Egyptians fought more effectively because their soldiers were fighting for territory they regarded as part of Egypt. Conversely, the Israelis were not fighting to defend Israeli territory until it looked as though the Arabs might breakthrough and threaten Israel itself. Similarly, the Israelis found that their invasion of Lebanon sparked a nationalist conflagration that eventually forced them to withdraw in virtual defeat. In short, nationalism provides a powerful explanation for the varying levels of military effectiveness in the different stages of the Arab-Israeli conflict.

Level of Development

The dramatically different levels of economic development between Israelis and Arabs certainly also account for their different levels of military effectiveness. Israel was essentially a developed country facing a number of underdeveloped adversaries.[231] Given that a higher level of economic development is associated with both democracy and military effectiveness, it is hardly any surprise that Israel was both a democracy and more militarily capable than its Arab neighbors. As Finance Minister David Horowitz observed, "The [Arabs'] standard of living is low: There are no parties, there is no democracy. There is nothing. That's because they're living at a precapitalist level. As for us, if we triple the population in a few years, our GNP will equal that of the entire Arab world put together. We shall have an industrialized country."[232] Table 4.5 makes this increasing difference in the wealth of the Jewish and Arab communities in Palestine very clear.

Israel was essentially born a developed country because it was founded by émigrés from developed parts of Europe. In particular, a major influx of capital came with German Jews in the Fifth Aliyah of 1932-39. Israel's high level of economic development helped it to produce a much more modern infrastructure compared to that of its Arab neighbors. This First World level of development

TABLE 4.5
National Income Distribution in Palestine (in millions of Palestinian pounds) (1936–47)

Year	National Income			Per Capita National Income		
	Palestine	Jews	Arabs	Palestine	Jews	Arabs
1936	34.8	10	15.8	25.5	47.5	16.3
1939	30.2	17.2	13.0	20.2	27.8	12.5
1942	84.0	48.0	36.0	51.4	94.0	32.0
1943	92.3	52.1	40.2	55.0	99.3	34.8
1944	125.5	70.6	54.9	72.0	128.6	46.0
1945	143.4	80.1	63.3	79.1	138.3	51.3
1946	170.0	96.0	74.0	90.0	157.4	57.8
1947	200.0	110.0	90.0	101.0	169.3	67.7

Source: Horowitz and Lissak, *Origins of the Israeli Polity,* 21, table 1.

has given the Jewish state still more advantages in its wars with its less developed adversaries and also made it more likely that Israel would be a democracy.[233]

Underdevelopment clearly reduced the Arab armies effectiveness compared to that of the IDF. As Israeli military analyst Zeev Schiff observes, "The Arab armies . . . were large but they were peasant armies, the vast majority of fighting men being illiterate and the gap between soldier and officer immense. Organization was faulty, ammunition stores ill-prepared, and medical facilities inadequate."[234] In contrast, Israel's relatively higher level of development conferred clear military advantages to the Jewish state. According to Luttwak and Horowitz, "Perhaps the most obvious [Israeli advantage] was the higher average level of technical skill of Israeli manpower. . . . In this respect Israel, as the more developed society, had a built in advantage over her Arab antagonists for, if ultramodern weapons can be acquired overnight, the skills required for their successful use can only be learned more slowly."[235] Israel had, in the words of one Israeli newspaper editor, "the only European army in the Middle East."[236] It also has its own defense industry, which is on a par with those of rest of the developed world. The most striking evidence of Israel's huge technological lead was the development of its own nuclear program.

Israel's technological lead provided it with important advantages in almost all its wars with the Arabs. Israel won the Suez War in part because it had a much more highly developed military.[237] Israel's nuclear weapons probably played a key role in preventing the Syrians from exploiting their breakthrough on Golan in 1973.[238] Finally, Israel's lopsided success in the air battle over the Bekkah Valley in 1982 was clearly the result of its technological advantage over the Syrians.[239] The imbalance in the level of economic development between the Israelis and Arabs made most of the confrontations between the two, in the words of one American defense analyst, akin to a war pitting "the *Wehrmacht* against the Apaches."[240]

CONCLUSIONS

At first glance, Israel appears to provide much evidence to support the triumphalists' argument that democracy confers military advantages upon states at war. A small state surrounded by millions of Arabs, İsrael nonetheless prevailed in major wars in 1948, 1967, and 1973. Many in Israel and around the world attribute this amazing record of military victory to the fact that Israel was democratic and its adversaries were not.

The problem with arguing that it was democracy that accounted for Israel's spectacular record in wartime is that it rests on a logical fallacy: Israel is a democracy; Israel has won many of its wars; ipso facto, democracy must have been the cause. This is an example of the fallacy of post hoc, ergo propter hoc. Moreover, to believe that it was Israel's democratic political system that explained its military track record, one would also have to endorse the implausible counterfactual argument that Israel would have performed equally well against non-Arab authoritarian regimes.

But a closer examination of the Israeli cases casts doubt on the claim that democracy was the root of Israel's military effectiveness. Triumphalists have not shown that Israeli democracy increased its likelihood of victory through any of the causal mechanisms they identify. Neither their selection effects nor their wartime effectiveness arguments actually explain the outcome in the Israeli cases. Other factors provide better explanations for the variation in Israel's military performance. If one wants to understand the roots of Israel's remarkable military record since 1948, it makes sense to look at other factors besides the fact that it was a democracy. This leads me to conclude that the correlation between Israel's regime type and its military effectiveness is spurious because none of the triumphalists' causal mechanisms operate in these cases.

CHAPTER 5

Democracy and Britain's Victory in the Falklands War

The 1982 Falklands War seems to offer strong support for the triumphalists' view that democracies enjoy an advantage over nondemocracies when they meet on the battlefield. On April 2, 1982, the Argentine military junta sent its armed forces to invade the Islas Malvinas in an effort to assert Argentine sovereignty. But by June 6, 1982, the Argentine garrison on the islands surrendered to a British task force sent to retake the Falkland Islands. The democratic United Kingdom, with fewer troops, comparable weapons and technology, and fighting nearly 8,000 miles from home, nonetheless decisively defeated military-ruled Argentina.[1]

As then U.S. secretary of state Alexander Haig remarked with respect to Britain's victory, "The British demonstrated that a free people have not only kept a sinewy grip on the values they seem to take for granted, but are willing to fight for them, and to fight supremely well against considerable odds."[2] Many scholars concurred with this assessment. "A military challenge such as this cannot but be a critical test for the presiding political system," Britain's official historian of the war, Sir Lawrence Freedman, observed, and its "eventual success in retrieving the islands was then held to reflect well on the political system."[3] The Falklands War certainly appears, at first glance, to be another prime example of a democracy's advantage over an autocracy during war.

Moreover, the war seems also to demonstrate that the various mechanisms advanced by triumphalists to explain why democracies should have a military advantage over nondemocracies operate as specified. The Falklands War, for example, seems to support that part of the triumphalists' selection effects argument that holds that the fate of leaders is inextricably linked to success in war.

According to a Liberal member of Parliament, "The facts speak for themselves. After unsuccessful foreign ventures, prime ministers have been replaced."[4] In Britain, Prime Minister Margaret Thatcher's decisive victory in the war apparently arrested the precipitous decline in her public approval rating and ensured her reelection the following year. Conversely, in Argentina the defeat sealed the fate of General Leopoldo Galtieri and his colleagues on the ruling military junta, who lost power soon after launching the ill-fated expedition.

The Falklands War also provides some evidence that democracies enjoy advantages over nondemocracies once the war has begun. This case seems to vindicate, for instance, the triumphalists' claims that democracies can count on a greater level of commitment from their democratic allies than nondemocracies can. In particular, the claim that audience costs in democracies make democratic alliances stronger and more durable seems to find some support. As Haig recalled cautioning General Leopoldo Galtieri early in the conflict, "In the United States, the support for Britain is widespread. In the liberal world sentiment is overwhelmingly in favor of Great Britain and would remain so if it comes to a confrontation."[5] The British secretary of state for foreign and commonwealth affairs, Francis Pym, similarly recollected that "I was greatly encouraged by the support that I encountered for Britain during my visit to the United States of America. The Americans are well aware that Argentina is the aggressor in this dispute and I imagine that they are greatly influenced by the ties of history and the shared ideals of freedom and democracy that link their country to ours. I have no doubt these are some reasons why public opinion polls in American have shown such solid support for the United Kingdom."[6] In contrast, despite Argentine beliefs to the contrary based on private assurances from Reagan's ambassador to the United Nations, Jeane Kirkpatrick, the United States did not support the junta against Great Britain.

In addition, the Falklands case also seems to support the triumphalists' view that democracies are better at strategic evaluation than nondemocracies. One member of Parliament remarked in the House of Commons that "If the Argentines believed that their aggression would present Her Majesty's Government with a *fait accompli* to which they would not react, clearly they have sadly misjudged the reaction of a democratic Government who have responsibilities that they intend to carry out for the sovereign parts of their territory. Perhaps all dictatorships are likely to make such a mistake, so no one should be surprised."[7] Conversely, democratic Britain appeared to have made all the right strategic decisions during the war.

The Falklands War also seems to support the argument that democracies prevail in war because they enjoy greater public support. One American diplomat concluded that "one cannot assume that democracies are at a disadvantage in a war because of the difficulty of holding public support. . . . [S]upport for Mrs. Thatcher actually increased after the casualty lists started coming in. Of course, it is also clear that once the public is enraged an elected government may have less room for compromise. Democracies can be formidable adversaries."[8] In Argentina, after an initial surge of patriotic frenzy at the beginning of the war, public enthusiasm for the war effort ebbed very quickly.

Finally, the Falklands campaign also appeared to demonstrate the superiority of democratic soldiers on the battlefield. British ground component commander Major General Jeremy Moore attributed Britain's victory to the superiority of the personnel in its armed forces, which he clearly thought was a function of the differences in the two countries' political systems:

> I think we neither of us appreciated that the conflict would so clearly depict the social and domestic characters of both contestants. In Argentina the officer class is highly motivated. They are privileged, indeed they have a major stake in the country, and they are politically involved, their ambition in this direction causing considerable interservice rivalry. The enlisted conscript has no such stake in the country or the service. He is not paid much, he is not cared for, he is pawn. Perhaps it is not surprising he does not always fight that hard. I think that this was most tellingly demonstrated at the negotiation of the surrender when the Argentine officers asked to keep their sidearms as a protection against their own men. All the well-publicised euphoria back home in Argentina did not seem to inspire them.
>
> Compare this with the unified response of our forces who are professional and motivated. When our front line infantry man or young sailor looked to his officer or NCO in the South Atlantic he was looking for guidance on how to improve his contribution. And this can be and was projected upwards. The ability to operate central joint command of our national force was war winning. Much was left unsaid because we knew our people and could rely on their flexibility, commonsense and sense of purpose. We were thus able to be truly joint. We won because we were unified, the enemy were not.[9]

This view was echoed by Britain's secretary of state for defense, John Nott: "The most decisive factors in the land war were the high state of individual training and fitness of the land forces, together with the leadership and initiative displayed especially be junior offices and NCOs."[10]

The Falklands War should therefore be an easy case for the triumphalists. Not only did democratic Britain triumph over authoritarian Argentina, but it apparently did so via the precise mechanisms that many triumphalists expect would give Britain an advantage. If, however, the casual mechanisms specified by the triumphalists' theories do not in fact explain the outcome of this case, there are additional grounds for doubts about the triumphalists' various theories of democratic military effectiveness.

I begin with a brief discussion of what the Falklands case says about that part of the triumphalists' selection effects argument that posits victory in war bolsters the standing of democratic leaders. I then consider what the Falklands case says about the triumphalists' wartime effectiveness arguments that attribute the propensity of democracies to win their wars to their larger economies, their stronger and more durable alliances, their superior strategic evaluation, their higher levels of public support, or their more effective soldiers. I also briefly assess whether the triumphalists' coding of Argentina as a high autocracy at the time of the war is justified. The Falklands case provides scant evidence of the operation of any of the triumphalists' causal mechanisms, and so I conclude that it provides little support for their larger argument that democracy conveys distinct advantages in war.

SELECTION EFFECTS

Because democratic Britain did not initiate the war, the Falklands/Malvinas War does not provide much direct support for the triumphalists' selection effects argument. The ruling military junta in Argentina made the decision on March 26, 1982, to invade the Falklands and then launched Operation Azūl (Blue), later renamed Rosario, on April 2 of that year. That the military regime initiated an unsuccessful war seems compatible with part of the triumphalists' selection effects argument that holds that authoritarian leaders lack caution about starting wars; but the fact that regime was quickly ousted after the war was over contradicts the other part of the triumphalists' selection effects argument that maintains that authoritarian regimes should be less careful about starting chancy wars because they can weather military defeats and still retain power. In fact, it is widely believed that one of the reasons the junta launched the invasion in the first place was to rally support from the Argentine people, which had been declining precipitously in the days immediately prior to the war.[11]

Triumphalists might counter that victory in the Falklands War also played an important role in restoring the declining fortunes of the Tory government of Prime Minister Margaret Thatcher and that this at least provides evidence that victory bolsters democratic leaders. In fact, some British political analysts believe that without that victory, the June 1983 parliamentary elections would not have returned the Conservative Party to power. In the best empirical study of the domestic political effect of the Falklands War, however, David Sanders, Hugh Ward, David Marsch, and Tony Fletcher find that, at most, the Falklands victory added only three percentage points for the three months of the war to Thatcher's popularity. They also demonstrate quite convincingly that the actual cause of the restoration of Thatcher's political fortunes was the dramatic rebound in the British economy throughout 1982.[12] Of course, victory in the Falklands certainly did not hurt Thatcher's public approval rating, but the experience of American president George H. W. Bush after the 1991 Gulf War shows that victory in war is no guarantee of electoral success and suggests, contrary to the selection effects argument, that the political fortunes of democratic leaders depend far more on domestic, rather than international, success.[13]

WARTIME EFFECTIVENESS
Rent Seeking

If the Falklands/Malvinas case tells us little about the triumphalists' selection effects argument, it does offer us a direct test of the triumphalist argument that democracies win their wars because they are wealthier. This wealth, triumphalists believe, accrues from the fact that democracies are more likely to have free market economies which generate superior wealth. This greater wealth, so the argument goes, can be translated into greater military resources, which in turn makes victory in war more likely.

There can be no doubt that Britain was far wealthier than Argentina. In 1980 Britain had a total GDP of $485 billion while Argentina had a GDP of only $62 billion. This better than nearly 13:1 preponderance in wealth certainly provided a decisive military advantage for the British. However, Britain was not wealthier because it had less state intervention in its economy, as this triumphalist argument holds. In fact, if one measures state rent seeking by the percentage of GNP consumed by the central government, Britain was more of a rent-seeking state than Argentina. According to World Bank figures for 1982, the democratic government of the United Kingdom spent about 42.4 percent of Britain's GNP, while the Argentine military government spent only 21.6 percent.[14] James Gwartney, Robert Lawson, and Walter Block note that Britain's government expenditures as a percentage of GNP and its transfer payments were "among the largest in the world."[15] By some estimates of economic freedom, the Argentine economy was more open under the military junta than was the British econ-

DEMOCRACY AND BRITAIN'S VICTORY IN THE FALKLANDS WAR   149

omy in the early Thatcher years.[16] In sum, it is hard to maintain, as the triumphalists would have to, that Britain's advantage in wealth was due to the fact that its government engaged in less rent-seeking behavior than the Argentine government.

Alliances

The Falklands/Malvinas case provides only limited evidence to test the triumphalists' proposition that democracies win their wars because they attract other democracies who make better alliance partners. The root of the problem is that Britain had no formal allies in the war against Argentina.[17] Moreover, as one British member of Parliament reminded his colleagues, "For all our alliances and for all our social politeness which diplomats so often mistake for trust, in the end in life it is self-reliance and only self-reliance that counts. Suez, when I first came into the House 25 years ago, surely taught us that not every ally is staunch when the call comes."[18] In fact, Britain had three "quasi" allies on its side in the Falklands War, and the behavior of these allies does not fully accord with the triumphalists' expectations.

The United States

Britain's first, and arguably most important, ally was the democratic United States. American behavior, at least initially, did not seem to accord with the triumphalists' expectation that democracies would be more reliable allies. The first response of the Reagan administration, and even its famously anglophile secretary of state, Alexander Haig, was to try to remain neutral in the conflict despite a clear majority of the American public who sympathized with Britain in the war. The United States regarded Britain as an important NATO ally but regarded the Argentine junta as a critical partner in its efforts to combat communism in Central America. The administration was deeply divided by the war, with the pro-Argentine faction led by the fiercely anticommunist ambassador to the United Nations, Jeane Kirkpatrick, and the pro-British faction, headed by Secretary of Defense Caspar Weinberger.[19] Given these deep divisions, reflective of the conflicting U.S. interests at stake, Haig kept the United States neutral through the first month of the war in order to foster a negotiated settlement.[20] As Haig recalled, "While my sympathy was with the British, I believed that the most practical expression of that sympathy would be impartial United States mediation in the dispute. The honest broker must, above all, be neutral."[21] This meant in practice that the United States did not supply Britain with intelligence early in the conflict.[22] Also, the United States did not provide Britain with extensive military assistance right away either.[23] Despite common democracy and very salient audience costs, the United States maintained a generally neutral stance until April 30, 1982.

British leaders recognized early on that because America's national interests were in conflict in this case, unqualified American support would be slow in coming.[24] Many feared that Jeane Kirkpatrick wielded excessive influence in the Reagan administration.[25] These concerns were so widespread that Thatcher's foreign minister, Francis Pym, could not assure the House of Commons that "the U.S. wouldn't be neutral between a democracy and a dictatorship."[26]

Haig's policy of neutrality infuriated many British leaders who believed that U.S. ambivalence caused the Argentine junta to "miscalculate" and launch the invasion.[27] Others blamed U.S. hesitation for prolonging the crisis. One member of Parliament complained that:

> If the United States Government took action in conformity with their own Organization of American States, they could stop the Argentine Government in their tracks within a week. But they will not do it because they have far too many vested interests in Argentina and in South and Central America as a whole. So it must be understood clearly that some of us do not trust the United States Government to deliver the goods, even though the Prime Minister has fallen over backwards ever since she took office to defend every action that the Reagan Administration has ever taken.[28]

Another MP ridiculed the U.S.'s effort to maintain an even-handed stance: "The United States described itself as an honest broker. . . . Given the facts of the dispute, an even-handed approach from the United States was never justified. If America had given a firm commitment and come in right from the start on the side of Britain—a democracy and a North Atlantic Treaty ally—the [crisis?] would never have reached this stage."[29] Throughout the conflict, American behavior seemed to British politicians eerily reminiscent of the 1956 Suez Crisis, in which the United State had not supported its allies in the democratic coalition of Britain, France, and Israel against authoritarian Egypt. Indeed, Suez became the dominant analogy for the many British politicians who doubted the credibility of America's commitment to its NATO ally Great Britain.[30]

Even after the collapse of the joint American-Peruvian peace initiative at the end of April, which marked the point at which the Reagan administration at last openly sided with Britain, it was still evident that the United States was hedging, trying to balance its interests in Latin America while honoring its obligation to the United Kingdom.[31] Minister of Defence John Nott suspected that the United States was even sharing intelligence about the movements of the British naval task forces and admitted that "it is a frightening thing . . . that our greatest ally is not wholly on our side."[32] As late as June 2, 1982, continuing U.S. ambivalence was evident when the American delegation to the United Nations changed its vote from veto to abstention on a U.N. cease fire initiative that the British opposed.[33] As Britain's UN ambassador Sir Anthony Parsons tartly noted, "It is ironic, in the light of my experience here, that our best support should have come from Africans, Asians and Caribbeans, with our partners and allies either useless or actively unhelpful."[34] Far from American democracy making it a more credible ally in British eyes, as the triumphalists' audience costs argument maintains, some British leaders thought that U.S. inconsistency was actually the result of its domestic political system. This view was nicely summarized by British ambassador Sir Nicholas Henderson, who reflected after the war that "the nature of the American Government makes it very difficult to have one clear-cut and comprehensive fount of policy."[35]

While triumphalists can point to rhetorical statements by American leaders to the effect that the U.S. public overwhelmingly sided with Britain against Argentina, the evidence suggests that the decisive factor in finally pushing the United States to support Britain was its realization that NATO was at stake,[36] which Thatcher made clear to President Reagan.[37] When forced to choose between its ally in the war against communism in the Western Hemisphere and one of its NATO allies in Europe, the United States went with its most important geopolitical interest. According to then assistant secretary of state for European affairs Lawrence Eagleberger, "I was driven essentially by one very simple argument—an ally is an ally. I believed . . . that one of our most serious general foreign policy problems was the growing perception—correct perception—that we are no longer as reliable partners and allies as we were, [and] under those circumstances, in a case that was so important to Mrs. Thatcher . . . we had no choice."[38]

Another aspect of the eventual U.S. tilt toward Britain that does not accord very neatly with the triumphalists' argument about the behavior of democratic allies is that the main impetus for the pro-British tilt came from the most undemocratic quarters. Much of the early support for the British war effort before April 30 was secretly arranged by Caspar Weinberger's Pentagon, perhaps without either Haig's or Reagan's knowledge.[39] The long-standing bureaucratic connections between the American and British militaries and intelligence communities provide additional explanation for the close cooperation between the United States and Britain during the war. The foundation of this very close bureaucratic relationship was the common interest of the two states in waging the Cold War.[40] This military and intelligence cooperation, however, produced an enormous bureaucracy which often operated with only minimal democratic oversight from either country.[41] It is a great irony, therefore, that the mechanisms by which the United States provided military and intelligence support to Britain were so undemocratic.

To be sure, U.S. support to Britain in these two areas was important to the war effort. The United States granted Britain access to a crucial base at Ascension Island, which made it possible for the British to support their operation in the South Atlantic without relying exclusively on facilities in the United Kingdom.[42] The United States also provided important intelligence support during the war, especially in the areas of signals intelligence and ocean surveillance.[43] Britain had access to data from the Fleet Ocean Surveillance Information Centre, a U.S. Navy facility in London that regularly provided data to the Royal Navy as part of day-to-day NATO operations. Britain also received intelligence from the U.S. Navy's Ocean Surveillance Satellites because important downlink facilities were based in the United Kingdom. Finally, Britain is part of a joint program with the United States that monitors all naval traffic around the world, which proved to be of great value during the Falklands War.[44] But there were also clear limits to U.S. support, even after April 30. For example, the United States would not supply Airborne Warning and Control System (AWACS) aircraft to Britain, which would have made a huge difference in Britain's ability to deal with the very serious threat to its ships posed by the Argentine air force.[45] It is important, therefore, to put U.S. aid in perspective. As Max Hastings and Simon Jenkins conclude, "America would hold Britain's coat, and even sew on some buttons, but the task force in the South Atlantic must fight its war alone."[46]

In sum, America was not really Britain's ally in the Falklands War; essentially, Britain fought it alone. After much hesitation, America did provide Britain with some important military and intelligence assistance. However, it did so not so much out of democratic obligation but rather because American leaders decided that aiding Britain was vital to the preservation of NATO. Moreover, much of the aid that was provided was done secretly and as the result of bureaucratic, rather than democratic, initiative. In short, the democratic United States was not as reliable an ally as the triumphalists expected, and the reasons it ultimately sided with the United Kingdom had less to do with democratic fraternity and more with common geostrategic interests and bureaucratic momentum.

The European Economic Community

The members of the democratic European Economic Community (EEC) also sided with Great Britain, and triumphalists might point to that fact as further evidence that democracies flock together. That would be a mistake, however. First, despite their strong initial support for Britain, which was manifested primarily through the imposition of economic sanctions and the restriction of military sales to Argentina, that support eroded very quickly during the war.[47] The key event that caused the erosion of EEC support for sanctions against Argentina was Britain's sinking of the Argentine warship *General Belgrano* on May 2.[48]

Second, the EEC members' motives for backing Britain had less to do with democratic fraternity and more to do with individual self-interest. Few other European powers with residual colonial holdings wanted to let stand a precedent by which other states could use force to settle such disputes.[49] Also, the EEC members had other self-interested reasons for backing Britain. Obviously, they had a greater economic stake in relations with Britain than they did with Argentina, and so siding with the Britain was in their economic interest. "I was not disappointed with the response from Europe, because I never expected anything better," a British member of Parliament observed, because "in this dispute our European partners have never lifted their eyes above the cash register."[50] Such cynicism may not have been unjustified because it was widely suspected that the French violated the embargo early in the war and helped Argentina get its Super Entendard / Exocet systems up and running.[51] Finally, some British politicians suspected that EEC support may have been motivated not by democratic fraternity but rather by European desires to moderate British actions. As another MP remarked, "we are fortunate in having the EEC's backing, but I suspect that it wants not only to provide us with support but to act as a restraining force on any over-adventurousness on our part."[52] Evidence on behalf of this theory is that European support for sanctions against Argentina faltered after the sinking of the *Belgrano* made clear that Britain would retake the islands by force.

European Economic Community support for Britain does not really accord with triumphalists' expectations either: it was motivated by factors other than common democratic solidarity, and it declined significantly over the course of the conflict.

Chile

A final reason the triumphalists cannot use the Falklands / Malvinas case as evidence that democracies win their wars because they attract more reliable alliance partners in other democracies is the fact that a crucial supporter of Britain's war effort was General Agosto Pinochet's authoritarian regime in Chile. Very early in the Falklands campaign, press reports suggested that Chile was providing Britain with significant aid in its war against Argentina, its traditional rival in South America. Opposition members of Parliament questioned Defence Minister John Nott on April 27, but he refused to confirm or deny these rumors of British-Chilean military cooperation.[53]

After the war, rumors of such cooperation persisted. In his early history of the war, Freedman characterized Chile as a "virtual ally" but did not elaborate upon what this meant.[54] In 1999, when Pinochet was detained in Britain facing extradition to Spain for human rights violations committed against Spanish citizens after the overthrow of Salvador Allende, Baroness Thatcher publicly opposed the cooperation of the Blair government with the Spanish court based on the extensive British-Chilean cooperation during the war.[55] As she wrote in the *Times* of London: "I have better cause than most to remember that Chile, led at that time by General Pinochet, was a good friend to this country during the Falklands War. By his actions the war was shortened and many British lives were saved."[56]

The exact nature of that cooperation was finally revealed in a March 2002 interview conducted by a Chilean newspaper with General Fernando Matthei, the former commander in chief of the Chilean air force and a member of Pinochet's military government. Chile and Britain negotiated a deal in which the United Kingdom gave Chile arms in return for intelligence support and access to Chilean military bases from which to conduct operations against Argentina. Specifically, the British transferred to Chile attack aircraft, radars, surface-to-air missiles, and reconnaissance and electronic intelligence gathering aircraft (which were manned during the war by Royal Air Force personnel).[57] In return, Chile provided the British military with intelligence on Argentine military dispositions and movements and allowed British Special Air Service teams to operate from Chile against Argentine air bases.[58]

Such Chilean support materially aided the British war effort. There is some evidence, for example, that Chile supplied intelligence that assisted Britain in the sinking of the Argentine warship *General Belgrano*.[59] More generally, the legacy of the recent Argentine-Chilean conflict over the Beagle Channel in 1978, plus the widely recognized fact in Buenos Aires that Chile was cooperating with Britain during the war, forced Argentina to fight the Falklands War with one hand tied behind its back.[60] Argentina could not deploy the bulk of its best troops to the islands because seven of Argentina's nine infantry brigades remained behind to guard the border with Chile.[61] The Twenty-fifth Infantry Regiment, which the Argentines deployed to the Falklands as their initial occupation force, was hardly an elite unit.[62] One U.S. government analyst later confirmed that the Argentines "were so worried that Chile would exploit the political situation that crack well trained Argentine Army units were stationed around Commodoro Rivadavia and near the Chilean border to prevent a Chilean attack in the Southern tip of Argentina."[63] Contrary to what triumphalists would expect, authoritarian Chile made a significant contribution to the British war effort. The British found the "unsavoury" authoritarian regime of Chilean strongman Agosto Pinochet to be a stalwart ally.[64]

In sum, given that the support of democracies like the United States and the EEC was inconsistent and self-interested and that an authoritarian regime like Pinochet's Chile was a "virtual ally" to democratic Great Britain, it is hard to hold up the Falklands case as providing clear-cut evidence that democracies make better allies and argue that is why democratic Britain prevailed over authoritarian Argentina.

Strategic Evaluation

The Falklands case also provides little support for the triumphalists' argument that democracies are more likely to win their wars because they are better at strategic evaluation. It is hard to maintain that Britain engaged in effective strategic evaluation prior to the war; but a better case can be made that during the conflict Britain fought the war relatively intelligently. However, a close examination reveals that this effective wartime strategic evaluation had little to do with either of the mechanisms the triumphalists suggest ought to make democracies better strategic evaluators.

There is a general consensus that Britain's prewar Falklands policy was a disaster. As Britain's ambassador to Argentina Anthony Williams pointedly minuted before closing the embassy in Buenos Aires:

> Knowing full well that current British policy with regard to the Islands could not
> lead to any satisfaction of Argentine aspirations and that the Argentines were becoming increasingly restive, we refused to face the fact that our encouragement of

total intransigence from the islanders involved physical risk to them, to counter which no adequate provision had been made or could have been made. Nor did we make adequately clear to the islanders the stark choice they faced. They were never really brought face to face with the full realities of their position.[65]

Many British politicians actually attributed this to the democratic nature of the British political system. The Foreign Office had long wanted to settle the issue with the Argentines but the small yet vocal pro-Falklands lobby made this impossible. Former foreign secretary Lord Carrington made clear that it was in Britain's interest to reach such a settlement:

> The Falklands represented no vital strategic or economic interest for Britain, and although nobody had questioned that the islanders' views on their future must carry proper weight it was clear that the only long-term solution to make sense must be one leading to peaceful co-existence with Argentina; while anybody could see that a protracted posture of defence against Argentina—if it were allowed to come to that—would be so intolerably expensive as to be an aberration of defence finance and priorities.[66]

Successive British governments, however, found that they could not settle the issue because of opposition in Parliament. The Franks Commission report, Parliament's postwar assessment of the Thatcher government's handling of the crisis, makes clear that Thatcher, like previous prime ministers, had little room to maneuver: "The British Government, on the other hand, had to act within the constraints imposed by the wishes of the Falkland Islanders, which had a moral force of their own as well as the political support of an influential body of Parliamentary opinion; and also by strategic and military priorities which reflected national defence and economic policies: Britain's room for policy manoeuvre was limited."[67] Far from encouraging a rational assessment of Britain's interests in the Falklands dispute with Argentina, the British political system actually made it harder for British leaders to think clearly about it.

Given the almost insurmountable obstacles to settling the Falklands issue amicably with Argentina, the actions taken by the Thatcher government in the month before the war seem particularly ill-advised. There were two interrelated failures. First, the Thatcher government's concern to save money led Britain to reduce its military forces, especially those forces that were particularly useful for defending distant holdings such as the Falklands.[68] In the years preceding the Falklands War, Britain announced that it would sell or scrap its aircraft carriers, and it planned to withdraw and not replace the one ship it regularly kept on station in the South Atlantic, the HMS *Endurance*. The other thrust of the Thatcher government's defense policy was to reconfigure British forces exclusively to deal with a NATO war. This may have made sense in principle, but given that Britain remained mired in the unresolved Falklands dispute for domestic political reasons, reshaping British military forces exclusively to fight a NATO war without provision for dealing with Argentina was a serious strategic mistake.

Second, the British grossly misjudged Argentine intentions vis-à-vis the Falkland Islands.[69] In particular, Britain's intelligence failure in not anticipating and detecting the Argentine occupation of the Falklands is widely recognized.[70] A good case can also be made that the British military underestimated the Argentines militarily before the war, expecting the Argentine armed forces to stand down once the British fleet set sail. According to one senior British military officer, "the Navy thought we were British and they were wogs, and that would make all the difference."[71] In sum, prewar British strategic evaluation was poor.

During the war itself, strategic evaluation in Britain was better. However, it is hard to find evidence that Britain made the right strategic decisions because it was a democracy. The triumphalists believe that democracies should make better strategic decisions for one of two reasons. Some believe that because democracies bring a larger number of people into the decision-making loop, and many of these are individuals who will pay the price for failure, they ought to produce better policies. Other triumphalists focus on the free discussion of strategy in democracies, arguing that, in this marketplace of ideas, the better policies should rise to the top. A close examination of the Falklands case shows that neither of those mechanisms accounts for Britain's victory.

It is hard to argue that a large number of people were involved in formulating Britain's wartime strategy because the key decisions affecting British strategy were made by a small, centralized group of decision makers in Thatcher's cabinet and the bureaucracy.[72] Many of the most important policies—such as sending British submarines to the South Atlantic early in the conflict—were made without much input from Parliament.[73] The following exchange between Thatcher and the leader of the opposition, Michael Foot, is quite illustrative of this point:

> *Mr. Foot:* . . . I say that the House as a whole should have the chance of passing judgement on that position. We want the House as a whole to dictate the situation, not 60 or 70 of the right hon. Lady's backwoodsmen off the leash.
>
> *The Prime Minister:* We really cannot have full debate on the military options with the House making a decision. Nothing would be more helpful to the enemy or more damaging to our boys.[74]

Therefore, the Falklands is not an example of a war won through the input of a large number of self-interested decision makers.

There is also very little evidence that British strategy was improved through debate about it in the marketplace of ideas. Opposition members of Parliament regularly complained about the lack of detailed discussion of Thatcher's diplomacy and strategy during the war.[75] As one MP lamented, "it is disgraceful that we should have to learn from outside what is happening when we have been elected to come to the House to learn whatever is happening."[76] To be sure, opposition leaders could get confidential briefings as privy councillors to the government, but then they were prevented from publicly discussing what they knew.[77] Nor was the Thatcher administration above lying to members of Parliament about matters of wartime strategy and operations, such as the sinking of the *Belgrano*.[78] Thus, there was really not much informed debate in the House of Commons about British strategy.

Britain's free press was quite limited in its access to hard information about the war. Even the representatives of the press with the fleet were kept largely in the dark.[79] Admiral Woodward characterized his media policy as "cooperation, yes; information, no."[80] The British press has been very constrained in wartime because of strict national security regulations and a tradition of deferring to the government.[81] Even given that, the Thatcher government aggressively tried to control the flow of information to the press about the war effort. For example, Defence Minister John Nott tried to prevent retired officers from offering expert commentary in the media during the conflict.[82] This, and similar efforts, led one MP to complain that "The Prime Minister was at pains to point out on the BBC that we are a democracy. If she really believes that, will she call off the dangerous vendetta against the BBC, because one of the tenets of democracy, law and liberty is the right of people to express their views publically, even if they happen to disagree with those in authority?"[83] The Thatcher government ultimately engaged in sound strategic evaluation during the Falklands War, if not in the period running up to it. However, neither the input of large numbers of self-interested citizens nor the marketplace of ideas played much of a role in Britain's victory over Argentina in the Falklands War.

Public Support

There was widespread public support for the war effort in Britain. According to one source, 83 percent of British respondents agreed the Falkland Islands were important and 78 percent supported using force to free them from Argentine occupation.[84] Clearly, this high level of public support for the war effort was a net benefit, as Ground Forces Commander Major General Jeremy Moore acknowledged after the war.[85] However, it is not clear that this level of public support was a function of the democratic nature of Britain's political system. As former prime minister Edward Heath noted, the primary reason the public supports wars is not because of the ideological issues at stake, but rather because there was a general sense that a British interest (in this case, reversing Argentine aggression) was at stake:

> Nor are we taking action because the Argentine Government can be described as Fascist or as one that has a disgraceful record of human rights. I sometimes feel that the attitude of some Opposition Members is motivated or colored by that. We are dealing with this because there has been aggression against the Falkland Islands. If other types of Governments had done that, we would have been in exactly the same position.
>
> Fascism or a disgraceful record on human rights should not be allowed to color the issue. We did not fight Hitler or Mussolini because they were dictators or because of their internal policies. We fought them because they had reached such a state of power that they were a menace to vital British interests. We must always consider vital British interest.[86]

Nor could a high level of public support have been sustained over the longer term if that had been necessary, in part because of the nature of British democracy. As Jenkins and Hastings observe, "the difficulty of persuading the civilian public to accept the horrific realities of war [like the *Sir Galahad* disaster at Bluff Cove] caused Sir Robin Day to ask, in a lecture some years ago, whether in the post-Vietnam age any western democracy with a free press and television can hope to sustain national support for any war, however necessary."[87] While there were high levels of public support for the war effort initially, as one would expect in response to Argentina's unexpected invasion of the islands, it is not clear that long-term public support is an asset democracies can count on in war. In other words, the duration of the war, rather than public support per se, probably plays as significant a role in accounting for Britain's victory.[88]

Troops

Finally, there can be little doubt that British soldiers fought better on the battlefield than did their Argentine counterparts. Their superior battlefield performance is probably the main reason that Britain defeated Argentina. It was not so much the nature of each side's political system but other factors that accounted for British armed forces' higher level of military effectiveness. These other factors included such things as differences in historical military experience, military format, unit cohesion, training, level of technology, logistics, and tactical decision making. Britain's superiority in these areas had little to do with the fact that it was a democracy.

One major advantage the British enjoyed was that they had a long tradition of fighting successful wars, often at great distance from England. As one U.S. military analyst noted,

> Both Argentines and British are profoundly loyal, patriotic, have a proud military heritage, deep religious conviction and an ingrained sense of valor or heroism. But the British long history of wars and battles over four hundred years and the armed forces' continuing training and preparation for NATO exercises combined with their living memory of World War II, Korea, Suez, Belize and constant duty in Northern Ireland makes the British forces more aware of battlefield tactics and quick response in combat. The Argentines did not lack for valor or loyalty but were woefully lacking in experience.[89]

Indeed, Britain's extensive operational experience at war throughout the twentieth century gave its soldiers real advantages on the battlefield.

Conversely, the last major war that Argentina fought was the War of the Triple Alliance in the nineteenth century. Prior to the Falklands War, the Argentine's military's most important campaign was the *guerra sucia* (dirty war) against domestic opponents of the regime inside of Argentina.[90] The dirty war gave the Argentine military little experience relevant to fighting a conventional war against a major power. Given the disparity in military experience between Britain and Argentina, it is hardly surprising that the outcome of the Falklands War was so lopsided.

Closely related to this difference in national military experience, was the very different military formats employed by each side. "The key differences between the two sides," argues Lawrence Freedman, "were in the organization of their military forces and their professionalism."[91] Ironically, the military of democratic Great Britain was actually a long-service, professional force (of the type that dominated Europe before the French Revolution), whereas the armed forces of Argentina were (like the armies of the French Revolution) made up largely of conscripts.[92] The conscript army of Argentina was no match for Britain's professional forces.[93]

Britain's enlisted soldiers served an average of six years, while officers and noncommissioned officers typically served for much longer. This system produced excellent soldiers. As one Royal Army officer colorfully put it, "The great quality of our toms is that they think. A lot of people don't given them credit for that—they think that they're just dozy, hairy-arsed parachute soldiers, all blood and thunder, but they think as well. There's no doubt about it, one's extremely fortunate to command that calibre of men. With that quality of soldier and a bit of luck, you can take on the world."[94] In truth, almost all the forces that Britain sent to the South Atlantic were first-rate professionals.[95]

Conversely, Argentina fielded, with few exceptions, a conscript, universal-service military.[96] While the officers were long-service professionals, most recruits served for only one year.[97] This clearly affected the performance of Argentina's armed forces on the battlefield. After the war, a common response from Argentine soldiers asked to explain their defeat was this difference in the character of the two armies. "There was nothing else to be done; it wasn't just the difference in weapons," one former conscript noted; the British "were real professionals, down to the last soldier."[98] Another Argentine ex-soldier agreed: "Just the fact that people were going to die made me feel bad. I prayed to God that peace would come, that there'd be no more deaths, English or Argentine. I suppose the English, who are professional, soldiers by choice, didn't have those kinds of problems or they'd take them more for granted. But I was civilian in the middle of war, dressed like a soldier, but a civilian in the final reckoning."[99]

Argentina's conscript army was notable for the lack of leadership provided by its officers and the lack of initiative shown by its soldiers.[100] Argentina had very few elite military formations, in part because of the fear that such units would pose the threat of a coup in Argentina's fractious political environment.[101] While not all British units fought superbly, and not all Argentine units fought abysmally, overall Argentina's short-service, conscript forces were no match for Britain's long-service professionals.[102]

One of the battlefield advantages of a long-service, professional military force is that it is likely to enjoy greater small-unit cohesion, one of the pillars of military effectiveness. The British army's regimental system was uniquely conducive to producing cohesive, and hence highly effective, combat units.[103] Also, there was surprisingly little connection between the larger political issues at stake and the cohesiveness of the respective militaries on the battlefield.[104] One British soldier interviewed after the war suggested that "When you're in a foxhole and there are tracers and grenades going off over your head, you don't really think about the Queen. You just worry about getting out alive and fighting for another day."[105] Another added that: "I don't believe that soldiers fight for political rea-

sons, we do it because that's what we're paid for and that's what we wanna do—
that's why I do it and because I get a kick out of it. It's a challenge. I don't like to
be beaten. Second best just ain't good enough."[106] The professional soldiers of
the British army fought more to survive and to win than for any of the larger political issues behind the war.

In contrast, the morale of the Argentine military was low from the very beginning of the war.[107] Argentine conscripts had very little time to bond either
with each other or with their officers.[108] Not surprisingly, the Argentine armed
forces, particularly the army, fought very poorly once ground operations commenced, because it suffered in the areas of leadership and cohesion.

Triumphalists might argue that the British army was so effective because it
came from a democratic society that valued leadership and initiative, two critical
elements in military effectiveness. However, as a U.S. Army study of small unit
effectiveness cautions, "We must not make the fallacious assumption that an
open climate is endemic exclusively to democratic societies. Even organizations
which appear, at first glance, to be rigid and inflexible, such as the Wehrmacht in
World War II and the North Vietnamese Army, showed that in battlefield situations and in small unit levels criticisms and suggestions were a part of an open
climate on the small unit level."[109] In other words, the fact that the British military manifested more of the traits in its officers and men that are key to military
success is not necessarily a function of its democratic political system.

Another decisive advantage the British had over the Argentines was that their
armed forces were much better trained.[110] The professionals of the British armed
forces engaged in a great deal of realistic and demanding training during the
course of their careers.[111] Conversely, the conscripts of the Argentine military
underwent very little real training during their brief terms of enlistment.[112] Realistic training was also not a major part of the Argentine military officer's professional development either. Compounding this dearth of regular training was
the fact that the Falklands operation caught the Argentine army between conscript class training cycles, and the incoming class of conscripts had only one
month of basic training before the Falklands War.[113]

This lack of training seriously undermined the effectiveness of the Argentine
soldiers on the battlefield. Another former Argentine soldier recalled:

> In the end we became quite friendly with some of the English soldiers. When I
> told them in one conversation that I'd done five shooting tests and had fifty days'
> training, they banged their heads on the walls. They couldn't understand it, and
> they understood still less how we could go off to fight without being paid a huge

wage as they were. For them, it was their profession, they'd come to work. All the English soldiers had had at least three years' training. And however much patriotism you put in, you can't fight that.[114]

Yet another Argentine conscript admitted that "we weren't prepared enough mentally, we weren't trained for war."[115] This lack of training was first apparent in the Argentine loss at the Battle of Goose Green on May 28, 1982, but was evident throughout the ground campaign to the final battle for Port Stanley.[116]

The Argentine armed forces looked good on paper. At least in terms of raw numbers, they stacked up well against British forces. Qualitatively, however, they were no match for the Royal Navy and Royal Army. Data in the appendix show that with few notable exceptions—like the deadly effective Super Entendard/Exocet combination—the bulk of the Argentine army, navy, air force, and marines was equipped with obsolete or obsolescent weaponry.[117] The British, in contrast, fielded a modern military force that gave them advantages in strategic and tactical mobility, air power, intelligence, night operations, electronic warfare, artillery, and small arms.[118] Though it is doubtful that this played much role in the actual course of operations, the fact that Britain had the world's fifth largest nuclear arsenal (200 warheads based primarily on Trident-2 submarine-launched ballistic missiles) is further indication of the huge technological advantage Britain had over Argentina.[119] In particular, Argentina's weakness in anti-submarine warfare capability meant that after the sinking of the *Belgrano* by the British nuclear submarine HMS *Conqueror,* the entire Argentine fleet had to remain in port, leaving the British fleet largely unmolested.[120] Also, Argentina's lack of helicopters meant that it had little tactical mobility on the battlefield.[121] These are just two illustrations of the more general consequences of Argentina's technological backwardness compared to Great Britain.

Similarly, given that Britain was fighting nearly 8,000 miles from home, and Argentina was operating about 400 miles from its coast, one would think that Argentina would have at least had the logistical advantage. Despite Argentina's proximity to the Falklands, however, Argentine forces were also operating at the "end of their tether" as the result of their extreme technological backwardness.[122] Britain's enforcement of its "maritime exclusion zone" meant that Argentina had to fly in most of its supplies to its forces on the islands with its very limited airlift capability.[123] The net result, as one former Argentine soldier recalled, was that the British "put ashore, in one week the same number of people as we had in a month, they distributed three times as much food and deployed ten times as much artillery and ammunition. They really did work in a coordinated fashion which was more than could be said for us."[124] Britain won the battle 8,000 miles from home, in the enemy's backyard, in part because it was logistically far more capable than Argentina.

A number of Argentine tactical mistakes affected the course of the war. To be sure, Britain had the advantage of being able to land anywhere it wanted to on the Falkland Islands, while Argentina had to defend nearly the entire coast line.[125] Also, despite its closer proximity to the Falklands, the Argentines still had to fly most of their fighter planes from bases on the mainland, which meant that they were at the edge of their operating range over the Malvinas.[126] In other words, geography hardly worked to Argentina's advantage.

The Argentines compounded these geographic disadvantages by committing three blunders.[127] First, the Argentine ground force commander, General Mario Menendez, guessed wrong about where the British were likely to land. The Argentine marines, who were trained by the U.S. Marine Corps, believed that the British would land over the shallow beaches on the east side of East Falkland Island near Port Stanley and so the bulk of the Argentine defense effort was concentrated there to counter that threat. However, the Royal Marines favor deep-water beaches, and they were able to land virtually unopposed at San Carlos on the west side of East Falkland.[128] Second, after the sinking of the *Belgrano,* the Argentines kept the rest of their navy out of the battle, conceding to the British fleet almost total freedom of operation in the seas east of the Falkland Islands. Finally, with the Navy restricted to ports within Argentine territorial waters, the only means the Argentines had for challenging the British Fleet and attacking the beachhead at Port San Carlos was their air force. However, the Argentines never took advantage of the skill and bravery of their pilots by coordinating their air attacks or focusing on the most lucrative British targets. "Bizarre really, the whole areo-strategy was bizarre," one Royal Navy officer remarked of Argentine's air strategy; "they showed such courage in some areas, such naivety in others; appalling professional naivety."[129] A Royal Marine officer agreed that the Argentine pilots "were extremely brave and very skillful. They came back again and again in full knowledge of the hazards they were running. They pressed home their attacks with vigour, skill and determination and achieved a number of notable successes. They could have won the war for the enemy if it had not been for the outstanding performance of our Harriers and the amazing Seawolf missiles."[130]

A key mistake the Argentines made in their air campaign was to focus their attacks on well-defended British warships rather than attacking the unarmed troop transports and supply ships that carried the British ground forces. The exceptions to this prove the rule: the Argentine air force sunk the British supply ship *Atlantic Conveyor* and nearly wiped out the ground forces' fleet of heavy transport helicopters, and its sinking of the landing ship *Sir Galahad* demonstrated the vulnerability of the British ships engaged in amphibious operations. A more systematic Argentine campaign against supply and transport vessels, rather than one targeting attractive but well-defended targets like Britain's aircraft carriers, could have made a significant difference in Britain's ability to conduct the ground war.[131]

While these tactical mistakes clearly hurt the Argentine war effort, like the French decision in May 1940 to defend northern Belgium rather than the Ardennes, it is hard to see they were the result of the fact that Argentina was not a democracy.

Finally, Argentina, under the control of a military dictatorship at the time of the war, had a democracy score of -8 according to the POLITY index. This would place it in the realm of a high autocracy. However, there is reason to regard Argentina not as an autocracy but rather as an "anocracy," a transitional form of rule between autocracy and democracy, because it was already moving from authoritarianism toward democracy. The instability of the Argentine regime, rather than its absolute level of democracy, certainly affected the outcome of the war. For example, the erosion of support for the regime prior to April 1982 undoubtedly played a part in encouraging the junta to launch the invasion prematurely: on the eve of winter and before Britain had completed its strategic reorientation, which would have made it more difficult to retake the Falklands by force. Also, the fact that the Argentine junta faced many domestic opponents led it to configure the military for internal security rather than external combat. As I discussed previously, this put Argentina at a disadvantage vis-à-vis the British military on the battle field.

Argentina was not, therefore, a consolidated authoritarian political system, as the POLITY codings suggest. Rather, it is better characterized as an unconsolidated, transitional regime.[132] Prior to the Falklands invasion, the junta was facing growing public pressure to step down because of a reenergized democracy movement. Also, far from being a consolidated dictatorship, the Argentine junta was falling apart.[133] The British ambassador to the United States, Nicholas Henderson, recounted a very telling anecdote from U.S. secretary of state Alexander Haig about the challenges of dealing with such a regime: "In a talk I had with Haig in Washington on April 21st, he described the irrationality and chaotic nature of the Argentine leadership. He said there seemed to be 50 people involved in the decisions. If he reached some sort of agreement on one of the points at issue with a member of the *junta,* this was invariably countermanded by a corps commander entering the room an hour or so later."[134] Because Argentina exhibited many of the characteristics of a transitional "anocracy," rather than those of a monolithic authoritarian regime, it is hardly surprising it fared so badly at war with Great Britain.

CONCLUSION

The Argentine case surely does not provide evidence that democracies are incapable of fighting and winning wars, as defeatists have long feared. Indeed, Lawrence Freedman argues that the Falklands case shows that democratic societies "are not allergic to the use of military might. It is still widely accepted that there are things worth fighting for. There is no evidence that the good society and the welfare state have had a softening effect, as many commentators have supposed. Nor despite the efforts of some sections of the press, was the public afflicted by a crude and belligerent nationalism that ignored the political context of the fight and the need for restraint in certain areas."[135] However, the Falklands case does not provide strong evidence for the contrary view that democracies have distinct advantages in fighting wars against nondemocracies. Britain was a democracy, and Britain clearly won the war. But a close look at the evidence demonstrates that Britain won for none of the reasons the triumphalists suggest, and the reasons why Britain actually won have little connection to the fact that Britain was a democracy. The link between Argentina's loss and its domestic political system is a little more plausible. Again, it is important to keep two points in mind: Argentina was not a consolidated autocracy but rather a transitional anocracy, and so the cause of its problems may be more a function of its transitional nature than its lack of democracy; and there were other reasons why Argentina lost that have no apparent connection with its domestic regime. In sum, regime type hardly mattered in the Falklands case.

Falklands War Order of Battle (1981–82)

	United Kingdom	Argentina
Population	55,968,000	28,000,000
Total armed forces	343,646	185,500
Estimated GDP (1980)	$485.14 billion	$62 billion
Defense expenditures (1980)	$27.77 billion	$3.38 billion
Nuclear arsenals	SLBM: Polaris A3 16X3 MIRV = 48 warheads (1964–81)	0
Main battle tanks	900 Chieftain, (60) reserve/ 1967	60 M-4 Sherman (US)/October 1941
Surface-to-air missiles	Blowpipe (portable) 1975), 108 Rapier/Blindfire	0
Attack submarine	Total = 28 13 Oberon [diesel] (1961) 3 Porpoise [diesel] (1958) 1 Dreadnought [nuclear] (1963) 3 Churchill [nuclear] (1973) 2 Valiant [nuclear] (1966) 6 Swiftsure [nuclear] (1973)	Total = 4 2 Guppy [US diesel] (1944) 2 Type 209 [FRG diesel] (1974)
Surface ships	Total = 62	Total = 13
Aircraft carriers	2 ASW aircraft carriers: *Invincible* (1980) and *Hermes* (1959)	1 *Colossus* (1945)
Destroyers	18 destroyers: 16 County (1966) 1 Type 82 (1973) 1 Type 42 (1976)	9 destroyers: 2 Type 42 [UK] (1976) 3 Fletcher [US] (1943) 3 Sumner [US] (1944) 1 Gearing [US] (1945)
Frigates and corvettes	45 frigates: 3 Type 22 (1979) 8 Type 21 (1974) 26 Leander (1975) 8 Rothsay (1960)	2 Corvettes: 2 A-69 [FR] (1978)
Cruisers	0	1 *Brooklyn* [US] (1937)
Naval aviation	20 Sea Harrier (1978)	11 A-4Q [US] (1954) [being replaced by FR Super Etendard]
Air force	17 squadrons/228 AC: 48 Vulcan B-2 (1960) 60 Buccaneer S-2A/B (1965) 72 Jaguar GR-1 (1969) 48 Harrier GR-3/T-4 (1966)	8 Squadrons/163 AC: 68 A-P4 Skyhawk [US] (1954) 26 Dagger [IS] (1969) 21 Mirage III EA/DA [FR] (1958) 2 T-64 (1964) 5 Super Etendard [FR] (1978) 9 B-62 Canberra [UK] (1949)
Air-to-Air missiles	Sidewinder (1953) Sparrow (1976) Red Top (1964) Firestreak (1951)	R-530 [FR] (1955?)

continued

APPENDIX *continued*

	United Kingdom	Argentina
Helicopters (land and naval)	Total = 641	Total = 159
	7 Alouette II [FR] (1957)	9 A-109 (1976)
	20 Sioux (1948)	7 Bell 206 [US] (1966)
	213 Gazelle (1967)	30 Bell UH-1H [US] (1967)
	65 Lynx (1971)	6 Bell 47G [US] (1945)
	106 Scout (1962)	10 Bell 212 [US] (1968)
	105 Sea King (1969)	5 CH-47C [US] (1967)
	41 Wasp (1962)	24 SA-315B Lama (1969)
	31 Puma (1968)	15 SA-330 Puma (1968)
	6 Chinook [US] (1962)	12 S-61 (1959)
	10 Whirlwind (1952)	4 Lynx [UK] (1971)
	37 Wasp/Lynx [naval]	9 Alouette II [FR] (1963)
	(1962/71)	14 Hughes 500M [US] (1963)
		2 S-58T (1952)
		6 UH-19 (1948)
		6 Unknown

CHAPTER 6

If Not Democracy, Then What?

Democratic defeatists maintain that democracy is a decided disadvantage for states in the preparation for and conduct of war. This long-standing argument—stretching from Thucydides in 406 B.C. to twentieth-century classical realists—has been very influential among scholars and policymakers. It suffers, however, from serious defects in both its logic and evidence. The most important problem with democratic defeatism is that it cannot account for the striking fact that over the past 200 years, democracies have been on the winning side of most of their wars. Democracy is obviously not an obstacle to success in war.

But does this mean that democracy is really an asset? Democratic triumphalists argue that it is and that democracies are more likely to win their wars precisely because of the nature of their domestic regimes. According to them, democracies start only wars they can win easily and enjoy important wartime advantages, such as greater wealth, stronger alliances, better strategic thinking, higher public support, and more effective soldiers. Their arguments begin with the correlation between democracy and victory over the past 200 or so years and then posit various causal mechanisms that they think make democracies more likely to win their wars.

But there is much more to establishing a causal link between democracy and victory than just identifying a statistical correlation and a plausible theoretical explanation for that association. We need to be sure that this correlation is not unduly sensitive to how the model is specified, the dataset used, or the disproportionate influence of a handful of cases. Beyond that, we also need to see that the hypothesized causal mechanisms really operate as specified in key cases.

After examining the data and methods that underpin these findings, I conclude that whether a state is democratic is not the *most important* factor to consider in determining a state's likelihood of victory. I argue that regime type plays, at best, a modest and inconsistent role compared to other factors such as military power and wealth, and there are grounds for thinking that the relationship between democracy and victory might actually be spurious.

Two final questions remain: what might account for both military victory and the statistical association of democracy with that outcome, and what are the policy implications of my claim that democracy is not the key to victory?

POWER AND OTHER EXPLANATIONS

In this section, I argue that explanations other than those associated with regime type better explain how states perform in war. For example, an advantage in military power is often a reliable indicator of which side is likely to win a war.[1] The nature of the conflict can also influence military outcomes. In particular, the opposing sides in a war often have asymmetrical interests in the outcome, and this asymmetry sometimes produces a paradoxical outcome in which the weaker state defeats its more powerful adversary.[2] Moreover, states that imitate the military organizations and doctrines of the leading states in the international system are likely to prevail in war over those that do not.[3] Nationalism has also proved to be a potent source of increased military effectiveness in democracies (revolutionary France, 1789-94) and in autocracies (Prussia and Spain, 1807-15).[4] Finally, whether a regime is consolidated could affect its performance in war.

In my view, national power is the most consistent and influential factor explaining why states win their wars. As we saw in chapter 2, the association between democracy and victory is very sensitive to model specification and the data employed. The case studies in chapters 3, 4, and 5 also show that the causal mechanisms triumphalists believe give democracies advantages in selecting and waging winnable wars do not operate either. Finally, employing a somewhat larger version of the COW dataset than Reiter and Stam's ($N = 268$ vs. 197), I offer additional evidence of the tenuousness of the triumphalists' finding. Specifically, when I control for a composite power variable—what I call "gross mismatches"—the democracy*initiation variable is no longer significant. Model 1 is a basic model to gauge the impact of democracy on the ability of states to select winnable wars. This approach essentially replicates Lake's findings in his original article. Model 2 controls for gross mismatches, a dummy variable coded

TABLE 6.1
Probit Model of Gross Mismatches and Victory

Variables	Model 1	Model 2
democracy	−.0047884	−.0019204
	(.002652)*	(.0037481)
initiate	.4079383	.2578242
	(.1781363)*	(.1852338)
democracy*initiate	.0123819	.0066406
	(.006074)*	(.0067368)
gross mismatch	—	.9068908
		(.1754944)***
gross mismatch*democracy	—	−.0068214
		(.0055754)
constant	−.1317465	−.5585584
	(.1018538)	(.1356381)***
Pseudo R2	.0212	.1263
Log likelihood	−181.75581	−162.25137
N	268	268

* ≤ .05 (all tests two-tailed and all standard errors are robust)
** ≤ .01
*** ≤ .001

"1" when one side has a 2:1 advantage in two out of three power categories such as iron and steel production, military manpower, and total population. The intuition behind this variable is that victory is likely to be a function of different combinations of military power that are in important respects fungible (i.e., wealth can substitute for manpower) and also often context-specific. This model also includes an interaction variable—democracy*gross mismatch—to make sure that democracy is not causing the gross mismatch. The results in table 6.1 show that controlling for gross mismatch, democracy*initiation is no longer a significant predictor of victory. Also, model 2 suggests that democracy does not interact with gross mismatches to produce victory, which is what would have been indicated if the second interaction variable were positive and significant. I want to be careful not to overemphasize these results inasmuch as there are some respects in which Reiter and Stam's truncated dataset is superior to this one (i.e., it desegregates the First and Second World Wars), and their models also employ control variables (i.e., the various strategies) that I cannot replicate in this dataset. Still, in combination with the findings in chapter 2, these models do further highlight the sensitivity of democracy as a significant predictor of victory to model specification and data. Power variables, in contrast, remain significant and powerful across specifications and datasets.

Second, a large body of scholarship argues that democracy takes root and flourishes as the result of a distinct set of preconditions. For example, one of the key covariates of both democracy and victory is wealth. Wealthy states are much

TABLE 6.2

Per Capita Gross Domestic Product and War Outcomes in Twentieth Century

Countries at War (per capita GDP) [years]	Per Capita GDP Wins
United States (3780) defeats Spain (1736) [1898]	X
France (2876), Japan (1180), Russia (1237), **United Kingdom**(4492), and **United States** (4091) defeat China (545) [1900]	X
Japan (1188) defeats Russia (1237) [1904–05]	
Serbia (1057), Turkey (?), Rumania (1741), and Greece (1592) defeat Bulgaria (1534) [1913]	X
Germany (3059) defeats Belgium (3923) [1914]	
United States (4799), **United Kingdom** (4927), **France** (3236), Bulgaria (1534), Italy (2543), and Greece (1592) defeats Germany (3059), Austria-Hungary (2876), and Turkey (?) [1917–18]	X
Czechoslovakia (1933) defeats Hungary (1709) [1919]	X
Poland (1739) defeats Soviet Union (1488) [1919–20]	X
Soviet Union (1386) defeats China (562) [1929]	X
Japan (1837) defeats China (569) [1931–33]	X
Soviet Union (2237) defeats Japan (2816) [1939]	
Germany (5403) defeats Poland (2182) [1939]	X
Germany (5403) defeats **Denmark** (5116) [1940]	X
Germany (5403) defeats **Belgium** (4562) [1940]	X
Germany (5403) defeats **Holland** (4831) [1940]	X
Germany (5403) defeats **France** (4042) [1940]	X
Germany (5403) defeats **Norway** (4088) [1940]	X
Greece (2223) defeats Italy (3505) [1940]	
Soviet Union (2237) defeats Finland (3408)	
Germany (5711) defeats Yugoslavia (1412) [1941]	X
Germany (5711) defeats Greece (1874) [1941]	X
Soviet Union (2114) defeats Germany (5711) [1941–45]	
United States (8206) defeats Japan (2873) [1941–45]	X
United States (9741) and **United Kingdom** (6856) defeat Germany (5403) and Italy (3505) [1941–45]	X
Israel (2817) defeats Egypt (910), Iraq (1364), Jordan (1663), and Lebanon (2429) [1948]	X
Israel (3860) defeats Egypt (905) [1956]	X
Soviet Union (3566) defeats Hungary (2906) [1956]	X
China (553) defeats India (758) [1962]	
Israel (6222) defeats Egypt (1151), Jordan (3059), and Syria (3291) [1967]	X
Israel (7723) defeats Egypt (1201) [1969–70]	X
India (856) defeats Pakistan (931)[1971]	
Israel (9645) defeats Egypt (1294) [1973a]	X
Israel (9645) defeats Iraq (3753), Jordan (2388), and Syria (4017) [1973b]	X
Ethiopia (608) and Cuba (2520) defeat Somalia (1421) [1977–78]	X
Tanzania (617) defeats Uganda (703) and Libya (6991) [1978–79]	
United Kingdom (12,955) defeats Argentina (7243) [1982]	X
Israel (11,390) defeats Syria (6,786) [1982]	X

Data from Angus Maddison, The World Economy: Historical Statistics (Paris: OECD, 2003).
Note: Side with highter per capita GDP wins 28/37 times, or 76%. Side with democracy score of ≥ 7 wins 16/21 times, or 76% (boldface indicates democracy).
Chi-squared = 0(2) = 1.

more likely to be democratic, and wealth is one of the key sinews of military power. As table 6.2 makes clear, per capita wealth and democracy seem to have been about equally good as predictors of victory over the past 100 years or so.

Disentangling the effects of wealth on both democracy and military effectiveness is a challenging task. In a recent paper, however, Errol Henderson and Resat Bayer have designed a very clever critical test that demonstrates that wealth is a much better predictor of victory than democracy. Specifically, after confirming that wealth is also a significant predictor of victory if added to Reiter and Stam's model 4, they show that while more democratic and wealthier states win 100 percent of their wars, more democratic but less wealthy states win only 47 percent of them. Conversely, less democratic but wealthier states win about 68 percent of their wars, while less wealthy and less democratic states win only 17 percent. In other words, wealth, rather than democracy, explains more of these victories.[5] This is further evidence that the correlation between democracy and victory is spurious. Certain preconditions that make it more likely that a state will be democratic—such as per capita wealth—also make it more likely that it will win most of its wars.[6]

If the preconditions argument is correct, there should also be little variation in the military effectiveness of states over time, especially those states before or after the adoption of democracy, but significant variation across cases with different preconditions. Some democracies, such as the United States and Israel, were born democratic so they are not useful for assessing the preconditions argument. However, two other democracies—Britain and France—have long predemocratic histories. They also have strikingly different records of military success since 1648. Britain has fought about forty-three wars since the end of the Thirty Years' War, winning thirty-five (81 percent) of them. Britain's record in the COW dataset is slightly better: it fought nine wars and won eight (89 percent).[7] The preconditions argument would attribute these results to the fact that Britain is a wealthy, geographically secure state with many allies, allowing it to win wars with little domestic mobilization. Conversely, France has few of the preconditions necessary for democracy and military success, and thus has been both an inconsistent democracy and a less successful belligerent. France fought thirty-one wars since 1648 and won eighteen of them (58 percent). In the COW dataset, it fought sixteen wars, winning only nine (56 percent). In other words, factors other than the level of democracy explain the different records of France and Britain during war.

A final possible explanation for how a state performs at war is whether its government is consolidated. The mean democracy score for Lake's winners is 0.59, which is well below the democracy range.[8] The average democracy score for winners in Reiter and Stam's dataset is even lower: –1.41. The distribution of winners in all wars since 1815 by democracy score shows that this remarkably low average is the result of the large numbers of the most authoritarian states that won their wars too (figure 6.1). This leads Reiter and Stam to propose that the effect of the level of democracy is curvilinear (i.e., the most democratic and most autocratic win, but those in the middle tend to lose).[9] This pattern, however, is also compatible with an argument that ascribes victory not to the level of democracy but to whether a regime has been politically consolidated, as one would expect with highly democratic and authoritarian states. The mixed regimes in between high democracy and high autocracy, which are referred to as "anocracies," may perform poorly in war because they are unconsolidated, transitional regimes.[10] Such regimes constitute 42 percent of the cases in Reiter and Stam's dataset. The primary reason for characterizing anocracies as transitional regimes is that they do not stay at this level as long as regimes do when they are in either the democracy or autocracy range.[11]

Figure 6.1 compares the average variance (how much does the regime type of countries vary over time [avar]) by level of democracy with the percentage of wins [pcwins] at each of those levels.[12] In other words, the lower the variance, the less change there is in the democracy score of the countries in the dataset. If the consolidation argument is correct, it should be the case that more consolidated regimes (e.g., those with less variance) have a higher percentage of wins than do less consolidated regimes. If my hypothesis is correct, variance in regime score should be higher among anocracies (those countries with democracy scores between –6 and 6), and they should win a lower percentage of their wars. Figure 6.1 suggests that this is in fact the case.

Obviously, much more work remains to done in terms of better specifying and testing these alternative explanations for the association between democracy and victory. But they are plausible explanations that are logically consistent and empirically well grounded.

In addition to helping us understand the interrelationship between regime type and success in war, this book has broader implications for the ongoing discussion of the sources of military effectiveness. Its findings do not contradict the widely held belief, as Voltaire observed long ago, that "God favors the big battalions." In other words, the most important powerful and consistent predictor of whether a state will win or lose a war is its share of the material indicators of national power.[13] The fact that high levels of wealth are the sinews of material power and one of the key preconditions of democracy may also account for the statistical association between democracy and victory. That being said, though, there is an important class of cases where states manifest superior military effectiveness without a significant power advantage. The classic case was Nazi Germany's Wehrmacht, which is widely regarded as a paragon of military effec-

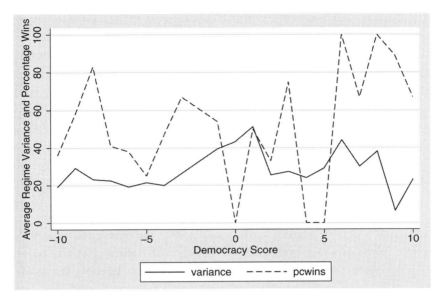

Figure 6.1. Variation in Democracy Scores and Percentages Wins

tiveness.[14] Today, many point to Israel as another example where a country at a significant disadvantage in numbers of soldiers, tanks, aircraft, and other material indices of power nonetheless managed to prevail in its wars. These and other cases have stimulated a growing body of literature that focuses on the nonmaterial constituents of military effectiveness.[15]

Democratic triumphalists focus on one particular nonmaterial factor—democracy—and argue that it helps states wisely choose and then effectively prosecute their wars. A number of these "fair-fight" cases constitute the core of the triumphalists' case. But, as my discussion in this book makes clear, only a handful of cases bolster their finding that nonmaterial factors such as regime type are important determinants of military effectiveness. And as table 6.3 makes clear, other factors aside from democracy actually explain why these democracies won their wars. Indeed, even in these cases, which ought to provide strong support for the proposition that democracy plays an important role in determining who wins or loses wars, other factors including the balance of forces, the nature of the conflict, nationalism, favorable geography, the level of economic development, and the willingness to emulate the dominant military formats really explain the outcome in these, the best cases for democratic triumphalism.

A good case can be made that, in even in these fair-fight cases, variables that realists emphasize play an important role in explaining the outcomes as well.

This argument starts from the fact that, over the past 200 years, the developed world has seen three important sociopolitical changes that have significant military consequences: industrialization, nationalism, and democratization. Democratic triumphalists believe that this last change has had the greatest impact upon military effectiveness, ignoring the role the first two play in both military effectiveness and democratization. Industrialization generates widespread wealth (a precondition of democracy and victory) and also militarily useful technologies. Nationalization helps harness these to the state. If we accept that industrialization and nationalism are the foundations of military success, as most realists maintain, then it becomes clear that even in the fair-fight cases these variables are important.

In terms of the nature of the conflict, for example, all of these cases, save perhaps for the Falklands, come down to nationalism as the primary factor explaining the asymmetry of interests. Of course, the nationalism cases themselves are self-evident. Three of the weak adversary cases (Israel in 1948 and 1967 and the Falklands) are about imbalances in wealth on the part of the defeated state. Wealth, or lack thereof, is also an important determinant as to whether and how geography matters. Finally, in a nationalist age, emulation of the dominant military formats and practices is the key to survival in an anarchic world. Given this, industrialization and nationalism account not only for the correlations of democracy and victory, but also for twenty-three out of twenty-eight of the boxes in table 6.3.

Therefore, if one wants to understand the sources of military effectiveness, either for one's own state or for potential allies and adversaries, whether that state is democratic is not the most important factor to consider. Although democracies and autocracies undoubtedly have different strengths and weaknesses that may affect some aspects of their performance in wartime, overall they seem to cancel each other out, and so regime type confers no clear advantage or disadvantage. Moreover, at least until recently, military power could be produced in a variety of ways, through many different combinations of social organization, economic potential, specific doctrinal and training decisions, and strategic choices. In other words, the "recipe" for effective military performance had a lot of variability, which meant that very different regimes could produce similar levels of capability by combining other ingredients in different ways. Given this fact, it is not surprising that democracies and nondemocracies are sometimes good at fighting and sometimes bad; regime type alone does not confer a clear advantage or disadvantage in selecting or fighting wars.

One might concede that regime type was relatively unimportant in the past

TABLE 6.3
Sources of Military Effectiveness in Cases of Democratic Fair Fights

Factor	Poland 1920	Israel 1948	Israel 1967	Israel 1973	Falklands 1982
Balance of forces	✓	✓	✓		
Nature of conflict	✓	✓	✓	✓	✓
Nationalism	✓	✓	✓	✓	
Weak adversary	✓	✓	✓		✓
Geography	✓	✓	✓		✓
Emulation		✓	✓	✓	✓
Development		✓	✓	✓	✓
Other	✓				

but argue that whether a state is democratic or not is now becoming more important. According to this line of reasoning, the lesson of the past fifteen years is that if a state wants to have a truly cutting-edge military fully capable of taking advantage of the so-called revolution in military affairs, it cannot do this in a centralized, coercive, and information-controlled society. In other words, if a country wants to be able to fight as successfully as the United States in the first Gulf War, it now must have an open democratic society where everyone is able to exchange ideas and knowledge freely and avail themselves without restriction of computer and communication technologies.[16] The collapse of the Soviet Union at the end of the Cold War, largely because it was a centralized and coercive political system that was unable to compete militarily with the West, lends credence to this view. However, China, which remains fairly centralized and undemocratic, suggests that it may be possible for a state to reform its economy and revitalize its technology base so as to produce an effective military without political democracy.[17] China is, therefore, one of the cases we need to watch to accumulate additional evidence about how much regime type may matter for military effectiveness in coming years.

Finally, an epistemological point: although this book has been critical of particular statistical studies that argue that democracy is the key determinant of victory, it should not, by any means, be read as a wholesale indictment of that approach. After all, I accept that the statistical association between democracy and victory clearly undercuts democratic defeatism. Rather, I argue that, while the statistical approach is necessary to gain an understanding what makes military victory more likely, by itself it is not sufficient. It should be read, therefore, as a corrective to those theorists who maintain that if they can specify a model in which the democracy variable is statistically significant and can tell a logically consistent story that explains that finding, their work is done.[18] In contrast, my argument is that, in order to accept the claim that democracy increases the likelihood of peace between states or victory in war, you also have to be able to specify and test causal mechanisms through in-depth process tracing in detailed case studies. Statistical correlation, no matter how logically and elegantly framed, does not, by itself, establish causation. We also ought to be able to see the hypothesized causal mechanisms actually operating in the cases.[19]

POLICY IMPLICATIONS

My skepticism about the importance of regime type for military effectiveness stands in direct contrast to the current trends in the U.S. government. As President George W. Bush's secretary of state, Condoleezza Rice, put it: "Our experience of this new world leads us to conclude that the fundamental character of regimes matters more today than the international distribution of power."[20] If I am right, intelligence analysts and national security decision makers should be wary of relying upon monocausal theories of military effectiveness, whether they are based on regime type or some other domestic-level factor.[21] Instead, they should look at a constellation of factors—including the balance of actual and potential military power resources, the nature of the conflict, the willingness and ability of states to emulate the most successful military practices, nationalism, whether states have the common preconditions for military effectiveness and democracy, and whether their regimes are consolidated or not—as indicators of how a state will do at war.[22]

Some democratic triumphalists today might point to the 2003 Iraq War as yet another example of how democracy confers military advantages on states. Before the war, President Bush boldly predicted the victory of democracy over autocracy: "Throughout the 20th century, small groups of men seized control of great nations, built armies and arsenals, and set out to dominate the weak and intimidate the world. In each case, their ambitions of cruelty and murder had no limit. In each case, the ambitions of Hitlerism, militarism, and communism were defeated by the will of free peoples, by the strength of great alliances, and by the might of the United States of America."[23] In a very impressive feat of arms, the United States and its democratic allies defeated a large and battle-hardened Iraqi military in little more than a month with only a handful of friendly casualties.

Although it is too early to say for sure what the Iraq case says about the role of democracy in this outcome, there are at least grounds for doubting that it will provide any support for democratic triumphalism.[24] First, by the fall of 2003, the stunning victory of May seemed to be giving way to a long and protracted insurgency. *New York Times* military correspondent Michael Gordon characterized

Iraq as a "catastrophic success": the U.S. won a tactical victory but is in danger of suffering a strategic defeat.[25] *Washington Post* military correspondent Thomas Ricks judged the result even more harshly in the title of his book *Fiasco*.[26] While few are willing to predict the United States will lose this war, fewer still are confident that it will decisively win it.[27]

Second, even if the United States and its democratic allies somehow succeed in achieving their goal of transforming Iraq into a stable and democratic country, it is not clear that democracy will have been the key factor producing that "victory." The role of democracy in helping the United States to wisely choose that war seems minimal. There was hardly a free and unfettered debate about the costs, benefits, and risks of the war, either publicly or even inside the administration. As former secretary of state Colin Powell's chief of staff, Lawrence Wilkerson, described the Bush administration's decision-making process in the run-up to the war: "Its insular and secret workings were efficient and swift—not unlike the decision-making one would associate more with a dictatorship than a democracy."[28] Indeed, the case for war could be made only by corrupting the marketplace of ideas, which is hardly compatible with the informational version of the selection effects theory.[29] True, there is evidence to suggest that some in the Bush administration saw an easy victory in Iraq as an electoral advantage. But Bob Woodward also makes clear that President Bush himself understood that rather than following public opinion in planning to attack Iraq, he would have to shape it, which certainly turns the logic of the institutional constraints version of the selection effects argument on its head. In an effort to bolster Italian prime minister Silvio Berlusconi's resolve, Bush reminded him that "We lead our publics. We cannot follow our publics."[30] The outcome of the 2004 election, in which a majority of voters regarded the war in Iraq as not going well but nevertheless voted to reelect the president, suggests that there is little danger of electoral punishment even for perceived failure in what is surely a costly war.[31] Even the result of the 2006 midterm elections, in which a majority of voters repudiated Bush's Iraq policies by giving over control of both houses of Congress to the Democrats, did not lead him to change course. Indeed, rather than rethink his policy, the president "surged" an additional 21,500 U.S. soldiers into Iraq. If democratic leaders do not fear electoral punishment for perceived failure in cases about which the public obviously cares deeply, then the triumphalists' argument that democratic leaders are more careful about the wars they start is also questionable.

There is also reason to think that the triumphalists' wartime effectiveness arguments are not operating as expected in the Iraqi case. While the United States is certainly wealthier than Saddam Hussein's Iraq, and this played a key role in the outcome of at least the first phase of the war, the fact that the Bush administration is running huge deficits to pay for the war, which will have the effect of increasing, rather than decreasing, the scope of the U.S. government's reach into the economy, conflicts with the triumphalists' claim that democracies win their wars because they suffer less state rent seeking.[32] Moreover, given that the Bush administration's "Coalition of the Willing" excluded a number of the major democracies around the world, it is hard to credit a democratic alliance with the victory. And as Chaim Kaufmann convincingly documents, the quality of the strategic debate in the United States in the run-up to the war was very poor: America's marketplace of ideas was bankrupt.[33] There was, to be sure, much public support for the war on Iraq, but this faded quickly as it became clear that the administration's case that Iraq had weapons of mass destruction and links to al-Qaeda crumbled.[34] Finally, there is also evidence that the enthusiasm of the troops for the Iraq war is waning as the recognition takes hold that they face a protracted insurgency.[35] In sum, it does not look like the United States will ultimately "win" in Iraq and, even if it does, there is little reason to think that American democracy will be the reason.

Because of the many defects with democratic triumphalism as an explanation of military effectiveness, I worry that it continues to influence U.S. policymakers and instill in them a false confidence in the capabilities of democracies in war. The key mechanism for this is democratic hubris: the unwarranted belief that democracy confers special advantages on a state such as extraordinary military prowess or exempts it from the normal dynamics of balance-of-power politics simply because of the virtues of its domestic political system.

The classic case of democratic hubris was Athens in the fifth century B.C. Many believe that Athens saved Greece by defeating the invading fleet of the Persian king Xerxes at the Battle of Salamis in 480 B.C. Reflecting on the Athenian victory in this decisive naval battle of the Persian War, democratic triumphalist historian and neoconservative pundit Victor Davis Hanson concludes: "Freedom turns out to be a military asset. It enhances the morale of the army as a whole; it gives confidence to even the lowliest of soldiers; and it draws on the consensus of officers rather than a single commander."[36] Many other scholars agree that this victory demonstrated the superiority of liberty over tyranny.[37]

It is doubtful, however, that democratic triumphalism really provides a plausible account of Athens' victory over the Persians inasmuch as Athens manifested hardly any of the traits contemporary democratic triumphalists suggest make democracies so successful in war. As Benjamin Constant observed in his famous essay comparing the liberty of the ancients and the moderns, the Athenians had a very different conception of the meaning of democracy than we have today: "The aim of the ancients was the sharing of social power among the citizens of the same fatherland: that is what they called liberty. The aim of the moderns is the enjoyment of security in private pleasures, and they call liberty the guarantees accorded by institutions to these pleasures."[38] In other words, ancient liberty is closer to what we would call nationalism, the freedom of the group; modern liberty, in contrast, is the freedom of the individual.

Nonetheless, because of its belief in the superiority of its democratic political regime, Athens fell victim to that most tragic of Greek flaws: hubris. Concern about the overweening postwar pride of the Athenians was evident in one the great tragic dramas of the day. Aeschylus, in his remarkable play *The Persians,* reminded his fellow citizens of the follies of their pride in a thinly veiled allegory told through the story of their recently defeated adversaries.[39] Aeschylus evidently feared that his fellow Athenians, like the defeated Persians before them, were in danger of losing sight of the limits of their power. The Greek historian Herodotus offered a similar caution against Athenian imperialism at the end of his account of the Greco-Persian War.[40]

The most dramatic evidence of Athenian democratic hubris came almost half a century later in the run-up to the Peloponnesian War. As Thucydides states at the beginning of his account, the roots of the war between democratic Athens, autocratic Sparta, and their respective alliances was the "growth of the power of Athenians, and the alarm which this inspired."[41] But democratic hubris kept the Athenians from coming to grips with the fact that, despite the many virtues of their democratic regime, their overwhelming power and overbearing behavior drove many of the other Greek city-states into the arms of autocratic Sparta.

As Thucydides describes in book 1, a delegation from Corinth came to Sparta to plead with the Spartans to join with them in an alliance to check the Athenian Empire. A group of Athenians also happened to be in Sparta at the same time and asked to respond to the Corinthians' charges in order to dissuade the Spartans from going to war against Athens. They offered two defenses of Athens' imperial behavior. They reminded the Spartans that, if not for Athens, the Greeks would have lost the war with the Persians. Without their ships, the leadership of the Athenian admiral Themistocles, and the commitment of the Athenian soldiers and sailors, the war would have gone badly for the Greeks.

"Surely, Spartans," the Athenians argued, "neither by the patriotism that we displayed at that crisis, nor by the wisdom of our counsels, do we merit our extreme unpopularity with the Hellenes, not at least unpopularity for our empire."[42]

In addition to arguing that they deserved their empire by virtue of their role in winning the Persian War, the Athenian delegation also boasted that due to the nature of their democratic regime, Athens was entitled to its empire because the Athenians ruled it more justly than other powers would: "And praise is due to all who, if not so superior to human nature as to refuse dominion, yet respect justice more than their position compels them to do."[43] The Athenians were blinded by the splendor of their democratic regime to the fact that their preponderant power and overbearing conduct were driving other city-states into the Spartan alliance, even though Sparta was hardly a democratic regime. Democratic hubris led Athens to make many other mistakes during the course of the Peloponnesian War—particularly the ill-fated Sicilian expedition—and these mistakes ultimately cost Athens the war. The link between democratic triumphalism and hubris was clear in the case of ancient Athens.

There are, indeed, worrisome similarities between the situations of ancient Athens and the contemporary United States. Like Athens, the United States can rightly claim to have played the key role in defeating two major threats to the democratic West: the Axis during the Second World War and the Soviet Union during the Cold War.[44] And, as with Athens, the United States gained its "empire" as a result of its victory in those two great conflicts.[45]

I also fear that, like Athens after its victory over the Persians, democratic triumphalism is today leading the United States to succumb to hubris. There have been, for example, clear echoes of democratic triumphalism in the rhetoric of the Bush administration in the global war on terrorism. The president himself put that effort in the context of previous American efforts to spread democracy: "Our commitment to liberty is America's tradition—declared at our founding; affirmed in Franklin Roosevelt's Four Freedoms; asserted in the Truman Doctrine and in Ronald Reagan's challenge to an evil empire. . . . The advance of freedom is the surest strategy to undermine the appeal of terror in the world. Where freedom takes hold, hatred gives way to hope. When freedom takes hold, men and women turn to peaceful pursuit of a better life. American values and American interests lead in the same direction: we stand for human liberty."[46] Sounding a lot like the Athenian delegation at Sparta as they argued that imperial Athens behaved better than it had to, President Bush also sought to reassure the world that American hegemony was benign despite widespread opposition abroad to the American war to topple Saddam Hussein: "We exercise power without conquest, and we sacrifice liberty for strangers."[47] Today, many sup-porters of the Bush administration now openly celebrate American hegemony, arguing that "just like the British Empire before it, the American empire unfail-ingly acts in the name of liberty."[48]

Proponents of an American empire may sincerely believe that because the United States is a democracy, it will rule its empire benignly and so it will be wel-comed by the rest of the free world. "I'm amazed, " President Bush confessed, "that there's such misunderstanding of what our country is about that people would hate us. I'm like most Americans, I just can't believe it because I know how good we are."[49] But even neoconservative pundit Robert Kagan admits that much of the democratic world has not in fact welcomed the advent of the Pax Americana.[50] Indeed, the 2003 war in Iraq, which the Bush administration touts as a noble and selfless undertaking, is viewed with much cynicism among the publics of even our staunchest democratic allies. Moreover, that war, which ap-peared initially to be such a stunning success for the democratic America, quickly became, like democratic Israel's Lebanon debacle, a Pyrrhic victory at best.[51] I fear that when future Gibbons write their histories of the decline and fall of the American empire, democratic triumphalism will no doubt figure prominently as the wellspring of our tragic hubris.

Notes

INTRODUCTION

1. Samuel P. Huntington, *The Third Wave: Democratization in the Late Twentieth Century* (Norman: University of Oklahoma Press, 1993), 26.

2. Francis Fukuyama, "The End of History?" *National Interest,* No. 16 (Summer 1989): 3–18. Also see his *The End of History and the Last Man* (New York: Free Press, 1992), xi.

3. See, for example, the responses by Allan Bloom, Pierre Hassner, Gertrude Himmelfarb, Irving Kristol, Daniel Patrick Moynihan, and Steven Sestanovich in the same issue of the *National Interest* and the pieces by Huntington, Leon Wieseltier, Timothy Fuller, David Satter, David Stove, and Frederick Will in the next issue. For Fukuyama's post-9/11 defense of his thesis, see his "History Is Still Going Our Way," *Wall Street Journal,* October 5, 2001.

4. For example, Immanuel Kant's "First Definitive Article of Perpetual Peace," in his *Perpetual Peace and Other Essay on Politics, History, and Morals,* trans. Ted Humphrey (Indianapolis: Hackett, 2004), 112. Also see Thomas L. Pangle and Peter J. Ahrensdorf, *Justice among Nations: On the Moral Basis of Power and Peace* (Lawrence: University of Kansas Press, 1999), 198–99.

5. Michael W. Doyle, "Kant, Liberal Legacies, and Foreign Affairs [Parts 1 and 2]," *Philosophy and Public Affairs,* Vol. 12, Nos. 3–4 (Summer–Fall 1983): 205–54 and 323–53.

6. Jack Levy, "Domestic Politics and War," *Journal of Interdisciplinary History,* Vol. 18, No. 4 (1988): 653–73. For a good overview of the state of the art in contemporary social science research on the democratic peace, see Bruce Russett, *Grasping the Democratic Peace: Principles for a Post–Cold War World* (Princeton, NJ: Princeton University Press, 1993).

7. A not wholly persuasive effort to distance the democratic peace from the Bush administration's policies in Iraq is Bruce Russett's "Bush Whacking the Democratic Peace," *International Studies Perspectives,* Vol. 6, No. 4 (November 2005): 395–408.

8. "A National Security Strategy of Engagement and Enlargement" (Washington, DC: The White House, February 1996), at www.fas.org/spp/military/docops/national/1996 stra.htm#II.

9. "State of the Union Address," January 20, 2004, at www.whitehouse.gov.news/ releases/2004/01/print/20040120-7.html.

10. "National Security Advisor Dr. Condoleezza Rice Discusses War on Terror at McConnell Center for Political Leadership," March 8, 2004, at www.whitehouse.gov/news/ releases/2004/03/print/20040308-15.html.

11. "President Bush Presses for Peace in the Middle East," May 9, 2003, at www.white house.gov/news/releases/2003/05/print/20030509-11.html.

12. "President Discusses Future of Iraq," February 26, 2003, at www.whitehouse.gov/ news/releases/2003/02/print/200030226-11.html.

13. "Interview of the Vice President by Wolf Blitzer, CNN," June 23, 2005, at www.white-house.gov/news/releases/2005/06/print/20050623-8.html.

14. "President Discusses War on Terror at Naval Academy Commencement," May 27, 2005, at www.whitehouse.gov/news/releases/2005/05/20050527.html.

15. www.whitehouse.gov/inaugural/index.html.

16. "President Sworn-In to Second Term," January 22, 2995, www.whitehouse.gov/ inaugural/index.html.

17. Quoted in Bob Woodward, *Plan of Attack* (New York: Simon and Schuster, 2004), 88.

18. "President Discusses Progress in Iraq," July 23, 2003, at www.whitehouse.gov/ news/releases/2003/07/print/20030723-1.html.

19. On the advantages of democracy generally, see Joseph T. Seigle, Michael Weinstein, and Morton Halperin, "Why Democracies Excel," *Foreign Affairs,* Vol. 83, No. 5 (September–October 2004): 57–71, and Paul Starr, *Freedom's Power: The True Force of Liberalism* (New York: Basic Books, 2007).

20. David A. Lake, "Powerful Pacifists: Democratic States and War," *American Political Science Review,* Vol. 86, No. 1 (March 1992): 24–37. See also Dan Reiter and Allan C. Stam, *Democracies at War* (Princeton, NJ: Princeton University Press, 2002).

21. Victor Davis Hanson, *Carnage and Culture: Landmark Battles in the Rise of Western Power* (New York: Doubleday, 2001), 4.

22. John Lewis Gaddis, *We Now Know: Rethinking Cold War History* (Oxford: Clarendon Press, 1997), 281–95.

23. "President Honors and Commemorates Veterans in the Netherlands" (Washington, DC: The White House, May 8, 2005), at www.whitehouse.gov/news/releases/2005/05/ print/20050508.html.

24. "Friedberg to Serve as Deputy National Security Adviser to Cheney," *News@Princeton,* May 5, 2003, at www.princeton.edu/main/news/archive/S04/17/61E20/index.xml?section=.

25. See Laura Secor, "The Farmer Classicist and Raisin-Grower Victor Davis Hanson Argues That the USA Needs a Dose of Ancient Greece's Warrior Culture. White House Hawks Are Listening," *Boston Globe,* May 25, 2003, D1; and Rone Tempest, "Right Way to Farm the Classics," *Los Angeles Times,* February 25, 2004.

26. Victor Davis Hanson, *The Soul of Battle: From Ancient Times to the Present Day, How Three Great Liberators Vanquished Tyranny* (New York: Free Press, 1999), 4. Also see 409.

27. "Vice President Cheney Salutes Troops," Remarks by the Vice President to the American Society of News Editors, April 9, 2003, at www.whitehouse.gov/news/releases/ 2003/04/print/20030409-4.html.

28. On these weaknesses, see the essays by Christopher Layne, David Spiro, and Henry S. Farber and Joanne Gowa in Michael E. Brown, Sean M. Lynn Jones, and Steven E. Miller, eds., *Debating the Democratic Peace: An International Security Reader* (Boston: MIT Press, 1996); and Sebastian Rosato, "The Flawed Logic of the Democratic Peace," *American Political Science Review,* Vol. 97, No. 4 (November 2003): 585–602.

29. See, for example, Allan R. Millett, Williamson Murray, and Kenneth H. Watman, "The Effectiveness of Military Organizations," *International Security*, Vol. 11, No. 1 (Summer 1986): 71; Stephen Biddle and Stephen Long, "Democracy and Military Effectiveness: A Deeper Look," *Journal of Conflict Resolution*, Vol. 48, No. 4 (August 2004): 525–46; Biddle, *Military Power: Explaining Victory and Defeat in Modern Battle* (Princeton, NJ: Princeton University Press, 2004); and Risa Brooks and Elizabeth Stanley-Mitchell, *Creating Military Power: The Impact of Culture, Society, Institutions, and International Forces on Military Effectiveness* (Stanford, CA: Stanford University Press, 2007).

30. Kenneth N. Waltz, "Fair Fights or Pointless Wars," *International Security*, Vol. 28, No. 3 (Winter 2003–4): 181.

CHAPTER 1: DEMOCRACY AND VICTORY:
WHY DEMOCRACY IS NOT A LIABILITY

1. Kenneth N. Waltz, *Foreign Policy and Democratic Politics: The American and British Experience* (Boston: Little, Brown, 1967), 298.

2. See the discussion of Plato's views of the weaknesses of democracy in Periclean Athens in Donald Kagan, *Pericles of Athens and the Birth of Athenian Democracy* (New York: Free Press, 1991), 268–69.

3. Quoted in Melvin Small, *Democracy and Diplomacy: The Impact of Domestic Politics on U.S. Foreign Policy, 1789–1994* (Baltimore: Johns Hopkins University Press, 1996), xvii.

4. Alexis de Tocqueville, *Democracy in America*, Vol. 1 (New York: Vintage, 1945), 243.

5. Quoted in Small, vii–viii.

6. Quoted in Small, 169.

7. Gabriel Almond, *The American People and Foreign Policy* (New York: Harcourt, Brace, 1950). Also Small, xiv, and Kenneth N. Waltz, "Electoral Punishment and Foreign Policy Crises," in James N. Rosenau, ed., *Domestic Sources of Foreign Policy* (New York: Free Press, 1967), 266.

8. George F. Kennan, *American Diplomacy: 1900–1950* (Chicago: University of Chicago Press, 1951), 61.

9. Hans J. Morgenthau, *American Foreign Policy: A Critical Examination* (London: Methuen, 1952), 222–23.

10. Walter Lippmann, *The Public Philosophy* (New York: Mentor, 1955), 19. Also cf. 23–24.

11. Tocqueville, 1:245.

12. Lippmann, 27.

13. Morgenthau, 224 (emphasis added).

14. Quoted in Small, 84.

15. Lippmann, 28.

16. Ole R. Holsti, "Public Opinion and Foreign Policy: Challenges to the Almond-Lippmann Consensus, Mershon Series: Research Programs and Debates," *International Studies Quarterly*, Vol. 36, No. 4 (December 1992): 440.

17. Holsti, 439–66. Also see Miroslav Nincic, "Domestic Costs, the U.S. Public, and the Isolationist Calculus," *International Studies Quarterly*, Vol. 41, No. (1997): 597.

18. Quoted in E. H. Carr, *The Twenty Years Crisis: 1919–1939; An Introduction to the Study of*

International Relations (New York: Harper and Row, 1939), 24. Of course, Carr himself did not endorse this view.

19. Bruce Russett, *Controlling the Sword: The Democratic Governance of National Security* (Cambridge, MA: Harvard University Press, 1990), 106.

20. Kant, *Perpetual Peace,* cited in Jack Levy, "Domestic Politics and War," *Journal of Interdisciplinary History,* Vol. 18, No. 4 (Spring 1988): 658–59; and Randolph Siverson, "Democracies and War Participation: In Defense of the Institutional Constraints Argument," *European Journal of International Relations,* Vol, 1, No. 4 (1995): 481–89.

21. Miroslav Nincic, *Democracy and Foreign Policy: The Fallacy of Political Realism* (New York: Columbia University Press, 1992), 42.

22. Niccolò Machiavelli, *The Discourses* (Harmondsworth: Penguin, 1974), book I, 58.

23. Waltz, *Foreign Policy and Democratic Politics,* 311.

24. Kenneth N. Waltz, *Theory of International Politics* (Reading, MA: Addison-Wesley, 1979), 96–97.

25. Thucydides, *The Peloponnesian War,* trans. Rex Warner (Middlesex: Penguin, 1954). See especially the discussion of the Sicilian debacle in book VII.

26. See the discussion of Mao's views in E. L. Katzenbach, "Time, Space, and Will: The Politico-Military Views of Mao Tse-tung," in T. N. Greene, ed., *The Guerrilla and How to Fight Him* (New York: Frederick A. Praeger, 1962), 155.

27. Quoted in Small, xiii.

28. Jean-François Revel, *How Democracies Perish* (Garden City, NY: Doubleday, 1984), 3.

29. See, for example, Revel, 3.

30. Donald Kagan and Frederick W. Kagan, *While America Sleeps: Self-Delusion, Military Weakness, and the Threat to Peace Today* (New York: St. Martin's, 2000), viii, 307; and Robert Kagan and William Kristol, "Getting Serious," *Weekly Standard,* November 19, 2001, at www .weeklystandard.com/Content/Public/Articles/000/000/000/518hrpmo.asp. For an influential philosophical discussion of the weakness of liberal democracy, see Leo Strauss's discussion of the Weimar Republic in his preface to the English translation of *Spinoza's Critique of Religion* (New York: Schocken Books, 1965), 1.

31. Thucydides, II, 65.

32. Alexander Hamilton, "No 6," in Hamilton, James Madison, and John Jay, *The Federalist Papers* (New York: Mentor, 1961), 58.

33. Gabriel Almond, "Public Opinion and National Security Policy," *Public Opinion Quarterly,* Vol. 20, No. 2 (Summer 1956): 371–78.

34. Lippmann, 28, and Carr, 133–34.

35. Edmund Ions, "Dissent in America: The Constraints on Foreign Policy," *Conflict Studies,* No. 18 (1971): 1–14; Revel, 3; and Morgenthau, 223. Also see the general discussion in Levy, 660–61.

36. Herodotus, *The Histories,* trans. David Grene (Chicago: University of Chicago Press, 1987), V, 78.

37. Quoted in Kagan, *Pericles of Athens,* 147.

38. On the advantages of consensual over coercive mobilization, see Aaron L. Friedberg, "Why Didn't the United States Become a Garrison State?" *International Security,* Vol. 16, No. 4 (Spring 1992): 109–42.

39. Indeed, the famous "bureaucratic politics" model was developed by Andrew Marshall at RAND to account for Soviet nuclear strategy in the 1950s. See Marc Tractenberg, *History and Strategy* (Princeton, NJ: Princeton University Press, 1991), 28–30.

40. Steven David's *Choosing Sides* (Baltimore: Johns Hopkins University Press, 1999) shows how alliance decisions in many nondemocratic states are shaped by the need to counter domestic opponents.

41. See Jack Snyder, *The Ideology of the Offensive: Military Decision Making and the Disasters of 1914* (Ithaca: Cornell University Press, 1984), whose three cases include one democracy (France) but two authoritarian states (Wilhelmine Germany and Czarist Russia).

42. Jack Snyder, *Myths of Empire: Domestic Politics and International Ambition* (Ithaca: Cornell University Press, 1991), chaps. 3, 4, and 6, shows how domestic disunity in Wilhelmine Germany, interwar Japan, and the Cold War Soviet Union produced irrational expansionary policies. Of course, none of those states were democratic.

43. The classic example of this was imperial Japan's decision to attack the United States at Pearl Harbor. On this see Snyder, *Myths of Empire,* 148–49.

44. On "most" and "least likely" cases see Harry Eckstein, "Case Study and Theory in Political Science," in Fred I. Greenstein and Nelson Polsby, eds., *Handbook of Political Science,* Vol. 7 (Reading, MA: Addison-Wesley, 1975), 118–19.

45. Classic accounts include William L. Shirer, *The Collapse of the Third Republic: An Inquiry into the Fall of France in 1940* (New York: Da Capo, 1994); Eugen Weber, *The Hollow Years: France in the 1930s* (New York: W. W. Norton, 1994); and Alistair Horne, *To Lose a Battle: France 1940* (New York: Penguin, 1988).

46. Marc Bloch, *Strange Defeat: A Statement of Evidence Written in 1940* (New York: Octagon Books, 1968), 157.

47. Shirer, 285–338. Also see and Eugen Weber, *The Hollow Years: France in the 1930s* (New York: W. W. Norton, 1994), 270; and Paul Marie de la Gorce, *The French Army: A Military Political History* (New York: Braziller, 1963), 197–98.

48. Anthony Adamthwaite, *France and the Coming of the Second World War* (London: Frank Cass, 1977), 125.

49. Shirer, 466–70. On the rigidity of the French military, see Bloch, 116.

50. Shirer, 458–59. There were also compelling geopolitical considerations as well, as I discuss in chapter 3.

51. Bloch, 35.

52. Robert Young, *In Command of France: French Foreign Policy and Military Planning, 1933–1940* (Cambridge, MA: Harvard University Press, 1978), 250–51.

53. For review of the various explanations of the "strange defeat," see John C. Cairns, "Some Recent Historians and the 'Strange Defeat' of 1940," *Journal of Modern History,* Vol. 46, No. 1 (March 1974): 60–85.

54. Young, 252–58.

55. Hans-Adolph Jacobsen, "Dunkirk 1940," in Jacobsen and Jürgen Rohwher, eds., *Decisive Battles of World War II: The German View* (London: Andre Deutsch, 1965), 65. Also see Andre Beaufre, *1940: The Fall of France* (New York: Alfred A. Knopf, 1968), 211; and Guy Chapman, *Why France Collapsed* (London: Cassell, 1968), 331.

56. Elizabeth Kier, "Culture and Military Doctrine: France between the Wars," *Interna-*

tional Security, Vol. 19, No. 4 (Spring 1995): 84; and Kier, "Culture and French Military Doctrine before World War II," in Peter Katzenstein, ed., *The Culture of National and Security* (New York: Columbia University Press, 1996), 187.

For a thoroughgoing critique of Kier's argument, see Douglas Porch, "Military 'Culture' and the Fall of France in 1940: A Review Essay," *International Security,* Vol. 24, No. 4 (Spring 2000): 157–80.

57. Len Deighton, *Blitzkrieg: From the Rise of Hitler to the Fall of Dunkirk* (New York: Alfred A. Knopf, 1980), 135.

58. See Don M. Alexander, "Repercussions of the Breda Variant," *French Historical Studies,* Vol. 8, No. 3 (Spring 1974): 488; Deighton, 172–73; and Erich von Manstein, *Lost Victories: The War Memoirs of Hitler's Most Brilliant General* (Novato, CA: Presidio Press, 1994), 101–2 and 126.

59. Alexander, 477.

60. Richard D. Challener, "The Military Defeat of 1940 in Retrospect," in Edward Mead Earle, ed., *Modern France: Problems of the Third and Fourth Republics* (Princeton, NJ: Princeton University Press, 1951), 412.

61. Jacobsen, 35.

62. Brian Bond and Martin Alexander, "Liddell Hart and de Gaulle: The Doctrines of Limited Liability and Mobile Defense," in Peter Paret, ed., *The Makers of Modern Strategy: From Machiavelli to the Nuclear Age* (Princeton, NJ: Princeton University Press, 1986), 622.

63. Alexander, 482 and 486.

64. Alexander, 477 and 485.

65. Jacobsen, 46.

66. Alexander, 487.

67. Deighton, 366.

68. Jacobsen, 33–35.

69. Manstein, 98.

70. Deighton, 275. Also see Barry R. Posen, *The Sources of Military Doctrine: France, Britain, and Germany between the World Wars* (Ithaca: Cornell University Press, 1984), 87.

71. Alistair Horne, *To Lose a Battle: France 1940* (London: Penguin, 1979), 221.

72. Eliot A. Cohen and John Gooch, *Military Misfortunes: The Anatomy of Failure in War* (New York: Free Press, 1990), 201.

73. Manstein, 102.

CHAPTER 2: DEMOCRACY AND VICTORY:
WHY REGIME TYPE HARDLY MATTERS

1. David A. Lake, "Powerful Pacifists: Democratic States and War," *American Political Science Review,* Vol. 86, No. 1 (March 1992): 24–37. See also Dan Reiter and Allan C. Stam, *Democracies at War* (Princeton, NJ: Princeton University Press, 2002).

2. Dan Reiter and Allan C. Stam, "Democracy and Battlefield Military Effectiveness," *Journal of Conflict Resolution,* Vol. 42, No. 3 (June 1998): 259. For similar sentiments, see Aaron L. Friedberg, *In the Shadow of the Garrison State: America's Anti-Statism and Its Cold War Grand Strategy* (Princeton, NJ: Princeton University Press, 2000), 340; and Victor Davis Hanson, *Carnage and Culture: Landmark Battles in the Rise of Western Power* (New York: Doubleday, 2001), 4.

3. Reiter and Stam, *Democracies at War*, 197, 205 (emphasis added).

4. William Reed and David H. Clark, "War Initiation and War Winners," *Journal of Conflict Resolution*, Vol. 44, No. 3 (June 2000): 378–95.

5. The COW dataset refers to J. David Singer and Melvin Small, *Correlates of War Project: International and Civil War Data, 1816–1992* (Ann Arbor, MI: ICPSR #9905, 1994). This dataset contains information about war participation, outcomes, various indices of military power, and who started the war. For discussion of the POLITY democracy index, see Keith Jaggers and Ted Robert Gurr, *Polity III: Regime-Type and Political Authority, 1800–1994* (Ann Arbor, MI: ICPSR #6695, 1996). From that data most analysts calculate a composite democracy score (-10 to 10) by subtracting their AUTOC from DEMOC scores.

6. On a 21-point scale from -10 to 10, 6 is the generally accepted cutoff point for democracy. Karen Rasler and William R. Thompson, "Predator Initiators and Changing Landscapes for Warfare," *Journal of Conflict Resolution*, Vol. 43, No. 4 (August 1999): 7.

7. Lake, "Powerful Pacifists," 24–37. Because there was often more than one state on each side in these wars, Lake actually has an N of 121. The Gulf War, which occurred subsequent to the publication of Lake's chapter, should also count according to his criteria.

8. The 1994 version of the COW dataset, including these wars, has an N of 269. Reiter and Stam, *Democracies at War*, 52–57, employ many, but not all of these wars, leaving them with an N of 197. Specifically, they do not include the following wars: First Schleswig-Holstein (1848–49), Spanish-Chilean (1865–66), Sino-French (1884–85), Franco-Thai (1893), Central American (1906), Lithuanian-Polish (1919–20), Franco-Turkey (1919–22), Sino-Japanese (1937–41), Chankufeng (1938), Franco-Thai (1940–41), Korean (1950–53), Second Kashmir (1965), Football War (1969), Sino-Vietnamese (1979), Iran-Iraq (1980–88), Gulf War (1990–91), and Azeri-Armenian War (1992–98). They also disaggregate World War I, World War II, the Vietnam War, and the Yom Kippur War into distinct phases.

9. Other scholars have recognized this problem too. See, for example, D. Scott Bennett and Allan C. Stam, "The Declining Advantages of Democracy: A Combined Model of War Outcomes and Duration," *Journal of Conflict Resolution*, Vol. 42, No. 3 (June 1996): 246.

10. Reiter and Stam, who do disaggregate the war in Europe, credit the United States and Britain with defeating Nazi Germany. Their dataset also credits democratic Israel with not one but two victories in the 1973 Yom Kippur War by dividing it into two wars: Israel versus Egypt and Israel versus Syria. This coding tilts the scale in favor of democracies, although it is balanced by their counting as separate victories Germany's defeats of Belgium, the Netherlands, Denmark, and France.

11. Bennett and Stam also identified this problem. It is not clear, however, given the large number of missing data points and the fact that capabilities may not measure real contribution to the war effort, that their solution of gauging each participant's role in the alliance based upon their individual capabilities solves the problem of who contributed what in a mixed alliance. Bennett and Stam, 248, n. 20.

12. Alan Clark, *Barbarossa: The Russian-German Conflict of 1941–45* (New York: Quill, 1965); Richard Overy, *Why the Allies Won* (New York: W. W. Norton, 1995), 63–100; and Richard Overy, *Russia's War: A History of the Soviet War Effort, 1941–45* (New York: Penguin, 1997).

13. W. Victor Madej, "Effectiveness and Cohesion of the German Ground Forces in World War II," *Journal of Political and Military Sociology*, Vol. 6, No. 2 (Fall 1978): 233–48.

14. Quoted in Martin van Creveld, *The Sword and the Olive: A Critical History of the Israeli Defense Force* (New York: Public Affairs, 1998), 215.

15. On Lebanon, see Ze'ev Schiff and Ehud Ya'ari, *Israel's Lebanon War* (New York: Simon and Schuster, 1984); and van Creveld, *The Sword and the Olive*, 296.

16. Martin Gilbert, *Israel: A History* (New York: William Morrow, 1998), 504.

17. On the importance of "crucial cases" for devising "fair tests" for comparative theory testing, see Arthur Stinchcombe, *Constructing Social Theories* (New York: Harcourt, Brace, and World, 1968), 24–28.

18. Because Reiter and Stam, *Democracies at War*, 58, reject other triumphalist arguments that democracies win wars because of a preponderance of power—either their own or their allies—they ought to be particularly eager to find cases of democracies being relatively evenly balanced with nondemocracies.

19. This adds thirteen cases to those listed in note 20. Five support the defeatists: the Ecuadorian-Columbian War (1863), Second Schleswig-Holstein War (1864), Central American War (1906), Sino-Soviet War (1929), and Chaco War (1932–35); and seven support the triumphalists: Pacific War (1879–83), Central American War (1885), Sino-Japanese War (1894–95), Russo-Japanese War (1904–5), Manchurian War (1931–33), Sino-Japanese War (1937–41), Changkufeng (1938), and the Football War (1969).

20. These are the first part of World War I (1914–17), the Battle of France (May–June 1940), and the Sino-Indian War (1962), which seemingly support the defeatists and the Russo-Polish War (1919–20), the Israeli War for Independence (1948), the Six Day War (1967), the Yom Kippur War (1973), and the Falklands War (1982), which appear to support the triumphalists.

21. Gary King, Robert O. Keohane, and Sidney Verba, *Designing Social Inquiry: Scientific Inference in Qualitative Research* (Princeton, NJ: Princeton University Press, 1994), 168–84.

22. Moreover, multiple case studies can be used to test probabilistic theories because they provide a great deal of information. Not only does this make them an efficient means of testing theories, but it also makes it possible to determine whether particular cases are outliers or not.

23. David Lake, "Fair Fights? Evaluating Theories of Democratic Victory," *International Security*, Vol. 28, No. 1 (Summer 2003): 164.

24. David A. Lake and Matthew A. Baum, "The Invisible Hand of Democracy: Political Control and the Provision of Public Services," *Comparative Political Studies*, Vol. 34, No. 6 (August 2001): 587–621.

25. Reiter and Stam, *Democracies at War*, 114–43.

26. Reiter and Stam, *Democracies at War*, 20, 138.

27. Dan Reiter and Allan C. Stam, "Understanding Victory: Why Political Institutions Matter," *International Security*, Vol. 28, No. 1 (Summer 2003): 170.

28. Donald P. Green, Soo Yeon Kim, and David H. Yoon, "Dirty Pool," *International Organization*, Vol. 55, No. 2 (Spring 2001): 441–68, and Michael D. Ward, Randolph M. Siverson, and Xun Cao, "Disputes, Democracies, and Dependencies: A Re-Examination of the Kantian Peace," *American Journal of Political Science*, Vol. 51, No. 3 (July 2007): 583–601.

29. John R. Oneal and Bruce M. Russett, "Clear and Clean: The Fixed Effects of the Liberal Peace," *International Organization*, Vol. 55, No. 2 (Spring 2001): 471.

30. Gary King, "Proper Nouns and Methodological Propriety: Pooling Dyads in International Relations Data," *International Organization,* Vol. 55, No. 2 (Spring 2001): 497–507.

31. Important cautions about overreliance upon correlational findings include Jack S. Levy, "Domestic Politics and War," *Journal of Interdisciplinary History,* Vol. 18, No. 4 (Spring 1988): 669; and David Dessler, "Beyond Correlations: Toward a Causal Theory of War," *International Studies Quarterly,* Vol. 35, No. 3 (September 1991): 337–55.

32. Samuel P. Huntington, *The Third Wave: Democratization in the Late Twentieth Century* (Norman: University of Oklahoma Press, 1991), 37–38. There is a burgeoning literature on democracy and both economic development and peace, which suggests that the statistical association between them is spurious, with other factors in fact causing them both. See James A. Robinson, "Economic Growth and Democracy," *Annual Review of Political Science,* Vol. 9 (2006): 503–27; and Azar Gat, "The Democratic Peace Reframed: The Impact of Modernity," *World Politics,* Vol. 58, No. 1 (October 2005): 73–100.

33. Brian M. Downing, *The Military Revolution and Political Change* (Princeton, NJ: Princeton University Press, 1992), 78–79. For the classic discussion of how a benign security environment is more conducive to democracy, see Otto Hintze's treatment of Great Britain in "Military Organization and the Organization of the State," in Felix Gilbert, ed., *The Historical Essays of Otto Hintze* (New York: Oxford University Press, 1975), 178–215.

34. This follows the discussion in Kenneth Schultz, "Do Democratic Institutions Constrain or Inform? Contrasting Two Institutional Perspectives on Democracy and War," *International Organization,* Vol. 52, No. 2 (Spring 1999), 233.

35. The logic of this argument, like so much of modern liberal international relations theory, finds its wellspring in the work of Immanuel Kant. This is nicely summarized in Randall L. Schweller, "Domestic Structure and Preventive War: Are Democracies More Pacific?" *World Politics,* Vol. 44, No. 2 (January 1992): 241–43.

36. Levy, "Domestic Politics and War," 658–59; Bruce Bueno de Mesquita and Randolph M. Siverson, "War and the Survival or Political Leaders: A Comparative Study of Regime Types and Political Accountability," *American Political Science Review,* Vol. 89, No. 4 (December 1995): 841–55; Kenneth A. Schultz, "Domestic Opposition and Signaling in International Crises," *American Political Science Review,* Vol. 92, No. 4 (December 1998): 830; Bennett and Stam, 346, 365; Dan Reiter and Allan C. Stam, "Democracy, War Initiation, and Victory," *American Political Science Review,* Vol. 92, No. 2 (June 1998): 378; and Bruce Bueno de Mesquita, Randolph M. Siverson, and Alistair Smith, "Policy Failure and Political Survival: The Contribution of Political Institutions," *Journal of Conflict Resolution,* Vol. 43, No. 2 (April 1999): 147–61.

For the claim that initiators are more likely to win wars, see Kevin Wang and James Lee Ray, "Beginners and Winners: The Fate of Initiators of Interstate Wars Involving Great Powers since 1495," *International Studies Quarterly,* Vol. 38, No. 1 (March 1994): 139–54.

37. For application of these logics to the democratic victory thesis, see Reiter and Stam, *Democracies at War,* 10, 19–20, 21, 23, 144, 146, 162.

38. Lake uses a logit model to measure the impact of two independent variables—democracy and initiation—on the dependent variable, which is the likelihood of winning or losing a war. Based on that, for example, going from a democracy score of 5 to 10 (e.g., from Syria in 1948 to the United States in 1941) more than doubles the likelihood of victory. Logit makes it possible to calculate the odds likelihood ratio by applying anti-logs to both sides

of the basic equation logit (π) = $\alpha + \beta X$ which yields the odds likelihood ratio from the formula

$$\frac{\pi}{1-\pi} = \varepsilon^{\alpha+\beta X} = \varepsilon^{\alpha}(\varepsilon^{\beta})^{X}.$$

This tells us the effect of a one unit increase in the democracy score on the likelihood of victory.

Reiter and Stam, *Democracies at War,* 45, table 2.2, particularly their model 4, which I think best captures the argument that democracies are better able to pick winning wars, employ more sophisticated probit models (including more control variables and a broader spectrum of cases). Unlike Lake, who measures the interaction effect between democracy and war initiation by simply including both variables in the same equation, Reiter and Stam assess selection effects by including an interaction term between democracy and war initiation in their equations along with various control variables.

39. Lake, "Fair Fights?"165–67, and Reiter and Stam, "Understanding Victory," 175–76.

40. Jeffrey M. Wooldridge, *Introductory Econometrics: A Modern Approach* (Mason, Ohio: South-Western College Publishing, 2000), 131.

41. Stephen Van Evera, *Guide to Methods for Students of Political Science* (Ithaca: Cornell University Press, 1997), 17.

42. I calculated these effects using STATA's "mfx compute" function, which holds the values of other variables at their mean in computing the marginal effect of each variable.

Reiter and Stam, *Democracies at War,* fig. 2.2, provide data on the marginal effects of increases in the democracy score but not the relative effect of democracy compared to those of other variables. In an earlier work, Allan C. Stam, *Win, Lose, or Draw: Domestic Politics and the Crucible of War* (Ann Arbor: University of Michigan Press, 1996), figs. 28, 45, does. Not surprisingly, my findings about democracy's relatively small marginal effect on the likelihood of victory are similar to his.

43. The elasticity for democracy*initiation is –0.0486938; for the state's capabilities it is 0.9587111; and for its allies capabilities it is 0.6250279.

44. A formal test of the difference of models 3 and 4 is H$_0$: $\beta_{\text{polini}} = \beta_{\text{poltarg}} = \beta_{\text{initiation}}$ = 0 versus H$_a$: At least one β differs from 0 would use the likelihood ratio statistic: G^2 = 2[log(L(complete model)) − log(L(reduced model))] = 2[−64.9 − (−69.3)] = 8.8. The p-value is P = Prob(χ^2_3> 8.8) = .0321, which implies that there is some evidence that at least one coefficient differs from zero and that the complete model improves somewhat on the reduced model. But the difference between models 1 and 4 is even larger: 2[log(L(complete model)) − log(L(reduced model))] = 2[−64.9 − (−28.3)] = 126.8. The p-value is P = Prob(χ^2_9> 126.88.8) < .0001. I thank Tom Wehrly for suggesting this approach to me.

The log likelihoods considered here come from Reiter and Stam, *Democracies at War,* 45, table 2.2.

45. This follows Erik Gartzke, "Preferences and the Democratic Peace," *International Studies Quarterly,* Vol. 44, No. 2 (June 2000): 205–7.

46. I thank an anonymous reviewer for suggesting this approach.

47. The classic brief for "rational ignorance" is in Anthony Downs, *An Economic Theory of Democracy* (New York: HarperCollins, 1957), 214–16. For an application of this to inter-

national affairs, see Mancur Olson, *The Rise and Decline of Nations: Economic Growth, Stagflation, and Social Rigidities* (New Haven: Yale University Press, 1982), 26.

48. Bueno de Mesquita and Siverson, 853. See also William R. Thompson, "Democracy and Peace," *International Organization,* Vol. 50, No. 1 (Winter 1996): 149.

49. H. E. Goemans, *War and Punishment: The Causes of War Termination and the First World War* (Princeton, NJ: Princeton University Press, 2000), 39–40. For a logically rigorous argument that the incentives facing democratic and authoritarian leaders are similar, see Gordon Tullock, *Autocracy* (Dordrecht: Kluwer, 1987), 19.

50. See Jack Levy, "The Causes of War: A Review of Theories and Evidence," in Phillip E. Tetlock, Jo L. Husbands, Robert Jervis, Paul C. Stern, and Charles Tilly, eds., *Behavior, Society, and Nuclear War,* Vol. 1 (New York: Oxford University Press, 1989), 270. I thank Hein Goemans for reminding me of this point.

51. For an accessible discussion of the limitations of selection models, see Anne E. Sales, Mary E. Plomondon, David J. Magi, John A. Spertus, and John S. Rumsfeld, "Assessing Response Bias from Missing Quality of Life Data: The Heckman Method," *Health Quality and Life Outcomes,* Vol. 2 (September 2004) at www.pubmedcentral.nih.gov/articlerender.fcgi?artid=521693; and Nancy L. Allen and Paul W. Holland, "Exposing Our Ignorance: The Only 'Solution' to Selection Bias," *Journal of Education Statistics,* Vol. 14, No. 2 (Summer 1989): 141–45.

52. I thank an anonymous reviewer for suggesting this approach. For a similar application, see Alastair Smith, "To Intervene or Not to Intervene: A Biased Decision," *Journal of Conflict Resolution,* Vol. 40, No. 1 (March 1996): 16–40.

53. Kenneth A. Schultz, "Looking for Audience Costs," *Journal of Conflict Resolution,* Vol. 45, No. 1 (February 2001): 35, 48, and 52.

54. See David Kinsella, "No Rest for the Democratic Peace," *American Political Science Review,* Vol. 99, No. 3 (August 2005): 454–55.

55. Schultz, "Looking for Audience Costs," 44, seems to acknowledge that "spinning" can be employed by democratic leaders to mitigate the consequences of bad decisions.

56. Giacomo Chiozza and H. E. Goemans, "International Conflict and the Tenure of Leaders: Is War Still *Ex Post* Inefficient?" *American Journal of Political Science,* Vol. 48, No. 3 (July 2004): 605.

57. This follows the related argument for assessing audience costs in Schultz, "Looking for Audience Costs," 53.

58. Eugene Gholz and Daryl Press, "Untangling Selection Effects in Studies of Coercion" (unpublished manuscript, Dartmouth College and the University of Texas, n.d.).

59. I get slightly different numbers than Reiter and Stam, because in appendix 2.2 they list the United States as initiating the European phase of World War II, but in my copy of their dataset they do not. Reiter and Stam, *Democracies at War,* 52–57.

60. Michael Clodfelter, *Warfare and Armed Conflicts: A Statistical Reference to Casualty and Other Figures, 1618–1991* (Jefferson, NC: McFarland, 1992), 643.

61. George Childs Kohn, *Dictionary of Wars,* rev. ed. (New York: Facts on File, 1999), 264; and R. Ernest Dupuy and Trevor N. Dupuy, *The Harper Encyclopedia of Military History: From 3500 B.C. to the Present* (New York: HarperCollins, 1993), 1091.

62. Thomas A. Bailey, *A Diplomatic History of the American People,* 10th ed. (Englewood

Cliffs, NJ: Prentice-Hall, 1970), 257; and Robert H. Ferrell, *American Diplomacy: A History* (New York: W. W. Norton, 1975), 190.

63. Bailey, *A Diplomatic History of the American People,* 256.

64. John J. Mearsheimer, *The Tragedy of Great Power Politics* (New York: W. W. Norton, 2001), 242–44.

65. Theodore George Tatsios, *The Megali Idea and the Greek Turkish War of 1897: The Impact of the Cretan Problem on Greek Irredentism, 1866–1897* (New York: Columbia University Press, 1984), 40, 48, and 115.

66. C. M. Woodhouse, *Modern Greece: A Short History* (London: Faber and Faber, 1986), 193.

67. Reiter and Stam, *Democracies at War,* 12–13. John J. Mearsheimer, *Conventional Deterrence* (Ithaca: Cornell University Press, 1983), examines cases of both democracies (Britain, France, India, and Israel) and nondemocracies (Egypt, Germany, North Korea, the Soviet Union, and Vietnam) who only started wars when they thought they had a high chance of victory.

68. Lake, "Powerful Pacifists," 24, and before him Frederic C. Lane, "The Economic Meaning of War and Protection," in his *Venice and History: The Collected Papers of Frederic C. Lane* (Baltimore Johns Hopkins University Press, 1996), 389, n. 10, applied this argument to military power. A related argument is that liberal institutions make it easier for governments to borrow money to wage war. See Kenneth A. Schultz and Barry Weingast, "Limited Governments, Powerful States," in Randolph M. Siverson, ed., *Strategic Politicians, Institutions, and Foreign Policy* (Ann Arbor: University of Michigan Press, 1998), 15–50.

For general arguments about democracies being less prone to rent seeking, see Mancur Olson, "Dictatorship, Democracy, and Development," *American Political Science Review,* Vol. 87, No. 3 (September 1993): 567–76; Barry Basinger, Robert B. Ekeland Jr., and Robert Tollison, "Mercantilism as a Rent-Seeking Society," in James M. Buchanan, Robert D. Tollison, and Gordon Tullock, eds., *Toward a Theory of the Rent-Seeking Society* (College Station: Texas A&M University Press, 1980), 235–68; and Mark Brawley, "Regime Types, Markets, and War: The Impact of Pervasive Rents in Foreign Policy," *Comparative Political Studies,* Vol. 26, No. 2 (July 1993): 178–97.

69. Lake, "Powerful Pacifists," 28.

70. "Democracy and Growth: Why Voting Is Good for You," *Economist,* August 27, 1994, 15–17; and Yi Feng, "Democracy, Political Stability, and Economic Growth," *British Journal of Political Science,* Vol. 27, No. 3 (July 1997): 391–418.

For a largely theoretical argument that democracy causes growth because of the greater credibility of democratic governmental institutions, see Douglass C. North and Barry Weingast, "Constitutions and Commitment: The Evolution of Institutions Governing Public Choice in Seventeenth-Century England," *Journal of Economic History,* Vol. 49, No. 4 (December 1989): 803–32.

71. John F. Helliwell, "Empirical Linkages between Democracy and Economic Growth," *British Journal of Political Science,* Vol. 24, No. 2 (April 1994): 225–48; Ross E. Burkhardt and Michael S. Lewis-Beck, "Comparative Democracy: The Economic Development Thesis," *American Political Science Review,* Vol. 88, No. 4 (December 1994): 903–10; Deane E. Neubaur, "Some Conditions of Democracy," *American Political Science Review,* Vol. 61, No. 4 (December 1967): 1002–9; John B. Londregen and Keith T. Poole, "Does Income Promote Democ-

racy?" *World Politics,* Vol. 49, No. 1 (October 1996): 2; and Larry Diamond, "Economic Development and Democracy Reconsidered," *American Behavioral Scientist,* Vol. 35, Nos. 4–5 (March–June 1992): 450.

72. Mark J. Gasiorowski, "Democracy and Macroeconomic Development in Underdeveloped Countries," *Comparative Political Studies,* Vol. 33, No. 3 (April 2000): 319–50.

73. James M. Buchanan, "Rent Seeking and Profit Seeking," in Buchanan, Tollison, and Tullock, 3–15; and Robert D. Tollison, "Rent Seeking: A Survey," *Kyklos,* Vol. 35, No. 4 (November 1982): 575–602.

74. Mancur Olson, "A Theory of Incentives Facing Political Organizations: Neocorporatism and the Hegemonic State," *International Political Science Review,* Vol. 7, No. 2 (April 1986): 165–89, and Tollison, 590.

75. This is a classic argument. See Alexis de Tocqueville, *Democracy in America,* Vol. 1 (New York: Vintage, 1945), 243. See also Reiter and Stam, "Democracy and War Initiation," 378, and Reiter and Stam, *Democracies at War,* 117–29.

76. See Jacek Kugler and William Domke, "Comparing the Strength of Nations," *Comparative Political Studies,* Vol. 19, No. 1 (April 1986): 39, 50, 66. See also Adam Przeworski and Fernando Limongi, "Political Regimes and Economic Growth," *Journal of Economic Perspectives,* Vol. 7, No. 3 (Summer 1993): 51–69; Erich Weede, "The Impact of Democracy on Economic Growth: Some Evidence from Cross-National Analysis," *Kyklos,* Vol. 36, No. 1 (February 1983): 35; and José Antonio Cheibub, "Political Regimes and the Extractive Capacity of Government: Taxation in Democracies and Dictatorships," *World Politics,* Vol. 50, No. 1 (April 1998): 372–73.

77. Randolph M. Siverson and Juliann Emmons, "Birds of a Feather: Democratic Political Systems and Alliance Choices in the Twentieth Century," *Journal of Conflict Resolution,* Vol. 35, No. 2 (June 1991): 285–300. The classic statement of the normative argument is Immanuel Kant, "Perpetual Peace," in Ted Humphrey, ed., *Perpetual Peace and Other Essays on Politics, History and Morals* (Indianapolis: Hackett, 1983), 107–45. More recent work combines normative and institutional arguments. See, for example, Kurt Taylor Gaubatz, "Democratic States and Commitment in International Relations," *International Organization,* Vol. 50, No. 1 (Winter 1996): 110–11.

78. On the greater durability of democratic alliances, see William Reed, "Alliance Duration and Democracy: An Extension and Validation of 'Democratic States and Commitment in International Relations,' " *American Journal of Political Science,* Vol. 41, No. 3 (July 1997): 1072–78; and D. Scott Bennett, "Testing Alternative Models of Alliance Duration, 1816–1984," *American Journal of Political Science,* Vol. 41, No. 3 (July 1997): 846–78.

79. Lake, "Powerful Pacifists," 24, and Anjin Choi, "Cooperation for Victory: Democracy, International Partnerships, and State War Performance, 1816–1992" (unpublished manuscript, John M. Olin Institute for Strategic Studies, Harvard University, April 2002).

80. For the institutional argument that because democracies have large audience costs (e.g., leaders cannot change policies because the public is wedded to them), their commitments (or threats) are more credible, see James Fearon, "Domestic Political Audiences and Escalation of International Disputes," *American Political Science Review,* Vol. 88, No. 3 (September 1994): 577–92; and Joe Eyerman and Robert A. Hart Jr., "An Empirical Test of the Audience Costs Proposition," *Journal of Conflict Resolution,* Vol. 40, No. 4 (December 1996): 597–616.

81. Michael W. Simon and Erik Gartzke, "Political System Similarity and the Choice of Allies," *Journal of Conflict Resolution*, Vol. 40, No. 4 (December 1996): 617–35; and Brian Lai and Dan Reiter, "Democracy, Political Similarity, and International Alliances, 1816–1992," *Journal of Conflict Resolution*, Vol. 44, No. 2 (April 2000): 203–28.

82. Siverson and Emmons, 300.

83. This observation about the time boundedness of the democratic "birds of a feather" phenomenon is similar to the finding that the so-called democratic peace is also a recent development. On this, see Henry S. Farber and Joanne Gowa, "Polities and Peace," in Michael Brown, Sean Lynn-Jones, and Steven Miller, *Debating the Democratic Peace* (Cambridge, MA: MIT, 1996), 239–62.

84. Compare Reiter and Stam, *Democracies at War*, 111–13, with Choi, 32.

85. Reiter and Stam, "Democracy and War Initiation," 378.

86. Simon and Gartzke, 617–35.

87. Mancur Olson Jr. and Richard Zeckhauser, "An Economic Theory of Alliances," in Julian R. Friedman, Christopher Bladen, and Steven Rosen, comp., *Alliance in International Politics* (Boston: Allyn and Bacon, 1970), 186.

88. Eyerman and Hart, 597–616. But see Stephen M. Walt, "Rigor or Rigor Mortis? Rational Choice and Security Studies," *International Security*, Vol. 23, No. 4 (Spring 1999): 33–35, for a discussion of the limits of this empirical support. For suggestions of other logical problems with the audience costs argument, see Schultz, "Do Democratic Institutions Constrain or Inform?" 237, n. 11.

89. This point is made by Walt, "Rigor or Rigor Mortis," 33–35.

90. Ole R. Holsti, "Public Opinion and Foreign Policy: Challenges to the Almond-Lippmann Consensus, Mershon Series: Research Programs and Debates," *International Studies Quarterly*, Vol. 36, No. 4 (December 1992): 447; and John Mueller, *War, Presidents, and Public Opinion* (Lanham, MD: University Press of America, 1985), 2.

91. Charles D. Tarlton, "The Styles of American International Thought," *World Politics*, Vol. 17, No. 4 (July 1965): 584–614. This trend has become even more pronounced since the end of the Cold War. The Chicago Council on Foreign Relations' most recent survey of public opinion finds that foreign policy is not even a top-ten issue for the American public. See John E. Reilly, ed., *American Public Opinion and U.S. Foreign Policy, 1999* (Chicago: CCFR, 1999), 7, fig. I-2, which finds that the public's concern about international problems is the lowest ever. See also John Mueller, "Eleven Propositions about American Foreign Policy and Public Opinion in an Era Free of Compelling Threats" (unpublished manuscript, Department of Political Science, Ohio State University, April 19, 2001).

92. Gaubatz, "Democratic States and Commitment in International Relations," 137.

93. Russett's reasoning follows Condorcet's jury theorem discussed in chapter 1. Bruce M. Russett, *Controlling the Sword: The Democratic Governance of National Security* (Cambridge, MA.: Harvard University Press, 1990), 106, 150.

94. Stephen Van Evera, "Primed for Peace: Europe after the Cold War," *International Security*, Vol. 15, No. 3 (Winter 1990–91): 27; and Jack Snyder, *Myths of Empire: Domestic Politics and International Ambition* (Ithaca: Cornell University Press, 1991), 18–19; and Reiter and Stam, *Democracies at War*, 23–24, 146, and 160.

95. Kurt Taylor Gaubatz, "Intervention and Intransitivity: Public Opinion, Social Choice, and the Use of Military Force Abroad," *World Politics,* Vol. 47, No. 4 (July 1995): 538. Kenneth Arrow originally laid out his "paradox of democracy" argument in *Social Choice and Individual Values* (New York: Wiley, 1951).

96. For cautionary notes from an early proponent of the "marketplace of ideas," see Stephen Van Evera, "Why States Believe Foolish Ideas: Non-Self-Evaluation by States and Societies" (unpublished manuscript, MIT, January 10, 2002), 11, n. 21.

97. Friedberg, *In the Shadow of the Garrison State,* and Aaron Friedberg, "Why Didn't the United States Become a Garrison State?" *International Security,* Vol. 16, No. 4 (Spring 1992): 109–42.

98. Friedberg, *In the Shadow of the Garrison State,* 30–31.

99. Karen A. Rasler and William R. Thompson, *War and State-Making: The Shaping of Global Powers* (Boston: Unwin and Hyman, 1989); and Bruce D. Porter, *War and the Rise of the State: The Military Foundations of Modern Politics* (New York: Free Press, 1994).

100. Overy, *Why the Allies Won,* 206, and Alan S. Milward, *War, Economy, and Society: 1939–1945* (Berkeley: University of California Press, 1977), 99–131.

101. Donna J. Nincic and Miroslav Nincic, "Commitment to Military Intervention: The Democratic Government as Economic Investor," *Journal of Peace Research,* Vol. 32, No. 4 (July 1995): 413–26.

102. See the discussion of resurgent Russian nationalism during World War II in Overy, *Why the Allies Won,* 290–93.

103. Reiter and Stam, "Democracy and Battlefield Military Effectiveness," 259–77; and Reiter and Stam, *Democracies at War,* 58–74.

104. See Management and Support Directorate, *Military History: A Data Base of Selected Battles, 1600–1973,* Vol. 1, *Main Report* (Bethesda, MD.: USACAA, September 1984), 2|211. See also John J. Mearsheimer, "Assessing the Conventional Balance: The 3:1 Rule and Its Critics," *International Security,* Vol. 13, No. 4 (Spring 1989): 66, n. 29.

105. Robert Helmbold, "Lesson Learned Regarding Battle Data Bases," January 14, 1987, Howard Whitley Archives, box 1, Center for Army Analysis, Ft. Belvoir, Virginia.

106. Discussions with Christopher Lawrence and Richard Anderson of the Dupuy Institute, McLean, Virginia, April 2000.

107. Letter (with attachments) to author from Chris Lawrence, executive director, Dupuy Institute, June 8, 2000.

108. Lawrence telephone conversation, June 19, 2000.

109. Reiter and Stam, *Democracies at War,* 71–72.

110. On the problems of bad data due to "measurement error," see W. H. Williams, "How Bad Can 'Good' Data Really Be?" *American Statistician,* Vol. 32, No. 2 (May 1978): 61–65. See also Gary King, Robert O. Keohane, and Sidney Verba, *Designing Social Inquiry: Scientific Inference in Qualitative Research* (Princeton, NJ: Princeton University Press, 1994), 158–63, concerning how nonsystematic error in the dependent variable reduces efficiency.

111. Risa Brooks, "Making Military Might: Why Do States Fail and Succeed?" *International Security,* Vol. 28, No. 2 (Fall 2003): 181–92.

112. Ido Oren, "The Subjectivity of the Democratic Peace," in Brown, Lynn-Jones, and

Miller, 226. For a thoughtful discussion of the other limitations of the POLITY dataset, see Kristian Gleditsch and Michael D. Ward, "A Reexamination of Democracy and Autocracy in Modern Politics," *Journal of Conflict Resolution,* Vol. 41, No. 3 (June 1997): 361–83.

113. Reiter and Stam, "Democracy and Battlefield Military Effectiveness," 264.

114. Allan R. Millett, Williamson Murray, and Kenneth Watman, "The Effectiveness of Military Organizations," *International Security,* Vol. 11, No. 1 (Summer 1986): 37.

115. John H. Cushman, "Challenge and Response at the Operational and Tactical Levels, 1914–45," in Williamson Murray and Allan R. Millett, eds., *Military Effectiveness,* Vol. 3, *The Second World War* (Boston: Allen and Unwin, 1988), 320–40. Cross-tabulations and χ^2 for POLITY III Democracy scores and Cushman's operational and tactical effectiveness grades for various countries covered in the three-volume study (A = 4, B = 3, C = 2, D = 1, F = 0) show no significant relationship between regime type and effectiveness.

116. Niall Ferguson, *The Pity of War* (New York: Basic Books, 1999), 290–303; and Timothy T. Lupfer, *The Dynamics of Doctrine: The Changes in German Tactical Doctrine during the First World War* (Fort Leavenworth, KS: Combat Studies Institute, U.S. Army Command and General Staff College, 1981).

117. For comparative discussion of the combat power of the German army, see Martin van Creveld, *Fighting Power: German and U.S. Army Performance, 1939–1945* (Westport, CT: Greenwood, 1982).

118. Van Creveld, *The Sword and the Olive,* xvii.

119. John A. Lynn, *The Bayonets of the Republic: Motivation and Tactics in the Army of Revolutionary France, 1791–94* (Boulder, CO: Westview, 1996).

120. Theodore Ropp, *War in the Modern World* (New York: Collier, 1962), 98–142.

121. Peter Paret, "Napoleon and the Revolution in War," in Paret, *Makers of Modern Strategy,* 123–42.

122. Michael Howard, *War in European History* (Oxford: Oxford University Press, 1976), 110–11, argues that democracy and nationalism are intimately related. However, Ropp, 126, 138, reminds us that the Spanish and the Prussian cases during the Napoleonic Wars demonstrate that nationalism and democracy and not necessarily linked.

123. Reiter and Stam, "Democracy and Battlefield Military Effectiveness," 264.

124. See Samuel Huntington, *The Soldier and the State: The Theory and Politics of Civil-Military Relations* (Cambridge, MA: Belknap, 1957), 143–62.

125. For discussion of this in the context of the American case, see Ole Holsti, "A Widening Gap between the U.S. Military and Civilian Society? Some Evidence, 1976–96," *International Security,* Vol. 23, No. 3 (Winter 1998–99): 5–42; and the essays in Peter D. Feaver and Richard H. Kohn, eds., *Soldiers and Civilians: The Civil-Military Gap and American National Security* (Cambridge, MA: MIT Press, 2001).

126. Hanson, *Carnage and Culture,* 446.

127. Dupuy and Dupuy, 946.

128. Lake also considers this an example of two democracies fighting each other and excludes it on those grounds. The most recent version of the POLITY III dataset does not count Spain as a democracy, nor does Michael Doyle, "Liberalism and World Politics," *American Political Science Review,* Vol. 80, No. 4 (December 1986): 1164, code Spain as Liberal. This is one example of inconsistency in coding of democracies.

129. Dupuy and Dupuy, 1098–99.

130. Ido Oren, "The Subjectivity of the Democratic Peace: Changing U.S. Perceptions of Imperial Germany," *International Security*, Vol. 20, No. 2 (Fall 1995): 147–84; and Ferguson, *The Pity of War*, 29, table 1, which shows that Germany was the second most highly enfranchised state in Europe in 1900.

131. Michael C. Desch, *When the Third World Matters: Latin American and U.S. Grand Strategy* (Baltimore: Johns Hopkins University Press, 1993), 39–44.

132. Dupuy and Dupuy, 1405.

133. This included satellite support and access to bases. See the Sunday Times Insight Team, *The Falklands War: The Full Story* (London: Sphere's Books, 1982), 137.

CHAPTER 3: DEMOCRACY AND THE RUSSO-POLISH WAR

1. Norman Davies, *White Eagle, Red Star: The Polish-Soviet War, 1919–20* (New York: St. Martins, 1972), 236; and Norman Davies, "The Genesis of the Polish-Soviet War, 1919-20," *European Studies Review*, Vol. 5, No. 1 (January 1975): 31.

2. Quoted in Thomas C. Fiddick, *Russia's Retreat from Poland, 1920: From Permanent Revolution to Peaceful Coexistence* (New York: St. Martin's Press, 1990), 9.

3. Richard M. Watt, *Bitter Glory: Poland and Its Fate, 1918–1939* (New York: Hippocrene Books, 1982), 93; and Maxime Weygand, "The Red Army in the Polish War," in B. H. Liddell Hart, *The Red Army* (Gloucester, MA: Peter Smith, 1968), 45.

4. Warren Lerner, "Poland in 1920: A Case Study in Foreign-Policy Decision Making under Lenin," *South Atlantic Quarterly*, Vol. 72 (1973): 408.

5. Richard C. Lukas, "The Seizure of Vilna, October 1920," *Historian*, Vol. 23, No. 2 (February 1961): 234–46.

6. Piotr S. Wandycz, "The Treaty of Riga: Its Significance for Interwar Polish Foreign Policy," *Polish Review*, Vol. 14, No. (Autumn 1969): 31–36; and Stanisław Dabrowski, "The Peace Treaty of Riga," *Polish Review*, Vol. 5, No. 1 (Winter 1960): 3–34.

7. M. B. Biskupski, "Piłsudski, Poland, and the War with Russia, 1919–1920," *Polish Heritage*, Vol. 35 (Winter 1984): 5–6.

8. Zygmunt J. Gasiorowski, "Joseph Piłsudski in the Light of British Reports," *Slavonic and East European Review*, Vol. 50, No. 121 (October 1972): 566.

9. Watt, 60–61.

10. Watt, 81.

11. Watt, 86–87. Also see M. B. Biskupski, "The Origins of the Paderewski Government in 1919: A Reconsideration in Light of New Evidence," *Polish Review*, Vol. 33, No. 2 (1988): 157–66.

12. Watt, 125, and Michael Palij, *The Ukrainian-Polish Defensive Alliance, 1919–1921–1921: An Aspect of the Ukrainian Revolution* (Edmonton: Canadian Institute of Ukrainian Studies Press, 1995), 118.

13. Watt, 189.

14. Norman Davies, *God's Playground: A History of Poland,* Vol. 2 (New York: Columbia University Press, 1982), 421.

15. Quoted in Watt, 99.

16. Watt, 105. Also cf. Serge Michiel Shewchuk, "The Russo-Polish War of 1920" (Ph.D.

diss., University of Maryland, 1966), 146; Adam Zamoyski, *The Battle for the Marchlands* (New York: Columbia University Press, 1981), 6; and Viscount D'Abernon, *The Eighteenth Decisive Battle of the World* (London: Hodder and Stoughton, 1931), 39.

17. Jozef Piłsudski, *Year 1920 and Its Climax Battle of Warsaw during the Polish-Soviet War, 1919–20* (London: Piłsudski Institute, 1972), 30–31, and Palij, 105.

18. Gasiorowski, "Joseph Piłsudski in the Light of British Reports," 559; and Norman Davies, "The Red Army's Only Defeat," *Kosciuszko Foundation Monthly Newsletter,* Vol. 29 (December 1974): 4.

19. Robert Szymczak, "Bolshevik Wave Breaks at Warsaw," *Military History,* Vol. 11, No. 6 (1995): 58–59.

20. John Erickson, *The Soviet High Command* (New York: St. Martin's Press, 1962), 85. Also see Taras Hunczak, "'Operation Winter' and the Struggle for the Baltic," *East European Quarterly,* Vol. 4, No. 1 (March 1970): 40–57.

21. J. F. C. Fuller, *A Military History of the Western World,* Vol. 3, *From the American Civil War to the End of World War II* (New York: Da Capo, 1956), 337–38; and Robert Jackson, *At War with the Bolsheviks: The Allied Intervention into Russia, 1917–20* (London: Tom Stacey, 1972), 228.

22. Zdzisław Musialik, *General Weygand and the Battle of the Vistula, 1920,* trans. Antoni Józef Bohdanowicz (London: Piłsudski Institute, 1987), 15.

23. Titus Komarnicki, *The Re-birth of Polish Republic* (London: William Heinemann, 1957), 583; and Fiddick, *Russia's Retreat from Poland,* 22 and 34.

24. Komarnicki, 724.

25. Komarnicki, 553. Also cf. Michael J. Fibich, "On the Polish-Bolshevik Front in 1919 and 1920," *Field Artillery Journal,* Vol. 13 (1923): 272–73.

26. Quoted in D'Abernon, *Eighteenth,* 14.

27. Palij, 5.

28. Sidney Brooks, "America and Poland, 1915–1925," *American Relief Bulletin Series* 2, No. 44 (April 1925): 25, and Komarnicki, 428 and 433.

29. D'Abernon, *Eighteenth,* 29.

30. Komarnicki, 435, and Zamoyski, 7.

31. Palij, 99.

32. Palij, 81.

33. Brooks, 40, and Komarnicki, 446.

34. Watt, 94; Sanislaw Kutrzeba, "The Struggle for the Frontiers, 1919–1923," in W. F. Reddaway et al., eds. *The Cambridge History of Poland* (Cambridge: Cambridge University Press, 1941), 521; Davies, "The Red Army's Only Defeat," 3; and Norman Davies, "The Missing Revolutionary War: The Polish Campaigns and the Retreat from Revolution in Soviet Russia, 1919–21," *Soviet Studies,* Vol. 27, No. 2 (April 1975): 181.

35. Zamoyski, 2; John P. Posey, "Soviet Propaganda as a Diplomatic Prelude to the Russo-Polish War, 1920," *Southern Quarterly,* Vol. 7, No. 2 (January 1969): 141; Mariusz Mazurek, "Great Britain, the United States and the Polish Soviet Peace Treaty of Riga, 1920–21," *Niepodleglosc,* Vol. 21 (1988): 55; Warren Lerner, "Attempting a Revolution from Without: Poland in 1920," *Studies on the Soviet Union,* Vol. 11, No. 4 (1971): 96; and M. K. Dziewanowski, "Polish-Soviet

War of 1919–21," in Joseph L. Wieczynski, ed., *The Modern Encyclopedia of Russian and Soviet History*, Vol. 28 (Gulf Breeze, FL: Academic International Press, 1982), 229.

36. Brooks, 63.

37. Quoted in Brooks, 78.

38. Brooks, 71.

39. Roman Debicki, *Foreign Policy of Poland, 1919–39* (New York: Frederick A. Praeger, 1962), 6. Also see M. B. Biskupski, "War and Diplomacy of Polish Independence, 1914–18," *Polish Review*, Vol. 35, No. 1 (1990): 5–17.

40. Piłsudski, 4.

41. Watt, 93; Norman Davies, "August 1920," *European Studies Review*, Vol. 3, No. 3 (July 1973): 271; and Norman Davies, "Lloyd George and Poland, 1919–20," *Journal of Contemporary History*, Vol. 6, No. 3 (1971): 139–40.

42. Palij, 89; Józef Garlinski, "The Polish-Ukrainian Agreement, 1920," in Paul C. Latawski, ed., *The Reconstruction of Poland, 1914–23* (New York: St. Martin's Press, 1992), 62; Piotr S. Wandycz, "Polish Federalism, 1919–20, and Its Historical Antecedents," *East European Quarterly*, Vol. 4, No. 1 (1970): 38; Davies, *God's Playground*, 401; J. F. C. Fuller, *Decisive Battles of the Western World*, Vol. 3 (London: Eyre & Spottiswoode, 1954–56), 248; and Davies, "The Genesis of the Polish-Soviet War," 53.

43. General Staff, German Army, *The Polish-Soviet Russian War, 1918–1920*, Vol. 1 (Washington, DC: U.S. Military History Institute, 1955), 45.

44. Shewchuk, 215; Komarnicki, 365; and Debicki, 32.

45. Shewchuk, 301.

46. Quoted in Watt, 107.

47. John James Flynn, "British Diplomacy and the Polish-Soviet War of 1920" (M.A. thesis, University of Virginia, 1983), 1; Kutrzeba, 517; and Davies, "Lloyd George and Poland," 133.

48. Davies, "Lloyd George and Poland, 136.

49. Flynn, 20.

50. Mazurek, 64.

51. Quoted in Watt, 63.

52. Shewchuk, 216.

53. Quoted in Shewchuk, 256.

54. Watt, 139.

55. Shewchuk, 275.

56. Komarnicki, 321, and Mazurek, 56–57. Also see Eugene Kyusielewicz, "New Light on the Curzon Line," *Polish Review*, Vol. 1, Nos. 2–3 (Spring–Summer 1956): 82–88.

57. Quoted in Shewchuk, 172.

58. Shewchuk, 29, and H. J. Elcock, "Britain and the Russo-Polish Frontier, 1919–1921," *Historical Journal*, Vol. 12, No. 1 (1969): 137–39.

59. Quoted in Flynn, 41.

60. Elcock, 145.

61. Posey, 152, and L. F. MacFarlane, "Hands Off Russia: British Labour and the Russo-Polish War, 1920," *Past and Present*, Vol. 38 (December 1967): 126–52.

62. Davies, "Lloyd George and Poland," 150.

63. Davies, "Lloyd George and Poland," 154.

64. Flynn, 42.

65. Stephen White, "Labor's Council of Action, 1920," *Journal of Contemporary History*, Vol. 9 (1974): 100.

66. Quoted in Shewchuk, 230. Also cf. Komarnicki, 528–30; Zamoyski, 49–50; D'Abernon, *Eighteenth*, 29; Davies, *God's Playground*, 393; and Davies, "Lloyd George and Poland," 138.

67. Elcock, 143.

68. Watt, 65; Shewchuk, 25; Komarnicki, 288 and 400; M. K. Dziewanowski, "Piłsudski's Federal Policy, 1919–1921," *Journal of Central European Affairs*, Vol. 10, No. 2 (July 1950): 117; and Michael Jabara Carley, "The Politics of Anti-Bolshevim: The French Government and the Russo-Polish War, December 1919 to May 1920," *Historical Journal*, Vol. 19, No. 1 (1976): 186.

69. Quoted in Komarnicki, 506.

70. Komarnicki, 409.

71. Shewchuk, 175.

72. Quoted in Fuller, *A Military History*, 348.

73. Debicki, 6.

74. Watt, 64, and Shewchuk, 25.

75. Watt, 55.

76. Bogusław Winid, "Polish Envoys in the United States of America, 1919–1929," *American Studies*, Vol. 9 (1990): 10.

77. Winid, "Polish Envoys in the United States of America," 13–14.

78. Zygmuynt J. Gasiorowski, "Joseph Piłsudski in the Light of American Reports, 1919–1922," *Slavonic and East European Review*, Vol. 49, No. 116 (July 1971): 425.

79. Shewchuk, 28.

80. Shewchuk, 253.

81. M. B. Biskupski, "Poland in American Foreign Policy, 1918–1945: 'Sentimental' or 'Strategic' Friendship—A Review Article," *Poland American Studies*, Vol. 38, No. 2 (1981): 6.

82. Komarnicki, 424; M. B. Biskupski, "Recreating Central Europe: The United States 'Inquiry' into the Future of Poland in 1918," *International History Review*, Vol. 12, No. 2 (May 1990): 275; and Boguslaw W. Winid, "After the Colby Note: The Wilson Administration and the Polish-Bolshevik War," *Presidential Studies Quarterly*, Vol. 26, No. 4 (Fall 1996): 1165.

83. Brooks, ii.

84. Biskupski, "Poland in American Foreign Policy," 14.

85. M. B. Biskupski, "Paderewski, Polish Politics, and the Battle of Warsaw, 1920," *Slavic Review*, Vol. 46, Nos. 3–4 (Fall–Winter 1987): 510.

86. Biskupski, "Recreating Central Europe," 257, 276, and 278; and Mieczysław Biskupski, "The Wilsonian View of Poland: Idealsim and Geopolitical Traditionalism," in John S. Micgiel, ed., *Wilsonian East-Central Europe* (New York: Piłsudski Institute, 1995), 129.

87. Davies, "August 1920," 276.

88. Fuller, *A Military History*, 348.

89. Musialik, 17–18.

90. Musialik, 19, and General Staff, 161.

91. Piłsudski, 206. Also see Shewchuk, 12, and Brooks, 282.

92. Quoted in Komarnicki, 445.

93. Piotr S. Wandycz, "French Diplomats in Poland, 1919–26," *Journal of Central European Affairs,* Vol. 23, No. 4 (January 1964): 99.

94. Piłsudski, 250.

95. Shewchuk, 235–36.

96. D'Abernon, *Eighteenth,* 47, 122–23. Also cf. Viscount d'Abernon, *Versailles to Rapallo: The Diary of an Ambassador* (Garden City, NY: Doubleday, Doran, 1929), 49–52.

97. Brooks, 45.

98. For a biography of Weygand, see Phillip Charles Farwell Bankwitz, *Maxime Weygand and Civil-Military Relations in Modern France* (Cambridge, MA: Harvard University Press, 1967).

99. Davies, "Lloyd George and Poland," 546.

100. Musialik, 47.

101. Shewchuk, 233; Komarnicki, 702; and Zamoyski, 124. On the Inter-Allied Military Mission generally, see F. Russell Bryant, "Lord D'Abernon, the Anglo-French Mission, and the Battle of Warsaw, 1920," *Jahrbücher für Geschichte Osteuropas,* Vol. 38, No. 4 (1990): 526–47.

102. Quoted in Watt, 150. Also cf. quotes in Komarnicki, 699.

103. D'Abernon, *Eighteenth,* 81.

104. Musialik, 24–25.

105. Dziewanowski, "Piłsudski's Federal Policy," 282.

106. Shewchuk, 265–66. Also see Julius Kaden-Bandrowski, *The Great Battle on the Vistula,* trans. Harriet E. Kennedy (London: Sampson Low, Marston, 1921).

107. D'Abernon, *Eighteenth,* 61–62.

108. Davies, *White Eagle,* 245. Also cf. Robert Jackson, *At War with the Bolsheviks: The Allied Intervention into Russia, 1917–20* (London: Tom Stacey, 1972), 233; and Komarnicki, 689.

109. Musialik, 94, and Piotr S. Wandycz, "General Weygand and the Battle of Warsaw of 1920," *Journal of Central European Affairs,* Vol. 19, No. 4 (1959–60): 363–64.

110. Watt, 67–68.

111. Brooks, 54.

112. Fiddick, *Russia's Retreat from Poland,* 254.

113. Fiddick, *Russia's Retreat from Poland,* 24, and Flynn, 49.

114. Shewchuk, 334–35; Palij, 170; and Konstantin Symmons-Symonolewicz, "Polish Political Thought and the Problem of the Eastern Borderlands of Poland (1918–1939)," *Polish Review,* Vol. 4, No. 2 (Winter–Spring 1959): 69–70.

115. Garlinski, 68.

116. Piłsudski, 172–73.

117. Shewchuk, 189.

118. General Staff, 53.

119. Piłsudski, 34, and Kutrzeba, 526.

120. Davies, *White Eagle,* 152.

121. On the Soviet view of the war, see James M. McCann, "Beyond the Bug: Soviet Historiography of the Soviet Polish War of 1920," *Soviet Studies,* Vol. 36, No. 4 (October 1984): 475–93.

122. Mikhail Tukhachevsky, "The March beyond the Vistula," in Piłsudski, 223–63.

123. Tukhachevsky, 226.

124. Zamoyski, 32–33. Also cf. Erickson, 101, and Elbart E. Farman Jr., "The Polish-Bolshevik Cavalry Campaigns of 1920," *Cavalry Journal,* Vol. 30, No. 124 (July 1921): 223–39.

125. John J. Mearsheimer, "Assessing the Conventional Balance: The 3:1 Rule and Its Critics," *International Security,* Vol. 13, No. 4 (Spring 1989): 54–89.

126. Shewchuk, 348, table 1. Also cf. Garlinski, 64.

127. Piłsudski, 223.

128. Zamoyski, 113–16.

129. Watt, 143; Piłsudski, 251; and Palij, 126–27. Shewchuk, 350–51, table 3, says the ratio in front of Warsaw was 1.3:1 in favor of the Poles; and Marian Kukiel, "The Polish-Soviet Campaign of 1920," *Slavonic Review,* Vol. 8 (June 1929): 62.

130. Zamoyski, 113 and 191.

131. Watt, 128; Shewchuk, 279; Palij, 126 and 132; Musialik, 30; and Norman Davies, "The Soviet Command and the Battle of Warsaw," *Soviet Studies,* Vol. 23, No. 4 (April 1972): 575–76.

132. Watt, 143, and Weygand, 51.

133. Davies, *White Eagle,* 135–36, and Shewchuk, 168.

134. Zamoyski, 50.

135. Weygand, 48–49, and Norman Davies, "The Missing Revolutionary War: The Polish Campaigns and the Retreat from Revolution in Soviet Russia, 1919–21," *Soviet Studies,* Vol. 27, No. 2 (April 1975): 178–95.

136. Piłsudski, 137; Fiddick, *Russia's Retreat from Poland,* 61, 63, 125; and Palij, 114.

137. Shewchuk, 201.

138. Shewchuk, 207, and Lerner, "Attempting a Revolution from Without," 98.

139. Quoted in Fiddick, *Russia's Retreat from Poland,* 227.

140. Isaac Deutscher, *The Prophet Armed,* Vol. 1, *Trotsky, 1879–1921* (New York: Vintage, 1965), 464; Shewchuk, 206; Lerner, "Poland in 1920," 411; and Robert Himmer, "Soviet Policy toward Germany during the Russo-Polish War, 1920," *Slavic Review,* Vol. 35, No. 4 (December 1976): 671.

141. Quoted in Fiddick, *Russia's Retreat From Poland,* 52. Also cf. 57.

142. Quoted in Shewchuk, 293.

143. Fibich, 273.

144. Watt, 26–28, and Palij, 30.

145. Quoted in Watt, 61.

146. Symmons-Symonolewicz, 68.

147. Shewchuk, 288; Zamoyski, 85; Fibich, 276 and 440; Davies, "The Soviet Command," 576; Davies, *God's Playground,* 401; and Weygand, 51.

148. Shewchuk, 226; Kukiel, 57.

149. Watt, 92.

150. Weygand, 51.

151. Watt, 144. For slightly different figures, see Fiddick, *Russia's Retreat from Poland,* 81.

152. General Staff, 163.

153. General Staff, 161, and Stephen Blank, "Soviet Nationality Policy and Soviet Foreign Policy: The Polish Case, 1917–1921," *International History Review,* Vol. 7, No. 1 (February 1985): 119.

154. Fiddick, *Russia's Retreat from Poland,* 15, 205.

155. Fiddick, *Russia's Retreat from Poland,* 264.

156. Quoted in Fiddick, *Russia's Retreat from Poland,* 229.

157. Quoted in Fiddick, *Russia's Retreat from Poland,* 227.

158. Quoted in Piotr S. Wandycz, "Secret Soviet-Polish Peace Talks in 1919," *Slavic Review,* Vol. 24, No. 3 (September 1965): 425.

159. Erickson, 102–03 and 107.

160. Fiddick, *Russia's Retreat from Poland,* 141.

161. Erickson, 96–97.

162. Fiddick, *Russia's Retreat from Poland,* 39.

163. Quoted in Fiddick, *Russia's Retreat from Poland,* 239.

164. Deutscher, 468; Fiddick, *Russia's Retreat from Poland,* 20, 30, 32, 84; and Thomas Fiddick, "The 'Miracle of the Vistula:' Soviet Policy versus Red Army Strategy," *Journal of Modern History,* Vol. 45, No. 4 (December 1973): 626.

165. Fiddick, *Russia's Retreat from Poland,* 21 and 138.

166. Shewchuk, 195 and 284–85, and Fiddick, *Russia's Retreat from Poland,* 28.

167. Fiddick, *Russia's Retreat from Poland,* 212.

168. Shewchuk, 282.

169. Fiddick, *Russia's Retreat from Poland,* 216–17; Shewchuk, 287. For a colorful account of life with Budenny's Fourth Cavalry Army, see Isaac Babel's "Red Cavalry Stories," in *Collected Stories,* trans. David McDuff (London: Penguin, 1994); and Isaac Babel, *1920 Diary,* trans. H. T. Willets (New Haven: Yale University Press, 1990).

170. Shewchuk, 83.

171. Fiddick, *Russia's Retreat from Poland,* 19.

172. Shewchuk, 262.

173. Fiddick, *Russia's Retreat from Poland,* 140, and Shewchuk, 263–64 and 278.

174. Komarnicki, 685, and Shewchuk, 268.

175. Watt, 143.

176. D'Abernon, *Eighteenth,* 161.

CHAPTER 4: DEMOCRACY AND ISRAEL'S MILITARY EFFECTIVENESS

1. Yigal Allon, *The Making of Israel's Army* (London: Vallentine, Mitchell, 1970), 63.

2. Ruth R. Wisse, "On Ignoring Anti-Semitism," *Commentary,* October 2002, 33.

3. Standard military histories of Israel include Edward Luttwak and Dan Horowitz, *The Israeli Army* (London: Allen Lane, 1975); Trevor N. Dupuy, *Elusive Victory: The Arab-Israeli Wars, 1947–1974* (New York: Harper and Row, 1978); and Chaim Herzog, *The Arab-Israeli Wars: War and Peace in the Middle East from the War of Independence through Lebanon* (New York: Vintage, 1982). Kenneth M. Pollack, *Arabs at War: Military Effectiveness, 1948–1991* (Lincoln: University of Nebraska Press, 2002), 2 and 4, argues that numbers and other traditional indices of power were irrelevant in the Israeli cases.

Israel's "new historians" provide ample evidence for challenging much of the received wisdom about the Jewish state's strategic situation in the years since 1948, and this chapter relies quite heavily upon them. For a good general discussion about how their work has changed our understanding of the Arab-Israeli conflict, see Jonathan B. Isacoff, "Writing the

Arab-Israeli Conflict: Historical Bias and the Use of History in Political Science," *Perspectives on Politics,* Vol. 3, No. 1 (March 2005): 71–88.

4. Geoffrey Wheatcroft, *The Controversy of Zion: Jewish Nationalism, the Jewish State, and the Unresolved Jewish Dilemma* (Reading, MA: Addison-Wesley, 1996), 308. For an argument that shared values and strategic interest are compatible, see "Remarks by the President to 1996 American-Israel Public Affairs Committee Policy Conference" (Washington Hilton Hotel, April 28, 1996).

5. Miriam Fendius Elman, "Israel's Invasion of Lebanon, 1982: Regime Change and War Decisions," in Fendius Elman, ed., *Paths to Peace: Is Democracy the Answer?* (Cambridge, MA: MIT Press, 1997), 329.

6. Howard M. Sacher, *A History of Israel: From the Rise of Zionism to Our Time,* 2nd ed. (New York: Knopf, 1996), 359; and Alan Dowty, "Is Israel Democratic? Substance and Semantics in the 'Ethnic Democracy' Debate," *Israel Studies,* Vol. 4, No. 2 (1999): 4.

7. Ira Sharkansky, "Israeli Democracy and Jewish History," *Journal of Church and State,* Vol. 37, No. 2 (Spring 1995): 1–17.

8. Dan Horowitz and Moshe Lissak, *Origins of the Israel Polity: Palestine under the Mandate* (Chicago: University of Chicago Press, 1978), 148.

9. Gerald M. Steinberg, "Interpretation of Jewish Tradition on Democracy, Land, and Peace," *Journal of Church and State,* Vol. 43, No. 1 (Winter 2001): 2; and Michael Bar-Zohar, *Ben-Gurion: The Armed Prophet,* trans. Len Ortsen (Englewood Cliffs, NJ: Prentice-Hall, 1967), 36 and 161.

10. Quoted in Golda Meir, *My Life* (New York: G. P. Putnam's Sons, 1975), 154.

11. Tom Segev, *1949: The First Israelis* (New York: Free Press, 1986), 285; and Peter Medding, *The Founding of Israel Democracy, 1948–1967* (New York: Oxford University Press, 1990), 181–82.

12. Sammy Smooha, "Ethnic Democracy: Israel as an Archetype," *Israel Studies,* Vol. 2, No. 2 (1997): 199–200.

13. Emanuele Ottolenghi, "Religion and Democracy in Israel," *Political Quarterly,* Vol. 71, No. 3 (2000): 44; and Nadav Safran, *Israel: Israel's Embattled Ally* (Cambridge, MA: Belknap Press of Harvard University Press, 1981), 207.

14. Ottolenghi, 43; Sharkansky, 17; and Ahmad H. Sa'di, "Israel as Ethnic Democracy: What Are the Implications for the Palestinian Minority?" *Arab Studies Quarterly,* Vol. 22, No. 1 (Winter 2000): 1–12.

15. Simha Flapan, *The Birth of Israel: Myths and Realities* (New York: Pantheon Books, 1987), 11; As'ad Ghanem, Nadim Rouhana, and Oren Yiftachel, "Questioning 'Ethnic Democracy': A Response to Sammy Smooha," *Israel Studies,* Vol. 3, No. 2 (1998): 253–67; and Baylis Thomas, *How Israel Was Won: A Concise History of the Arab-Israeli Conflict* (Lanham, MD: Lexington Books, 1999), 289.

16. Eva Etzioni-Halevy, "The Religious Elite Connection and Some Problems of Israeli Democracy," *Government and Opposition,* Vol. 29, No. 4 (Autumn 1994): 480.

17. Steinberg, 4.

18. Sacher, 1014. This is a continuing concern. See Daniel Ben Simon, "A Joke unto the Nations," *Ha'aretz,* March 12, 2007 (electronic version), http://www.haaretz.com/hasen/spages/835910.html.

19. Medding, 226. Also cf. 108–9; Benny Morris, *Righteous Victims: A History of the Zionist-*

Arab Conflict, 1881–1999 (New York: Knopf, 1999), 662; Dan Horowitz and Moshe Lissak, "Democratic National Security in a Protracted Conflict," *Jerusalem Quarterly,* No. 51 (Summer 1989): 30; Amos Perlmutter, "Israel's Fourth War, October 1973: Political and Military Misperceptions," *Orbis,* Vol. 19, No. 2 (Summer 1975): 435; and Ze'ev Schiff, *A History of the Israeli Army: 1874 to the Present* (New York: Macmillan, 1985), 232.

20. Sacher, 430.

21. Gad Barzilai, "War, Democracy, and Internal Conflict: Israel in a Comparative Perspective," *Comparative Politics,* Vol. 31, No. 3 (April 1999): 318.

22. Quoted in Medding, 123.

23. Avi Shlaim, *The Iron Wall: Israel and the Arab World* (New York: W. W. Norton, 2001), 149, and Sacher, 478.

24. Seymour M. Hersh, *The Samson Option: Israel's Nuclear Arsenal and American Foreign Policy* (New York: Random House, 1991), 78.

25. Quoted in Michael B. Oren, *Six Days of War: June 1967 and the Making of the Modern Middle East* (New York: Oxford University Press, 2002), 134.

26. Quoted in Oren, *Six Days of War,* 229 and 152.

27. Shlaim, *The Iron Wall,* 397, and Schiff, *A History of the Israeli Army,* 237.

28. Ze'ev Schiff and Ehud Ya'ari, *Israel's Lebanon War* (New York: Simon and Schuster, 1984), 43.

29. Schiff and Ya'ari, 302.

30. Richard Gabriel, *Operation Peace for Galilee: The Israeli-PLO War in Lebanon* (New York: Hill and Wang, 1984), 158.

31. Michael Brecher, *Decisions in Israel's Foreign Policy* (New Haven: Yale University Press, 1975), 544–46.

32. Michael N. Barnett, *Confronting the Costs of War: Military Power, State, and Society in Egypt and Israel* (Princeton, NJ: Princeton University Press), 157, and Safran, 127.

33. Hugh Thomas, *Suez* (New York: Harper and Row, 1966), 16; Avner Yaniv and Robert J. Lieber, "Personal Whim or Strategic Imperative? The Israeli Invasion of Lebanon," *International Security,* Vol. 8, No. 2 (Fall 1983): 140; and Brecher, 65.

34. Oren, *Six Days of War,* 89.

35. Quoted in Martin Gilbert, *Israel: A History* (New York: William Morrow, 1998), 375.

36. On this, see Roland Popp, "Stumbling Decidedly into the Six Day War," *Middle East Journal,* Vol. 60, No. 2 (Spring 2006): 297–98.

37. Schiff and Ya'ari, 34, 55, 57, 127, 163; Schiff, *A History of the Israeli Army,* 239–40; Gilbert, *Israel,* 504; Yaniv and Lieber, 137; and Trevor N. Dupuy and Paul Martell, *Flawed Victory: The Arab-Israeli Conflict and the 1982 War in Lebanon* (Fairfax, VA: HERO Books, 1986), 60, 148.

38. Quoted in Schiff and Ya'ari, 57.

39. Schiff and Ya'ari, 25, 34, 39, 220; Howard Sachar, *A History of Israel: From the Rise of Zionism to Our Time,* 2nd ed. (New York: Alfred A. Knopf, 1996), 900, 913, 916, 920; Dupuy and Martell, 15; and Gabriel, 25.

40. Schiff and Ya'ari, 41.

41. Shlaim, *The Iron Wall,* 183–85; Sacher, *A History of Israel,* 513–14; and Thomas, *How Israel Was Won,* 125.

42. Schiff and Ya'ari, 284; Sachar, *A History of Israel,* 920; and Shlaim, *The Iron Wall,* 419.

43. Wheatcroft, 241.

44. Quoted in Segev, *1949*, 229.

45. Quoted in Gilbert, *Israel*, 346. Also cf. Sacher, *A History of Israel*, 412; Barnett, 159; and Safran, 111–12.

46. Medding, 109.

47. Sacher, *A History of Israel*, 807, and Martin van Creveld, *The Sword and the Olive: A Critical History of the Israeli Defense Force* (New York: Public Affairs, 1998), 252–53.

48. Horowitz and Lissak, "Democratic National Security," 4.

49. See Kim R. Holmes, Bryan T. Johnson, and Melanie Kirkpatrick, *1997 Index of Economic Freedom* (Washington, DC: Heritage Foundation and the *Wall Street Journal*, 1997), xxx, 242–44, and 255–57.

50. Brecher, 326.

51. Flapan, 236.

52. On the use of the Holocaust, see Tom Segev, *The Seventh Million: The Israelis and the Holocaust* (New York: Hill and Wang, 1993), 472; and Shlaim, *The Iron Wall*, 23.

53. Meir, 460.

54. Quoted in Allon, 185.

55. Shlaim, *The Iron Wall*, 17–18 (emphasis added).

56. Moshe Dayan, *Moshe Dayan: Story of My Life* (New York: William Morrow, 1976), 184.

57. Oren, *Six Days of War*, 213 and 217.

58. Anthony H. Cordesman, *The Arab-Israeli Military Balance and the Art of Operations* (Washington, DC: AEI, 1987), 4; and Gabriel, 14.

59. Meir, 446.

60. Sacher, *A History of Israel*, 790–91; Safran, 496–97; and Schiff, *A History of the Israeli Army*, 220.

61. Meir, 414–19.

62. Safran, 571.

63. Yoav Ben-Horin and Barry Posen, "Israel's Strategic Doctrine," *RAND Report 2845-NA* (Santa Monica, CA: RAND, September 1981), 9 and 24.

64. Van Creveld, *The Sword and the Olive*, 252, and Gilbert, *Israel*,165, 225, 326, 367, 407, and 445.

65. Yair Evron, *War and Intervention in Lebanon: The Israeli-Syrian Deterrence Dialog* (Baltimore: Johns Hopkins University Press, 1982), 30. More recently see Stephen J. Glain, "For Some Israelis, U.S. Aid Is a Burden, Some Say Strings Attached to Military Assistance Aren't Worth the Money," *Wall Street Journal*, October 26, 2000, A23.

66. Sacher, *A History of Israel*, 724. Also see John Mearsheimer and Stephen Walt, "Israel and American Foreign Policy," *London Review of Books*, Vol. 28, No. 6 (March 23, 2006), at www.lrb.co.uk/v28/n06/mear01_.html.

67. On this mixed influence of the lobby, see Warren Bass, *Support Any Friend: Kennedy's Middle East and the Making of the U.S.-Israel Alliance* (New York: Oxford University Press, 2003); and Adam Garfinkle, "The Israel Lobby, Part II," *Prospect*, August 29, 2002 (electronic version), http://www.prospect-magazine.co.uk/article_details.php?id=5357.

68. Ahron Bregmand and Jihan El-Tahri, *The Fifty Year's War: Israel and the Arabs* (New York: T.V. Books, 1998), 28 and 38–39.

69. Thomas, *How Israel Was Won,* 37, 64–65, and Flapan, 158.

70. Schiff, *A History of the Israeli Army,* 38.

71. Michael I. Handel, "Israel's Political-Military Doctrine," *Occasional Papers in International Affairs,* No. 30 (Cambridge: CFIA, July 1973), 19.

72. Quoted in Segev, *1949,* 35. Also cf. Bar-Zohar, 28, and Brecher, 330.

73. Gilbert, *Israel,* 273.

74. Quoted in Allon, 188.

75. Flapan, 30, and Moshe Dayan, "Why Israel Strikes Back," in Donald Robinson, ed., *Under Fire: Israel's Twenty Year Struggle for Survival* (New York: W. W. Norton, 1968), 18.

76. Safran, 371.

77. Quoted in Shlaim, *The Iron Wall,* 204.

78. Hersh, 17.

79. Quoted in Hersh, 40. Also see, Avner Cohen, *Israel and the Bomb* (New York: Columbia University Press, 1998), 123; and Efraim Inbar, "Contours of Israel's New Strategic Thinking," *Political Science Quarterly,* Vol. 111, No. 1 (Spring 1996): 45.

80. Quoted in Hersh, 42. Also see Cohen, *Israel and the Bomb,* 174.

81. Quoted in Cohen, *Israel and the Bomb,* 212.

82. Quoted in Oren, *Six Days of War,* 77, and Shlaim, *The Iron Wall,* 240.

83. Dayan, *Moshe Dayan,* 379. Also see 319–20 and 342–43.

84. James M. Ennes Jr., *Assault on the Liberty: The True Story of the Israeli Attack on an American Intelligence Ship* (New York: Random House, 1979) is the primary indictment. See A. Jay Cristol, *The Liberty Incident: The 1967 Israeli Attack on the U.S. Navy Spy Ship* (Washington, DC: Brassey's, 2002), for the case it was an accident.

85. James Bamford, *Body of Secrets: Anatomy of the Ultra-Secret National Security Agency from the Cold War through the Dawn of a New Century* (New York: Doubleday, 2001), 201–4.

86. Peter Novick, *The Holocaust in American Life* (New York: Houghton Mifflin, 1999).

87. Hersh, 127.

88. Cohen, *Israel and the Bomb,* 236 and 240.

89. Dupuy, 408, n. 3.

90. Hersh, 227; Safran, 483; and van Creveld, *The Sword and the Olive,* 252.

91. Quoted in van Creveld, *The Sword and the Olive,* 224.

92. Dayan, *Moshe Dayan,* 543; Safran, 505–9; and Schiff, *A History of the Israeli Army,* 226.

93. Dayan, *Moshe Dayan,* 512–13.

94. Zeev Schiff, "The Green Light," *Foreign Policy,* No. 50 (Spring 1983): 81.

95. Yaniv and Lieber, 136–37.

96. Dupuy and Martell, 142.

97. Hersh, 16.

98. Hersh, 297.

99. On the Pollard case, see Wolf Blitzer, *Territory of Lies: The Exclusive Story of Jonathan Jay Pollard: The American Who Spied on His Country for Israel and How He Was Betrayed* (New York: Harper and Row, 1989).

100. Quoted in Schiff, *A History of the Israeli Army,* 87.

101. Quoted in Brecher, 263–64.

102. Shlaim, *The Iron Wall*, 162–64; Sacher, *A History of Israel*, 484; and Hugh Thomas, *Suez* (New York: Harper and Row, 1966), 20.

103. Hersh, 30.

104. Shlaim, *The Iron Wall*, 164.

105. Quoted in Oren, *Six Days of War*, 100.

106. Sacher, *A History of Israel*, 878–79.

107. Sacher, *A History of Israel*, 98–100; Morris, 73; Safran, 25; and Thomas, *How Israel Was Won*, 6.

108. Moshe Brilliant, "Israel's Policy of Reprisals," *Harpers*, Vol. 210 (March 1955): 72.

109. For an even stranger twist, see Stuart A. Cohen, "Still Stranger Aspect of Suez: British Operational Plans to attack Israel, 1955–1956," *International History Review*, Vol. 10, No. 2 (May 1988): 261–81.

110. Quoted in Brecher, 271.

111. Segev, *The Seventh Million*, 212.

112. Quoted in Brecher, 104.

113. Sacher, *A History of Israel*, 426.

114. Quoted in Gilbert, *Israel*, 150.

115. Meir, 231.

116. Flapan, 159.

117. Segev, *1949*, 101 and 173.

118. Avi Kober, "Great Power Involvement and Israeli Battlefield Success in the Arab-Israeli Wars, 1948–1982," *Journal of Cold War Studies*, Vol. 8, No. 1 (Winter 2006): 35–36.

119. Uri Bialer, "The Czech-Israeli Arms Deal Revisited," *Journal of Strategic Studies*, Vol. 8, No. 2 (June 1985): 308.

120. Meir, 230–31, and Sacher, *A History of Israel*, 329.

121. Quoted in Bregmand and El-Tahri, 43.

122. Quoted in Schiff, *A History of the Israeli Army*, 37.

123. Hersh, 263–83.

124. Flapan, 37 and 136.

125. Pollack, 271.

126. Shlaim, *The Iron Wall*, 30.

127. Dayan, "Why Israel Strikes Back," 121.

128. Eric Hammel, *Six Days in June: How Israel Won the 1967 Arab-Israeli War* (Pacifica, CA: Pacifica Military History, 1992), 21.

129. Thomas, *How Israel Was Won*, and Schiff, *A History of the Israeli Army*, 172.

130. Bregmand and El-Tahri, 142.

131. Quoted in Brecher, 340.

132. Flapan, 166, and Saul Friedlander, "Policy Choices before Israel," in Paul Y. Hammond and Sidney S. Alexander, eds., *Political Dynamics in the Middle East* (New York: American Elsevier, 1972), 116.

133. Van Creveld, *The Sword and the Olive*, 250.

134. Safran, 327.

135. Shlaim, *The Iron Wall*, 108.

136. Flapan, 10.

137. Van Creveld, *The Sword and the Olive*, 247.

138. Brecher, 232–34 and 275, n. 3; and Schiff, *A History of the Israeli Army*, 93.

139. Quoted in Brecher, 273–74.

140. Cohen, *Israel and the Bomb*, 72–73, 145, and 344.

141. Oren, *Six Days of War*, 209–10, and Schiff, *A History of the Israeli Army*, 231.

142. Shlaim, *The Iron Wall*, 55, and Segev, *1949*, 19.

143. Gilbert, *Israel*, 396; Wheatcroft, 312; and Safran, 102.

144. Sacher, *A History of Israel*, 745, and Perlmutter, 441.

145. Bregmand and El-Tahri, 130.

146. Bregmand and El-Tahri, 144, and Avi Shlaim, "Failures in National Intelligence Estimates: The Case of the Yom Kippur War," *World Politics*, Vol. 28, No. 3 (April 1976): 348.

147. Handel, 31; Chaim Herzog, *The Arab-Israeli Wars: War and Peace in the Middle East from the War of Independence through Lebanon*, rev. and updated (New York: Vintage, 1984), 228; and Shlaim, "Failures in National Intelligence Estimates," 348–80.

148. Sacher, *A History of Israel*, 752; Safran, 312–14; Luttwak and Horowitz, 346; Herzog, *The Arab-Israeli Wars*, 254–55; and Chaim Herzog, *The War of Atonement: October 1973* (Boston: Little, Brown, 1975), 31 and 278.

149. Ezer Weizman quoted in Brecher, 466.

150. Herzog, *The War of Atonement: October 1973*, 31 and 278; Herzog, *The Arab-Israeli Wars*, 236–39; Perlmutter, 434–60; "Chief of Military Resigns in Israel; Blamed in Inquiry," *New York Times*, April 3, 1974, 1 and 5; and Pollack, 106–7.

151. Schiff and Ya'ari.

152. Shlaim, *The Iron Wall*, 398.

153. Schiff and Ya'ari, 33, 39, 41, 58, 97, 100, 101, 103, 113, 266–68, 303, 304; Shlaim, *The Iron Wall*, 397; Schiff, *A History of the Israeli Army*, 246; Gabriel, 68; and Dupuy and Martell, 96, 142.

154. Schiff and Ya'ari, 48.

155. Quoted in Flapan, 51–52.

156. Herzog, *The War of Atonement*, 282.

157. Van Creveld, *The Sword and the Olive*, 125, 153, 197, and 241; John Laffin and Mike Chappell, *The Israeli Army in the Middle East Wars, 1948–73*, Men-at-Arms Series (Wellingborough: Osprey, 1982), 4; Handel, 9; Barzilai, 327; and Schiff, *A History of the Israeli Army*, 116.

158. Moshe Dayan, "Israel's Border and Security Problems," *Foreign Affairs*, Vol. 33, No. 1 (January 1955): 252–53.

159. Meir, 233. Also see similar comments by David Ben Gurion and Moshe Dayan in Dayan, *Moshe Dayan*, 92, 396, and 441; and van Creveld, *The Sword and the Olive*, 153.

160. Segev, *The Seventh Million*, 18 and 389; Segev, *1949*, 286; Safran, 63; Inbar, 43; and Friedlander, 116.

161. Segev, *The Seventh Million*, 328.

162. Oren, *Six Days of War*, 18; Wheatcroft, 246; and Safran, 165.

163. Dayan, *Moshe Dayan*, 92.

164. Quoted in Allon, 191.

165. Quoted in Morris, 311.

166. Meir, 359–60, and Safran, 63.

167. Quoted in Brecher, 334.

168. Barzilai, 323, and Jonathan Shimshoni, *Israel and Conventional Deterrence: Border Warfare from 1953 to 1970* (Ithaca: Cornell University Press, 1988), 171 and 186.

169. Quoted in Gilbert *Israel,* 445.

170. Shlaim, *The Iron Wall,* 421; Schiff and Ya'ari, 127; Barzilai, 324; Schiff, *A History of the Israeli Army,* 255–57; Dupuy and Martell, 59–60; Shai Feldman and Heda Rechnitz-Kijner, "Deception, Consensus and War: Israel in Lebanon," *Jaffee Center for Strategic Studies Paper No. 27* (Tel Aviv: JCSS, October 1984), 5 and 44; and Evron, *War and Intervention in Lebanon,* 105.

171. Wheatcroft, 302.

172. Allon, 250. Also cf. Cordesman, 10 and 21.

173. Van Creveld, *The Sword and the Olive,* 197. Also cf. van Creveld, *The Sword and the Olive,* 125–26; Oren, *Six Days of War,* 17; Schiff, "The Green Light," 37–38; and Brecher, 324.

174. Quoted in Schiff, *A History of the Israeli Army,* 153.

175. Luttwak and Horowitz, 70 and 74.

176. Allon, 36–37.

177. Oren, *Six Days of War,* 97.

178. Quoted in Handel, 40.

179. Quoted in Oren, *Six Days of War,* 179. Also cf. Laffin and Chapell, 3, and Morris, 662-63.

180. Quoted in Sacher, *A History of Israel,* 660.

181. Hammel, 133–34.

182. Schiff and Ya'ari, 215–12.

183. William Claiborne, "Israel Studies Lessons of Lebanon War," *Washington Post,* March 31, 1986, 1 and 18; and Yezid Sayigh, "Israel's Military Performance in Lebanon, June 1982," *Journal of Palestine Studies,* Vol. 13, No. 1 (Autumn 1983): 42.

184. Quoted in Feldman and Rechnitz-Kijner, 52.

185. Cordesman, 107.

186. Schiff, *A History of the Israeli Army,* 170–71.

187. Medding, 226; Smooha, 207; Ruth Gavison, "Jewish and Democratic: A Rejoinder to the 'Ethnic Democracy' Debate," *Israel Studies,* Vol. 4, No. 1 (1999): 44; and Peter Preston, "Why Israeli Democracy Passes Litmus Test," *IPI Report* (June–July 1996): 6.

188. See van Creveld, *The Sword and the Olive,* 242-43.

189. Safran, 266.

190. Shimshoni, 123 and 170.

191. Shlaim, *The Iron Wall,* 296–97; van Creveld, *The Sword and the Olive,* 215; and Schiff, *A History of the Israeli Army,* 189; and Pollack, 98.

192. Morris, 437.

193. Shlaim, *The Iron Wall,* 320–21, and Dupuy, 544.

194. Schiff and Ya'ari, 293; Morris, 590; Cordesman, 55–56; and Dupuy and Martell, 154.

195. Schiff, *A History of the Israeli Army,* 250.

196. Schiff, *A History of the Israeli Army,* 259–61; Feldman and Rechnitz-Kijner, 3; and Gabriel, 116–17 and 126.

197. Shlaim, *The Iron Wall,* xxviii–xix. Also cf. Morris, 540.

198. For examples of the conventional wisdom, see Pollack, 3 and 5, and Laffin and Chapell, 7.

199. Quoted in Allon, 3 and 34.

200. On Israel's advantages in military-age manpower and troops at various periods, see van Creveld, *The Sword and the Olive,* 32, and Dupuy, 19, 93, 121, and 231.

201. Shlaim, *The Iron Wall,* 36; Flapan, 197; van Creveld, *The Sword and the Olive,* 82; and Morris, 219.

202. Quoted in Allon, 185.

203. Dupuy, 93; Shlaim, *The Iron Wall,* 35; Morris, 217; Flapan, 10; and Safran, 44–50.

204. Luttwak and Horowitz, 143.

205. Cited in Popp, 303–4.

206. Dupuy, 231.

207. Hammel, 149.

208. Dupuy and Martell, 86–91.

209. Gilbert, *Israel,* 504.

210. Allon, 10–11 and 18; van Creveld, *The Sword and the Olive,* 359.

211. Hammel, 50–51.

212. Van Creveld, *The Sword and the Olive,* 106; Morris, 302; and Cordesman, 13–14.

213. Hammel, 107, and van Creveld, *The Sword and the Olive,* 169. But Luttwak and Horowitz, 54, claim this is a uniquely Israeli mode of military operations.

214. Van Creveld, *The Sword and the Olive,* 112 and 141, and Luttwak and Horowitz, 121.

215. Handel, 18.

216. Van Creveld, *The Sword and the Olive,* 65, 123, and 169; Dupuy, 335; Hammel, 84; Sacher, *A History of Israel,* 477; and Luttwak and Horowitz, 92 and 130.

217. Pollack, 284.

218. Cordesman, 10.

219. Pollack, 547.

220. Quoted in Flapan, 238. Also see Y. Harkabi, "Basic Factors in the Arab Collapse during the Six Day War," *Orbis,* Vol. 11, No. 3 (Fall 1967): 678–79.

221. Norvell De Atkine, "Why Arab Armies Lose Wars," *Middle East Review of International Affairs,* Vol. 4, No. 1 (March 2000): 6, and Hammel, 390 and 423.

222. Yesoshat Harkabi, "Basic Factors in the Arab Collapse during the Six Day War," *Orbis,* Vol. 11, No. 4 (Fall 1967): 680, and Gilbert, *Israel,* 174.

223. Norman G. Finkelstein, *Image and Reality of the Israel-Palestine Conflict* (London: Verso, 2001), 1.

224. Harkabi, "Basic Factors in the Arab Collapse," 680.

225. Morris, 192. Also see Luttwak and Horowitz, 28; Hammel, 8; and Sacher, *A History of Israel,* 164.

226. Flapan, 75, and Schiff, *A History of the Israeli Army,* 173.

227. Quoted in Flapan, 73.

228. Flapan, 126.

229. Flapan, 132.

230. Hammel, 8.

231. Van Creveld, *The Sword and the Olive,* 70. Also see Luttwak and Horowitz, 63; Flapan, 41; Horowitz and Lissak, *Origins of the Israel Polity,* 16; Safran, 108; Schiff, *A History of the Israeli Army,* 117–18; Friedlander, 123; and Dan Horowitz, "Flexibile Responsiveness

and Military Strategy: The Case of the Israeli Army," *Policy Sciences,* Vol. 1, No. 2 (1970): 191–205.

232. Quoted in Segev, *1949,* 38.

233. Luttwak and Horowitz, 170, and Cordesman, 8–9.

234. Schiff, *A History of the Israeli Army,* 41.

235. Luttwak and Horowitz, 283–84.

236. Quoted in Segev, *1949,* 267.

237. Allon, 59.

238. Van Creveld, *The Sword and the Olive,* 232 and 280–81; Morris, 404–5; and Shlomo Aronson, "The Nuclear Dimension of the Arab-Israeli Conflict: The Case of the Yom Kippur War," *Jerusalem Journal of International Relations,* Vol. 7, Nos. 1–2 (1984): 116–29. But for a contrary view, see Yair Evron, "The Relevance and Irrelevance of Nuclear Options in Conventional Wars: The 1973 October War," *Jerusalem Journal of International Relations,* Vol. 7, Nos. 1–2 (1984): 144–45.

239. Gabriel, 92-100.

240. Quoted in Clifford A. Wright, "The Israeli War Machine in Lebanon," *Journal of Palestine Studies,* Vol. 12, No. 2 (Winter 1983): 39.

CHAPTER 5: DEMOCRACY AND BRITAIN'S VICTORY IN THE FALKLANDS WAR

1. Lawrence Freedman, *Britain and the Falklands War* (London: Basil Blackwell, 1988), 48–49. For the definitive history, see Lawrence Freedman, *The Official History of the Falklands Campaign:* Vol. 1, *The Origins of the Falklands War,* and Vol. 2, *War and Diplomacy* (London: Routledge, 2005).

2. Alexander M. Haig Jr., *Caveat: Realism, Reagan, and Foreign Policy* (New York: Macmillan, 1984), 297.

3. Freedman, *Britain and the Falklands War,* 2.

4. Quoted in Haig, 265.

5. Haig, 279. Also cf. "America's Falklands War: A Relationship Sweet and Sour," *Economist,* March 3, 1984, 29.

6. Quoted in House of Commons, *The Falklands Campaign: A Digest of Debates in the House of Commons, 2 April to June 1982* (London: HMSO, 1982), 177. Also cf. Chaim D. Kaufmann, *U.S. Mediation in the Falklands/Malvinas Crisis: Shuttle Diplomacy in the 1980s* (Washington, DC: Pew Case Studies Center/Georgetown University, 1988), 16.

7. House of Commons, 86.

8. David Gompert, "Diplomacy and the Haig Mission," in Alberto R. Coll and Anthony C. Arend, eds., *The Falklands War: Lessons for Strategy, Diplomacy, and International Law* (Boston: G. Allen & Unwin, 1985), 114.

9. Jeremy Moore and John Woodward, "The Falklands Experience," *Journal of the Royal United Services Institute,* Vol. 128, No. 1 (March 1983): 31.

10. The Secretary of State for Defence, *The Falklands Campaign: The Lessons* (London: HMSO, December 1982), para. 212.

11. Jack Levy and Lily Vakili, "Diversionary Action by Authoritarian Regimes: Argentina

in the Falklands/Malvinas Case," in Manus I. Midlarsky, ed., *The Internationalization of Communal Strife* (New York: Routledge, 1992), 127, 135–36.

12. David Sanders, Hugh Ward, David Marsch, and Tony Fletcher, "Government Popularity and the Falklands War: A Reassessment," *British Journal of Political Science,* Vol. 17, No. 3 (July 1987): 281–313.

13. Rick Atkinson, *Crusade: The Untold Story of the Persian Gulf War* (New York: Houghton Mifflin, 1993), 496–97.

14. World Bank, *World Development Report* (New York: Oxford University Press, 1985), 225.

15. James Gwartney, Robert Lawson, and Walter Block, *Economic Freedom of the World: 1975–1995* (Vancouver, BC: Frasier Institute, 1996), 219.

16. Raymond Gastil, *Freedom in the World: Political Rights and Civil Liberties, 1982* (Westport, CT: Greenwood Press, 1982), 33–34, table 7.

17. Freedman, *Britain and the Falklands War,* 71–72.

18. House of Commons, 10.

19. Freedman, *War and Diplomacy,* 127–29.

20. Freedman, *Britain and the Falklands War,* 42-42.

21. Haig, 266.

22. House of Commons, 14; Lawrence Freedman and Virginia Gamba-Stonehouse, *Signals of War: the Falklands Conflict of 1982* (Princeton, NJ: Princeton University Press, 1991), 86.

23. Haig, 284–85.

24. House of Commons, 59, 81; Geoffrey Edwards, "Europe and the Falkland Islands Crisis, 1982," *Journal of Common Market Studies,* Vol. 12, No. 4 (June 1984): 299.

25. House of Commons, 108.

26. Quoted in Max Hastings and Simon Jenkins, *The Battle for the Falklands* (New York: W. W. Norton, 1983), 109.

27. Philip Windsor, "Diplomatic Dimensions of the Falklands Crisis," *Millennium: Journal of International Studies,* Vol. 12, No. 1 (1983): 91. For some evidence to support this belief, see Carlos Moneta, "The Malvinas Conflict: Analyzing the Argentine Military Regime's Decision-Making Process," in Heraldo Muñoz and Joseph S. Tulchin, eds., *Latin American Nations in World Politics* (Boulder, CO: Westview Press, 1984), 127; Gerald W. Hopple, "Intelligence and Warning: Implications and Lessons of the Falklands Islands War," *World Politics,* Vol. 36, No. 3 (April 1984): 351–52; and Lord Franks, *Falklands Islands Review: Report of the Committee of Privy Counsellors* (London: HMSO, January 1983), para. 276.

28. Quoted in House of Commons, 93.

29. Quoted in House of Commons, 288.

30. Freedman and Gamba-Stonehouse, 346.

31. Nicholas Henderson, "America and the Falklands: Case Study in the Behaviour of an Ally," *Economist,* November 12, 1983, 34–35.

32. Quoted in Freedman, *War and Diplomacy,* 233. Also see 360.

33. Freedman and Gamba-Stonehouse, 258–59, 334, 355.

34. Quoted in Freedman, *War and Diplomacy,* 523.

35. Henderson, 42.

36. Peter Calvert, "Latin America and the United States during and after the Falklands

Crisis," *Millennium: Journal of International Studies,* Vol. 12, No. 1 (1988): 69; and Freedman and Gamba-Stonehouse, 156.

37. Windsor, 94.

38. Quoted in Freedman and Gamba-Stonehouse, 155–56.

39. Freedman and Gamba-Stonehouse, 190, and "America's Falklands War," 29.

40. Jeffrey T. Richelson and Desmond Ball, *The Ties That Bind: Intelligence Cooperation between the UKUSA Countries—the United Kingdom, the United States of America, Canada, Australia and New Zealand* (Boston: Allen and Unwin, 1985), 307.

41. Richelson and Ball, *The Ties That Bind,* 308–11.

42. Freedman, *Britain and the Falklands War,* 72; Hastings and Jenkins, 142; and "America's Falklands War," 30–31.

43. Richelson and Ball, 304.

44. Duncan Campbell, "How We Spy on Argentina," *New Statesman,* April 30, 1982, 5.

45. Hastings and Jenkins, 142.

46. Hastings and Jenkins, 142.

47. Edwards, 296; Freedman, *Britain and the Falklands War,* 41.

48. Freedman, *Britain and the Falklands War,* 55; Freedman and Gamba-Stonehouse, 247.

49. Freedman and Gamba-Stonehouse, 152.

50. Quoted in House of Commons, 288.

51. Martin Middlebrook, *The Fight for the "Malvinas": The Argentine Forces in the Falklands War* (London: Viking, 1989), 121.

52. Quoted in House of Commons, 85.

53. House of Commons, 134–35, 316.

54. Freedman, *Britain and the Falklands War,* 42, 117, and Hastings and Jenkins, 142 and 162.

55. Margaret Thatcher, "Pinochet Was This Country's Staunch, True Friend," *Guardian Unlimited,* October 6, 1999, at www.guardian.co.uk/Archive/Article/0,4273,3909976,00.html.

56. Baroness Thatcher, "Thatcher Speaks Out for Pinochet," *The Times* (London), October 22, 1998, 27.

57. "Matthei Rompe el Silencio Sobre el Pacto Secreto Chile-Argentine en la Guerra de las Malvinas," *La Tercera,* March 24, 2002, at www.tercera.cl/diario/2002/03/24/24.00.REP.MATTHEI_TFP.html.

58. Philip Webster and Michael Binyon, "Thatcher Calls for Release of Pinochet," *The Times* (London), October 22, 1998, 1; House of Commons, 140; and Freedman, *War and Diplomacy,* 390–99.

59. Freedman and Gamba-Stonehouse, 261, and Walter Pincus, "British Got Crucial Data in Falklands, Diary Says," *Washington Post,* December 23, 1984, A20.

60. Hastings and Jenkins, 47, 323–24.

61. Middlebrook, 56.

62. Middlebrook, 40.

63. Nora Kinzer Stewart, *South Atlantic Conflict of 1982: A Case Study in Military Cohesion* (Alexandria, VA: U.S. Army Research Institute for Behavioral and Social Sciences, April 1988), 61.

64. Freedman, *Britain and the Falklands War,* 111.

65. Quoted in Freedman, *The Origins of the Falklands War,* 218.

66. Peter Lord Carrington, *Reflecting on Things Past: The Memoirs of Peter Lord Carrington* (New York: Harper and Row, 1989), 349–50. Also cf. 354.

67. Lord Franks, para. 338.

68. James D. Hessman, "The Lessons of Falklands," *Sea Power,* July 1982, 15.

69. House of Commons, 8–9; Richard Ned Lebow, "Miscalculation in the South Atlantic: The Origins of the Falkland War," *Journal of Strategic Studies,* Vol. 6, No. 1 (March 1983): 5; Guilermo A. Malkin, "Argentine Approaches to the Falklands/Malvinas: Was the Resort to Violence Foreseeable?" *International Affairs,* Vol. 59, No. 3 (Summer 1983): 391–403; Freedman and Gamba-Stonehouse, 19, 29; and Hastings and Jenkins, 42, 115, 117–19, 326–27.

70. Freedman, *Britain and the Falklands War,* 32, 37; Robert Andrew Burns, *Diplomacy, War and Parliamentary Democracy: Further Lessons from the Falklands or Advice from Academe* (Lanham, MD: University Press of America, 1985), 21; and "Matthei Rompe el Silencio Sobre," 367; Lord Carrington, 358, 362.

71. Quoted in Hastings and Jenkins, 120.

72. Freedman, *Britain and the Falklands War,* 13; Hastings and Jenkins, 13, 329.

73. Hastings and Jenkins, 71, and 334–35.

74. House of Commons, 236.

75. House of Commons, 130, 157.

76. House of Commons, 203, and Hastings and Jenkins, 331–35.

77. House of Commons, 184.

78. "All Out War," *New Statesman,* August 24, 1982, 14; Duncan Campell and John Rentoul, "The Belgrano Cover-Up," *New Statesman,* August 31, 1984, 8–10.

79. Freedman, *Britain and the Falklands War,* 90.

80. Quoted in Freedman, *War and Diplomacy,* 35.

81. Gastil, 357.

82. House of Commons, 199.

83. Quoted in House of Commons, 236.

84. Freedman, *Britain and the Falklands War,* xi, 94, 97.

85. Moore and Woodward, 27.

86. Quoted in House of Commons, 247.

87. Hastings and Jenkins, 283.

88. John Mueller, *War, Presidents and Public Opinion* (New York: Wiley, 1973), 266. To be fair, at least some democratic triumphalists recognize this fact, though their effort to turn it into a virtue (e.g., democratic leaders will try to find wars they can win quickly) is not fully persuasive. See Dan Reiter and Allan C. Stam, *Democracies at War* (Princeton, NJ: Princeton University Press, 2002), 172-78.

89. Stewart, 72.

90. Stewart, xii, and Middlebrook, 229–30.

91. Freedman, *Britain and the Falklands War,* 72-73.

92. Middlebrook, 271.

93. Stewart, 35; "Military Lessons of the Falklands Campaign," in *Strategic Survey: 1982/83* (London: IISS, 1983), 122; Freedman, *Britain and the Falklands War,* 91; Middlebrook, 182; and Hastings and Jenkins, 319.

94. Quoted in Max Arthur, *Above All Courage: The Falklands Front-Line: First-Hand Accounts* (London: Sidgwick and Jackson, 1985), 148.

95. Stewart, 116.

96. Stewart, 41, and Arthur, 144.

97. Stewart, 42, and Daniel Kon, *Los Chicos de la Guerra: The Boys of the War* (Sevenoaks, UK: New English Library, 1983), 126–27.

98. Quoted in Kon, 101, and Hastings and Jenkins, 322-23.

99. Quoted in Kon, 28.

100. Stewart, 44.

101. Middlebrook, 62.

102. Stewart, 53.

103. Stewart, 34, and Arthur, 299.

104. Stewart, 23.

105. Quoted in Stewart, 75. Also cf. Arthur, 1, 143.

106. Quoted in Arthur, 255.

107. H. M. Rose, "Toward an Ending of the Falkland Islands War, June 1982," *Conflict*, Vol. 7, No. 1 (1987): 1–13.

108. Kon, 74–88.

109. Quoted in Stewart, 114.

110. Freedman, *Britain and the Falklands War*, 61.

111. Stewart, 56.

112. Stewart, 56.

113. Stewart, 95, and Middlebrook, 49–50.

114. Quoted in Kon, 39.

115. Quoted in Kon, 17.

116. David Aldea, "Blood and Mud at Goose Green," *Military History*, Vol. 19 , No. 1 (April 2002): 45–46.

117. Moore and Woodward, 25–26; House of Commons, 132; and Jeffrey Record, "The Falklands War," *Washington Quarterly*, Vol. 5, No. 4 (Autumn 1982): 43.

118. Jose Teofilo Goyret, "El Ejercito Argentino en la Guerra de las Malvinas," *Armas y Geostrategica*, Vol. 2, No. 6 (May 1983): 19–57.

119. "All Out War," *New Statesman*, August 24, 1982, 9.

120. Robert L. Scheina, "The Malvinas Campaign," *Proceedings of the United States Naval Institute*, Vol. 109, No. 5 (1983): 117.

121. Scheina, 117.

122. Freedman, *Britain and the Falklands War*, 48.

123. Middlebrook, 70.

124. Quoted in Kon, 28–29.

125. Middlebrook, 142.

126. Scheina, 108–9 and 114, and Middlebrook, 91.

127. "Military Lessons of the Falklands Campaign," 122.

128. Stewart, 57.

129. Quoted in Arthur, 127.

130. Quoted in Arthur, 283. Also see Hastings and Jenkins, 199.

131. Freedman and Gamba-Stonehouse, 361.

132. Hastings and Jenkins, 111.

133. Gastil, 264, and Michael C. Desch, *Civilian Control of the Military: The Changing Security Environment* (Baltimore: Johns Hopkins University Press, 1999), 104–5.

134. Malkin, 304. Also cf. Haig, 288–89.

135. Freedman, *Britain and the Falklands War,* 90–91.

CHAPTER 6: IF NOT DEMOCRACY, THEN WHAT?

1. Ivan Arreguín-Toft, "How the Weak Win Wars: A Theory of Asymmetric Conflict," *International Security,* Vol. 26, No. 1 (Summer 2001): 97, finds that in interstate wars between 1800 and 1998, the stronger actor won nearly 71 percent of the time. See also John J. Mearsheimer, "Assessing the Conventional Balance: The 3:1 Rule and Its Critics," *International Security,* Vol. 13, No. 4 (Spring 1989): 54–89; and John Mearsheimer, *The Tragedy of Great Power Politics* (New York: W. W. Norton, 2001). Patricia L. Sullivan, "War Aims and War Outcomes: Why Powerful States Lose Limited Wars," *Journal of Conflict Resolution,* Vol. 51, No. 3 (June 2007): 496–524, argues that the effect of power varies with the issue at stake in wars, a finding not inconsistent with my argument. Still, it is striking that even when the balance of interests favors weaker states, the more powerful state still prevails over 60 percent of the time.

2. Andrew M. Mack, "Why Big Nations Lose Small Wars," *World Politics,* Vol. 27, No. 2 (January 1975): 175–200; and Arreguín-Toft, 93–128.

3. Kenneth N. Waltz, *Theory of International Politics* (Reading, MA: Addison-Wesley, 1979), 76–77, 127–28. See also João Resende-Santos, "Anarchy and the Emulation of Military Systems: Military Organization and Technology in South America, 1870–1914," *Security Studies,* Vol. 5, No. 3 (Spring 1996): 193–260.

4. Aside from Carl Maria von Clausewitz, *On War,* ed. Anatol Rapoport (Middlesex: Penguin, 1968), 384–85, the best general discussions of military consequences of increasing nationalism are Peter Paret, "Nationalism and the Sense of Military Obligation," *Military Affairs,* Vol. 34, No. 1 (February 1970): 2–6; R. R. Palmer, "Frederick the Great, Guibert, Bülow: From Dynastic to National War," in Peter Paret, ed., *Makers of Modern Strategy: From Machiavelli to the Nuclear Age* (Princeton, NJ: Princeton University Press, 1986), 91–122; Barry R. Posen, "Nationalism, the Mass Army, and Military Power," *International Security,* Vol. 18, No. 2 (Fall 1993): 80–124; and Stephen Van Evera, "Hypotheses on Nationalism and War," *International Security,* Vol. 18, No. 4 (Spring 1994): 30.

5. Errol Henderson and Resat Bayer, "Bringing Them to Their Knees: Death, Wealth, and the Transformation of Warfare as Determinants of Victory and Defeat in International War" (paper presented to the annual conference of the American Political Science Association, Chicago, September 2004).

6. John Mueller makes a similar argument about the spurious relationship between democracy and peace in "Is War Still Becoming Obsolete?" (paper presented to the annual meeting of the American Political Science Association, Washington, DC, August 1991), 50–52. See also John Mueller, *Quiet Cataclysm: Reflections on the Recent Transformation of World Politics* (Reading, MA: Addison-Wesley, 1995).

7. British and French military track records since 1648 were calculated from R. Ernest

Dupuy and Trevor N. Dupuy, *The Harper Encyclopedia of Military History: From 3500 B.C. to the Present,* 4th ed. (New York: HarperCollins, 1993).

8. David A. Lake, "Powerful Pacifists: Democratic States and War," *American Political Science Review,* Vol. 86, No. 1 (March 1992): 31, n. 31.

9. Dan Reiter and Allan C. Stam, *Democracies at War* (Princeton, NJ: Princeton University Press, 2002), 25, 129.

10. This logic parallels Edward D. Mansfield and Jack Snyder, "Democratization and the Danger of War," *International Security,* Vol. 20, No. 1 (Summer 1995), 35, who suggest that an alternative explanation for their finding about the increased likelihood of international conflict in democratizing states is that states undergoing any sort of political change are more likely to engage in war.

11. For evidence that anocracies are short-lived, see Hårvard Hegre, Tanja Elligson, Scott Gates, and Nils Peter Gleditsch, "Toward a Democratic Civil Peace? Democracy, Political Change, and Civil War, 1816–1992," *American Political Science Review,* Vol. 95, No. 1 (March 2001): 34.

12. This figures was calculated for each country in Reiter and Stam's dataset by calculating the variance for the same countries over time in the POLITY IV dataset.

13. Arreguín-Toft, 97, finds that in interstate wars between 1800 and 1998, the stronger actor won nearly 71 percent of the time.

14. Martin van Creveld, *Fighting Power: German and U.S. Army Performance, 1939–1945* (Westport, CT: Greenwood, 1982).

15. See, for example, Allan R. Millett, Williamson Murray, and Kenneth H. Watman, "The Effectiveness of Military Organizations," *International Security,* Vol. 11, No. 1 (Summer 1986): 71; Stephen Biddle and Stephen Long, "Democracy and Military Effectiveness: A Deeper Look," *Journal of Conflict Resolution,* Vol. 48, No. 4 (August 2004): 525–46; Stephen Biddle, *Military Power: Explaining Victory and Defeat in Modern Battle* (Princeton, NJ: Princeton University Press, 2004); and Risa Brooks and Elizabeth Stanley-Mitchell, *Creating Military Power: The Impact of Culture, Society, Institutions, and International Forces on Military Effectiveness* (Palo Alto, CA: Stanford University Press, 2007).

16. For the logical underpinning this argument, see Stephen Van Evera, "Primed for Peace: Europe after the Cold War," *International Security,* Vol. 15, No. 3 (Winter 1990–91): 14–16; and Aaron L. Friedberg, *In the Shadow of the Garrison State: America's Anti-Statism and Its Cold War Grand Strategy* (Princeton, NJ: Princeton University Press, 2000), 304.

17. For evidence that China may be able to liberalize economically while forestalling political opening for some time to come, see Bruce Bueno de Mesquita and George Downes, "Richer but Not Freer," *Foreign Affairs,* Vol. 84, No. 5 (September–October 2005): 77–86. For an example of how China has been able to modernize without across-the-board liberalization, see Evan A. Feigenbaum, "Who's behind China's High-Technology 'Revolution'? How Bomb Makers Remade Beijing's Priorities, Policies, and Institutions," *International Security,* Vol. 24, No. 1 (Summer 1999): 119.

18. This is the approach that Branislav L. Slantchev, Anna Alexandrova, and Erik Gartzke take in their response to Sebastian Rosato's critique of democratic peace theory in their "Probabilistic Causality, Selection Bias, and the Logic of the Democratic Peace," *American Political Science Review,* Vol. 97, No. 4 (November 2003): 459–62.

19. I thank Sebastian Rosato for this point.

20. Condoleezza Rice, "The Promise of the Democratic Peace," *Washington Post,* December 11, 2005, B7.

21. "Culture as Tool in National Security Analysis: A Roundtable," sponsored by the Strategic Assessments Group, Directorate of Intelligence, U.S. Central Intelligence Agency, Langley, Virginia, April 29, 1999.

22. See, for example, Jeffrey A. Isaacson, Christopher Layne, and John Arquilla, *Predicting Military Innovation,* documented briefing (Santa Monica, Calif.: RAND, 1999); and Ashley J. Tellis, Janice L. Bially, Christopher Layne, Melissa McPherson, and Jerry Solinger, *Measuring National Power in the Post-Industrial Age,* RAND Report 1818-A (Santa Monica, Calif.: RAND, July 1999).

23. "President Delivers 'State of the Union' " (Washington, DC: Office of the Press Secretary, January 28, 2003), at www.whitehouse.gov/news/releases/2003/01/print/20030128-19.htm.

24. Others, recognizing that the war has gone very badly, are now trying to distance democracy from it. Paul Starr, "War and Liberalism," *New Republic,* March 5–12, 2007, 21–24, argues that the reason the Bush administration is failing is precisely because it has abandoned liberalism in its conduct of the global war on terror. That, of course, begs the question of why America's democratic political system did not prevent the debacle and whether American liberalism itself might be implicated in the fiasco. For on argument on behalf of the latter proposition, see my "America's Liberal Illiberalism," *International Security* (forthcoming).

25. Michael R. Gordon, "The Strategy to Secure Iraq Did Not Foresee a 2nd War," *New York Times,* October 19, 2004, at www.nytimes.com/2004/10/19/international/19war.html; Gordon, "Poor Intelligence Misled Troops about Risk of Drawn-out War," *New York Times,* October 20, 2004, at www.nytimes.com/2004/10/20/international/20war.html; and Gordon, "Debate Lingering on Decision to Dissolve Iraqi Military," *New York Times,* October 21, 2004, at www.nytimes.com/2004/10/21/international/21war.html. Also see Michael R. Gordon and Bernard E. Trainor, *Cobra II: The Inside Story of the Invasion and Occupation of Iraq* (New York: Pantheon, 2006).

26. Thomas E. Ricks, *Fiasco: The American Military Adventure in Iraq* (New York: Penguin Press, 2006).

27. This seems to be the assessment of Israeli analysts who feel they have a large stake in a U.S. victory in Iraq and so are watching developments there very closely. See Yossi Sarid, "At Least the U.S. Admits Its Mistakes," *Ha'aretz,* December 28, 2005 (English edition-online), http://www.haaretz.co.il/hasen/spages/663139.html.

28. Lawrence B. Wilkerson, "The White House Cabal," *Los Angeles Times,* October 25, 2005, at www.latimes.com/news/opinion/commentary/la-oe-wilkerson25oct25,0,7455395.story?coll=la-news-comment-opinions.

29. Michael Massing, "Now They Tell Us," *New York Review of Books,* Vol. 51, No. 3 (February 26, 2004) (on-line edition), http://www.nybooks.com/articles/article-preview?article_id=16922.

30. Bob Woodward, *Plan of Attack* (New York: Simon and Schuster, 2004), 296. Also see 377.

31. According to Katherine Seeyle, "Moral Values Cited as Defining Issue of the Elec-

tion," *New York Times,* November 4, 2004, 4, 52 percent of voters thought the war in Iraq was "going badly." For further evidence of the willingness of the public to "forgive" the Bush administration, see "A Matter of Trust," *Economist,* April 1, 2004, at www.economist.com/PrinterFriendly.cfm?Story_ID-2253350.

32. Edmund L. Andrews, "Deficit Analysis and Bush Differ," *New York Times,* September 8, 2004, 1, which discusses how the Bush administration has gone from a surplus of $150 billion to a projected deficit of $500 billion in 2009.

33. Chaim Kaufmann, "Threat Inflation and the Failure of the Marketplace of Ideas: The Selling of the Iraq War," *International Security,* Vol. 29, No. 1 (Summer 2004): 5–48.

34. For clear evidence of declining public support for the war in Iraq from 60 to 48 percent over the past few years, see www.pollingreport.com/iraq.htm.

35. According to a 2006 *Military Times* poll, less than half of service personnel now think we should have gone to war in the first place and only 35 percent approve of how President Bush is handling of it. See the results at www.militarycity.com/polls/.

For evidence of declining troop morale in Iraq, see Neela Banerjee and Ariel Hart, "Inquiry Opens after Reservists Balk in Baghdad," *New York Times,* October 16, 2004, 1; Thom Shanker and Eric Schmitt, "Armor Scarce for Heavy Trucks Transporting U.S. Cargo in Iraq," *New York Times,* December 10, 2004, 1; and Tom Lasseter, "Among Soldiers, Growing Doubts about Mission," *Philadelphia Inquirer,* July 21, 2004. For discussion of recruitment and retention problems, see Eric Schmitt and Thom Shanker, "Army to Call Up Recruits Earlier," *New York Times,* July 22, 2004, at www.intimes.com/2004/07/22/politics/22recruit.html; and Dave Moniz, "Strained Army National Guard Having Tough Time Recruiting," *USA Today,* July 20, 2004, 5.

36. Victor Davis Hanson, *Carnage and Culture: Landmark Battles in the Rise of Western Power* (New York: Doubleday, 2001), 55. Also cf. 46–59.

37. Seth Bernadette, introduction to *Aeschylus II,* ed. David Grene and Richard Lattimore (Chicago: University of Chicago Press, 1991), 44; and J. Peter Euben, "The Battle of Salamis and the Origins of Political Theory," *Political Theory,* Vol. 14, No. 3 (August 1986): 359.

38. Benjamin Constant, "The Liberty of the Ancients Compared with That of the Moderns," in *Political Writings,* ed. Biancamaria Fontana (Cambridge: Cambridge University Press, 1998), 317. This sentiment is clearly expressed by Pericles in his "Funeral Oration": "Our public men have, besides politics, their private affairs to attend to, and our ordinary citizens, though occupied with the pursuits of industry, are still fair judges of public matters; for, unlike any other nation, we regard the citizen who takes no part in these duties not as unambitious but as useless." *The Landmark Thucydides: A Comprehensive Guide to the Peloponnesian War,* ed. Robert B. Strassler (New York: Free Press, 1996), II, 40.

39. Aeschylus, *The Persians,* 77, lines 819–29. The Passage is quoted in the book's epigraph.

40. Herodotus, *The Histories,* trans. David Grene (Chicago: University of Chicago Press, 1987), IX, 122.

41. Thucydides, I, 23.

42. Thucydides, I, 75.

43. Thucydides, I, 88.

44. For the best triumphalist account of the role of democracy in the United States' vic-

tory in the Cold War, see John Lewis Gaddis, *We Now Know: Rethinking Cold War History* (New York: Oxford University Press, 1997), 281–95.

45. Niall Ferguson, "America: An Empire in Denial," *Chronicle Review,* March 28, 2003, at http://chronicle.com/free/v49/i29/29b00701.htm.

46. "President Bush Announces Major Combat Operations in Iraq Have Ended" (Washington, DC: Office of the Press Secretary, May 1, 2003), at www.whitehouse.gov/news/releases/2003/05/iraq/20030501-15.htm.

47. "President Delivers 'State of the Union,'" January 28, 2003, http://www.whitehouse.gov/news/releases/2003/01/20030128-19.html. Also see Robert Kagan, *Of Paradise and Power: America and Europe in the New World Order* (New York: Knopf, 2003), 41.

48. Ferguson, "America: An Empire in Denial," 11. Also see Paul Johnson, "America's New Empire for Liberty," *Hoover Digest,* No. 4 (2003), at http/www/hooverdigest.org/034/johnson.html.

49. Quoted in Anatol Lieven, *America Right or Wrong: An Anatomy of American Nationalism* (New York: Oxford University Press, 2004), 52.

50. Kagan, *Of Paradise and Power,* 73.

51. Michael Desch, "Ominous Precedent," *American Conservative,* May 5, 2003, 8–11.

Index

Abdullah, King (of Jordan), 103, 122, 140
Abernon, Lord d', 82, 83
Abu Nidal, 100
Acheson, Dean, 9
Adenauer, Conrad, 119, 120
Aeschylus, 181
Agrov, Shlomo, 100
Alexander, Don, 16
Allende, Salvador, 154
alliances, 30, 53–55; in Falklands War, 149–55; in Israel's wars, 105–23; in Russo-Polish War, 77–84
Allon, Yigal, 95, 123, 130–31, 135
Almond, Gabriel, 9, 12
Amer, Abdel Haim, 104
anti-Semitism, in Poland, 80–81
Arab armies, weaknesses of, 139
Arab leaders, and political costs of war, 103–4
Arafat, Yassir, 127, 134
Argentina: economy of, 148–49; military forces of, 160–63. See also Falklands War
Arrow, Kenneth, 56
Athens, Greece: as analogous to U.S. role in Iraq, 182–83; hubris of, in victory over Persians, 180–82

Badran, Shams, 104
Bailey, Thomas A., 10
Balfour Declaration, 118
Balkan War, First (1912–13), 50
Bamford, James, 112
Bayer, Resat, 173
Begin, Menachem, 100, 102, 103, 115, 127
Ben-Eliezer, Arye, 129
Ben-Gurion, David, 98, 99–100, 101, 102, 109, 139, 140; alliances sought by, 106, 117, 123; and

distrust of Britain, 119; and relations with Germany, 120; and Suez War, 124–25
Bentham, Jeremy, 10
Berlusconi, Silvio, 179
Black September, 123
Bloch, Marc, 14
Block, Walter, 148
Bolsheviks, role of, in Russo-Polish War, 74
Boxer Rebellion, 49, 65
Brandt, Willy, 107
Brecher, Michael, 101
Brilliant, Moshe, 118
Britain: as ally of Israel, 117–19; democracy in, 173; and Russo-Polish War, 78–79. See also Falklands War
Brooks, Risa, 60
Brooks, Sidney, 76, 84
Budenny, Semyon, 91
Bueno de Mesquita, Bruce, 44
Bush, George H. W., 148
Bush, George W., on spread of democracy, 2, 3, 4, 178, 182–83

Caillaux, Joseph, 51
capitalism, and democracy, 4
Carrington, Lord, 156
Carter, Jimmy, 9, 114
Cheney, Dick, 4; on future of Iraq, 2–3
Chile, as ally to Britain in Falklands War, 154–55
China, 177
Chiozza, Giacomo, 48
Christopher, Warren, 9
Churchill, Winston, 70, 74, 78
Clemenceau, Georges, 79–80
Cold War: democratic alliances during, 54; factors contributing to U.S. success during,

Vistula, Battle of the, 71, 86
Voltaire, 135, 174

Waltz, Kenneth, 6, 8, 11
war: political consequences of, to leaders, 44–45,
    54–55; probability of victory as factor in initi-
    ating, 38–39; public support for, 56–58; vari-
    ables affecting likelihood of victory, 39–43
Ward, Hugh, 148
Watman, Kenneth, 60
Watt, Richard, 73, 89
wealth: and democracy, 52, 53, 171–72; and mili-
    tary power, 5, 35–36, 52. *See also* rent seeking
Weinberger, Caspar, 149, 151
Weizeman, Ezer, 30
Weygand, Maxime, 82–83, 86, 89–90
Wheatcroft, Geoffrey, 130
Wilkerson, Lawrence, 179
Williams, Anthony, 155–56
Wilson, Woodrow, 10; and Russo-Polish War, 80,
    81
Wingate, Orde, 138

Wisse, Ruth, 95
Woodward, Bob, 179
World War I, 58
World War II, 6, 29–30, 31, 49. *See also* France,
    Battle of; Nazi Germany; Soviet Union
Wrangel, Piotr, 90, 91, 92

Ya'ari, Ehud, 100–101, 103
Yariv, Aharon, 102
Yishuv, 118, 140
Yom Kippur War (1973), 61, 62, 96, 103, 107, 116,
    123, 128, 137, 141; outcome of, 134; public sup-
    port for, 130; strategic evaluation as factor in,
    126
Yoram, Yair, 132
Young, Robert, 15

Za'im, Husni, 103
Zamyoski, Adam, 74–76
Zeckhauser, Richard, 54
Zionism, 107, 139; British involvement with,
    117–18